# The Kabalistic and Occult Tarot of Éliphas Lévi

Taken from the books and writings of:

Abbé Alphonse Louis Constant
(Éliphas Lévi)

EDITOR'S NOTE:

The material in this Study Guide has been taken from a variety of sources and is intended for Educational use only.

The Editor's Appendix includes objects of interest or for reference which are not given in Eliphas Levi's books, but which he may reference or which may be helpful to the student of the Kabalah.

First Edition June 2013
Second Edition December 2013
Third Edition August 2014
Fourth Edition April 2015
Fifth Edition January 2016
Sixth Edition August 2016

# Table of Contents

Editor's Introduction ........................................................................ 1

Explanation of the Layout and Sources of the Materials ................... 10

**The Kabalistic and Occult Tarot of Eliphas Levi** ............................... 13
   1. Aleph and The Juggler / Magician ............................................. 15
   2. Beth and The Popess / Priestess ............................................... 19
   3. Gimel and The Empress ........................................................... 23
   4. Dalet and The Emperor ............................................................ 29
   5. Heh and The Pope/Hierophant ................................................. 37
   6. Vau and The Lovers ................................................................. 43
   7. Zain and The Chariot of Hermes ............................................. 49
   8. Cheth and Justice ..................................................................... 57
   9. Teth and The Hermit ............................................................... 61
  10. Yod and The Wheel of Fortune ............................................. 65
  11. Kaph and Force / Fortitude / Strength ................................... 71
  12. Lamed and The Hanged Man ................................................ 77
  13. Mem and Death ..................................................................... 81
  14. Nun and Temperance ............................................................. 87
  15. Samech and The Devil .......................................................... 91
  16. Ayin and The Tower of God / The Tower of Babel .............. 95
  17. Peh and The Star ................................................................... 99
  18. Tzadik and The Moon ......................................................... 103
  19. Qoph and The Sun .............................................................. 109
  20. Resh and Judgment ............................................................. 113
  21. Shin and The Unwise Man ................................................. 119
  22. Tav and The World ............................................................. 123
     The Kabalistic Prayer ............................................................ 128
     The Conclusion ...................................................................... 136
     Occult and Religious Maxims ................................................ 137

**The Key of Secondary Causes by Johannes (John) Trithemius** ......... 139

**Editor's Appendix** .............................................................................. 157
     Various Plates (Drawings) from the Books and Writings of Eliphas Levi ....................................................................................... 159
     The Minor Arcana from the Writings of Eliphas Levi ........... 255
     The Esoteric Egyptian Tarot from Eliphas Levi's Descriptions ..... 271
     Some Objects for Reference .................................................. 287

# Editor's Introduction

The associations that Eliphas Levi gives to the Tarot have been questioned by many English readers, some even saying that he does not give the correct attributes in his books and that there is some other esoteric association that must be made in order to understand them. We suggest these readers seriously study his books again because he emphasizes the same ideas over and over.

In the Preface to his famous *History of Magic* (1860) Levi says that we should "carefully study" his three books *Dogma and Ritual of High Magic*, the *History of Magic* and the *Key to the Great Mysteries* for a complete course on "the science of the ancient Magi".

> "...our discovery of the great mysteries of this science rests entirely upon the signification that the ancient hierophants attached to numbers."[1]

Because of the importance of the symbolic value of numbers, it follows that numbers are equivalent to letters, symbols or figures which represent some principle(s).

> "There is subject to believe that this comes from the ancient manner of explaining by numbers and by figures, as were the hieroglyphics among the Egyptians before letters were invented."[2]

> "The absolute hieroglyphical science has as its foundation an alphabet in which deities were represented by letters, letters represented ideas, ideas were convertible into numbers, and numbers were perfect signs. This hieroglyphic alphabet was what Moses used to make the great secret of his kabalah and which he took from the Egyptians..."[3]

Levi always emphasizes the importance of symbolism:

> "All religions have preserved the remembrance of a primitive book from the earliest centuries of the world written with figures by the sages, and from which these symbols (simplified and vulgarized later on) have provided Writing with its letters, provided the Verb with its characters, and provided occult Philosophy with its mysterious signs and its pentacles.

> This book, attributed to Enoch (the seventh master of the world after Adam) by the Hebrews; to Hermes Trismegistus by the Egyptians; to Cadmus, the mysterious builder of the Holy City, by the Greeks, this book was the symbolic summary of the primitive tradition, called since then "Kabalah" or "Cabala", a hebrew word which is equivalent to 'tradition'."[4]

---

[1] From the Preface to *History of Magic* (1860)
[2] From the article 'Allegory' in *Dictionary of Christian Literature* (1851)
[3] From Ch.4 of Book 1 in *History of Magic* (1860)
[4] From Ch.10 of *Dogma of High Magic* (1861)

"The doctrines of Hermes can never be lost for those who know the keys of symbolism."[5]

"The symbolism of numbers and the allegory of figures easily gives the key to the poetry of the prophets, as those from the past knew who were versed in oriental literature.

These oriental traditions are incontestably extremely ancient. The prophets often spoke through signs and hieroglyphics, and put their words into action. Their writings were full of figures which could seem strange to those who do not penetrate their meaning…"[6]

"Beautiful poetry is exactly what we call true philosophy, and that poetic measure obeys (like geometry) the laws of number and of comparison. Great poets are mathematicians without knowing it, since the incontestable beauty of their production is the result of their exactitude.

Words are the numbers of thought, and figures are the algebra of genius.

There is only beauty in that which is true, and that which is true is just or right. Rightness or accuracy in literature, is exactitude, and exactitude is the property of the mathematical sciences. Therefore the good poet is then a veritable mathematician…"[7]

"To be a poet, it is to create; it is not to dream nor to lie. God was a poet when he made the world, and his immortal epic is written with the stars.

The sciences have received from God the secrets of poetry, because the keys of harmony were delivered into their hands.

Numbers are poets, because they sing with notes that are always exact, which gives rapture to the genius of Pythagoras.

Poetry that does not accept the world such as God made it, and which seeks to invent another, is but the delirium of the spirits of darkness…"[8]

Going further, Levi says that we must be careful of the danger of literal interpretation of symbols, because often times this misses the point:

"…words, numbers and figures have their mystery, which explains how the letter kills while the spirit vivifies…"[9]

"…almost all popular superstitions are profane interpretations of some great axiom or of some marvellous arcanum of occult wisdom.

---

[5] From Ch.4 of Book 1 in *History of Magic* (1860)
[6] From the article 'Allegory' in *Dictionary of Christian Literature* (1851)
[7] Paraphase from the article 'Allegory' in *Dictionary of Christian Literature* (1851)
[8] From the Preliminary Discourse to the 2nd edition of *Dogma of High Magic* (1861)
[9] From the article 'Allegory' in *Dictionary of Christian Literature* (1851)

> Did not Pythagoras, in writing his admirable symbols, devise a perfect philosophy to the wise, and a new series of vain observances and ridiculous practices to the vulgar?
>
> Thus, when he said: "Do not pick up what falls from the table, do not cut down trees on the great highway, do not kill the serpent which has fallen into your garden", was he not giving the precepts of charity, either social or personal, under transparent allegories?
>
> And when he said: "Do not look at yourself by torchlight in a mirror", was he not teaching in an ingenious manner about the true knowledge of self, which does not know how to exist with artificial lights and with the prejudgments of systems?
>
> It is the same with the other precepts of Pythagoras, who, as it is known, were followed literally by a flock of stupid disciples, to the point that, among the superstitious observances of our provinces, there are a great number which apparently originate from the primitive misunderstanding of the symbols of Pythagoras.
>
> Superstition comes from a latin word which signifies 'survival'. It is the sign which survives the thought; it is the cadaver of a religious practice. Superstition is to initiation what the idea of the devil is to that of God.
>
> It is in this sense that the worship of images is forbidden and that the most holy dogma in its first conception may become superstitious and impious when it has lost its inspiration and its spirit.
>
> It is then that religion (always one like supreme reason) changes its clothes and abandons the ancient rites to the greed and deception of fallen priests, transformed by their wickedness and their ignorance into charlatans and puppeteers."[10]

Therefore, we must study the signs or symbols in order to understand their 'poetry', and grasp their meaning or 'spirit'. Luckily, these are available to us in the form of the Tarot:

> "Now, the tarot that we have today ... has come to us from Egypt passing through Judea.
>
> The keys of this tarot, in fact, correspond with the letters of the hebraic alphabet, and some of its figures even reproduce the same form of the characters of this sacred alphabet."[11]

So if the Tarot corresponds with the Hebrew alphabet, then we should study the Numeric and Kabalistic significance of the Hebraic letters in order to grasp symbolic value contained in them.

---

[10] Paraphrase from Ch.18 of *Dogma of High Magic* (1861)
[11] Paraphrase from Ch.2 of Book 5 in *History of Magic* (1860)

## Introduction

One of the first things one will notice when studying the Hebrew letters is that they correspond directly to numbers. Then it becomes clear that these letters (which are also numbers) are directly related to the Tarot cards.

| Hebrew Numeric Value | Modern Hebrew Letter | Hebrew Letter Name | Translation of Levi's Tarot Card Name | Hebrew Numeric Value | Modern Hebrew Letter | Hebrew Letter Name | Translation of Levi's Tarot Card Name |
|---|---|---|---|---|---|---|---|
| 1 | א | Aleph | The Juggler | 12 | ל | Lamed | Hanged Man |
| 2 | ב | Beth | The Popess | 13 | מ | Mem | Death |
| 3 | ג | Gimel | The Empress | 14 | נ | Nun | Temperance |
| 4 | ד | Daleth | The Emperor | 15 | ס | Samech | The Devil |
| 5 | ה | Heh | The Pope | 16 | ע | Ain | The Tower |
| 6 | ו | Vau | The Lovers | 17 | פ | Peh | The Star |
| 7 | ז | Zain | The Chariot | 18 | צ | Tzadi | The Moon |
| 8 | ח | Cheth | Justice | 19 | ק | Qoph | The Sun |
| 9 | ט | Teth | The Hermit | 20 | ר | Resh | Judgement |
| 10 | י | Yod | The Wheel | 21 | ש | Shin | The Lunatic |
| 11 | כ | Caph | Strength | 22 | ת | Tav | The Crown |

Table 1 – Tarot Card Name taken from Ch. 22 of *Ritual of High Magic* (*Note the alphabetical ordering)

Levi attributes the Hebrew letters to the Tarot cards based on the Hebrew alphabet. This can be seen in Ch. 10 of *Dogma of High Magic*, and in Ch. 22 of *Ritual of High Magic,* as well as in Levi's manuscript *The Magic Ritual of the Sanctum Regnum* given to his student Baron Spédalieri and published by W. Wynn Westcott in 1896. This last document is republished in the present study guide (excluding Westcott's notes) along with other materials from Levi's writings related to the Hebrew letters.

The correspondence of the Hebrew letter & number to the Tarot cards has been a cause for confusion for many Kabalists and most often this is because of the last 2 Tarot cards (although plenty of other diviations are also perpetuated). The value of these last 2 Tarot cards has been altered to conceal a mystery related to the symbolism of the Hebrew letter Shin ש. Levi has explained this mystery (the mystery of the Great Arcanum) in his books and it is summarized with the statement given in Ch. 10 of *Dogma of High Magic* for Shin ש: "Where the mortals who lack a brake descend in herds".

The 21st letter of the Hebrew alphabet is Shin ש and the corresponding Tarot card (the Lunatic or Fool) is sometimes given the value of 0, instead of 21. Careful study of the symbolism associated with Shin ש will explain why 0 might make sense for this letter individually, although this value causes confusion with Tav ת and therefore becomes problematic when used along with other letters.

The 22nd and last letter of the Hebrew alphabet is Tav ת and the corresponding Tarot card (the Crown or World) is often given the value of 21, instead of 22, when the 0 value is given to the Shin ש card. [See Table 2]

| Alternate Numeric Value | Modern Hebrew Letter | Hebrew Letter Name | Translation of Tarot Card Name | Alternate Numeric Value | Modern Hebrew Letter | Hebrew Letter Name | Translation of Tarot Card Name |
|---|---|---|---|---|---|---|---|
| 1 | א | Aleph | The Juggler | 12 | ל | Lamed | Hanged Man |
| 2 | ב | Beth | The Popess | 13 | מ | Mem | Death |
| 3 | ג | Gimel | The Empress | 14 | נ | Nun | Temperance |
| 4 | ד | Daleth | The Emperor | 15 | ס | Samech | The Devil |
| 5 | ה | Heh | The Pope | 16 | ע | Ain | The Tower |
| 6 | ו | Vau | The Lovers | 17 | פ | Peh | The Star |
| 7 | ז | Zain | The Chariot | 18 | צ | Tzadi | The Moon |
| 8 | ח | Cheth | Justice | 19 | ק | Qoph | The Sun |
| 9 | ט | Teth | The Hermit | 20 | ר | Resh | Judgement |
| 10 | י | Yod | The Wheel | 0 | ש | Shin | The Lunatic |
| 11 | כ | Caph | Strength | 21 | ת | Tav | The Crown |

Table 2 – Alternate Numeric values used for Tarot Cards (*Note the value of 0 for ש and of 21 for ת )

Further confusion has been caused by a complication of the previously mentioned association of Tav ת with 21. Since the card for Tav ת (the Crown or World) has been known as 21, when the card for Shin ש (the Lunatic or Fool) is added back to the deck: it mistakenly becomes the new 22. [See Table 3] This is common in many modern Tarot decks. Besides the previous example (given in Table 3), another mistaken Modern Tarot Card association is that the Hebrew *letters* are given in alphabetical order correctly, but the Tarot *cards* for Shin ש and Tav ת remain reversed.

| Modern Tarot Numeric Value | Modern Hebrew Letter | Hebrew Letter Name | Translation of Tarot Card Name | Modern Tarot Numeric Value | Modern Hebrew Letter | Hebrew Letter Name | Translation of Tarot Card Name |
|---|---|---|---|---|---|---|---|
| 1 | א | Aleph | The Juggler | 12 | ל | Lamed | Hanged Man |
| 2 | ב | Beth | The Popess | 13 | מ | Mem | Death |
| 3 | ג | Gimel | The Empress | 14 | נ | Nun | Temperance |
| 4 | ד | Daleth | The Emperor | 15 | ס | Samech | The Devil |
| 5 | ה | Heh | The Pope | 16 | ע | Ain | The Tower |
| 6 | ו | Vau | The Lovers | 17 | פ | Peh | The Star |
| 7 | ז | Zain | The Chariot | 18 | צ | Tzadi | The Moon |
| 8 | ח | Cheth | Justice | 19 | ק | Qoph | The Sun |
| 9 | ט | Teth | The Hermit | 20 | ר | Resh | Judgement |
| 10 | י | Yod | The Wheel | 21 | ת | Tav | The Crown |
| 11 | כ | Caph | Strength | 22 | ש | Shin | The Lunatic |

Table 3 – Mistaken Modern Tarot Card Associations (*Note the confusion of 22 for ש and of 21 for ת )

The solution to all of this is to just remember the alphabetical ordering and that alphabetically Shin ש = 21 and Tav ת = 22, then we will not fall into confusion regarding the ordering of the Tarot cards. [See Table 1] The alphabetical ordering is what Levi has given and explains in all his books, and is therefore the ordering used in this study guide.

"We have said that the 22 keys of the tarot are the 22 letters of the primitive kabalistic alphabet."[12]

When all of this becomes clear, then we understand why Levi has done the following:

"Our *Dogma* and our *Ritual* are each divided into twenty-two chapters marked by the twenty-two letters of the hebrew alphabet.

We have put at the head of each chapter the letter which is related to the latin words which (according to the best authors) indicate the hieroglyphic signification.

Thus, at the head of the first chapter, for example, we read:

1 א A

THE RECIPIENT,

Disciplina,

Ensoph,

Keter.

Which signifies that the letter aleph, who's equivalant in latin and french is A, the numerical value 1 signifies the recipient, man called to initiation, the skilled individual (the *bateleur* [or juggler] of the tarot), which also signifies the dogmatic syllepsis (disciplina), the being in its general and first conception (Ensoph [Ain Soph]); and finally the first and obscure idea of divinity expressed by *kether* (the crown) in kabbalistic theology.

The chapter is the development of the title and the title hieroglyphically contains the whole chapter. The whole book is composed following this combination." [13]

If we look at the chapters of *Dogma of High Magic*, we will see that Ch. 21 is associated with Shin ש, and Ch. 22 with Tav ת.

In Ch. 22 of *Ritual of High Magic*, which Levi has named "The Book of Hermes" and where he gives (among other things) a description of all 22 Hebrew letters and their 'hieroglyphs', there is the following description for Shin ש:

---

[12] From Ch.22 of *Ritual of High Magic* (1861)
[13] From the Preface to *History of Magic* (1860)

"THE LUNATIC: a man dressed as a lunatic, walking aimlessly, burdened with a satchel which he carries behind him, and which is no doubt full of his follies and vices; his disordered clothes allow the discovery of what should be concealed, and a tiger who follows him also bites him without him wondering how to escape or defend himself."

And in Chapter 22 of *Dogma of High Magic*, Levi describes the figure of 'the Crown or World', again showing the association of Tav ת, saying:

"This universal arcanum, the final and eternal secret of high initiation, is represented in the Tarot by a naked girl, who touches the earth by only one foot, has a magnetic wand in each hand, and seems to be running in a crown held up by an angel, an eagle, a bull and a lion."

In the 'Introduction' to *Ritual of High Magic*, Levi says the following:

"But here, Fabre d'Olivet is just missing the true interpretation, because he is ignorant of the great keys of the kabalah.

The word Nahash [והנש], explained by the symbolic letters of the Tarot, rigorously signifies:

- 14 נ Nun. — The force which produces mixtures.

- 5 ה He. — The recipient and passive producer of forms.

- 21 ש Shin. — The natural fire and central equilibrium through double polarization."

Here, again, Levi gives 21 as the numeric value of Shin ש and associates the "letters of the Tarot" with the Hebrew letters.

And in Ch. 19 of *Ritual of High Magic*:

"Whosoever wants to achieve an understanding of the great word and possession of the great Arcanum must (after studying the principles of our dogma) read the hermetic philosophers carefully, and he will doubtless attain initiation, as others have attained it; but one must take as the key of their allegories the unique dogma of Hermes, contained in his emerald tablet, and follow (in order to classify the knowledge and in order to direct the operation) the order indicated in the kabalistic alphabet of the Tarot..."

So we can see that Levi is using the alphabetical association of the Hebrew letters & numbers with the Tarot cards.

So let's study this wonderful book (the original book of the ancients that synthesizes their profound wisdom), 'letter' by 'letter', in order to access the secret science contained within.

"The science of signs begins with the science of letters. Letters are absolute ideas. Absolute ideas are numbers. Numbers are perfect signs.

In using ideas with numbers, one can operate upon the ideas like one can operate upon numbers and arrive at the mathematics of truth. The tarot is the key of letters and numbers…"[14]

"Each letter represents a number: Each assemblage of letters [is then] a series of numbers.

The numbers represent absolute philosophical ideas.

The letters are abridged hieroglyphs.

Now let's see the hieroglyphic and philosophic significations of each of the twenty-two letters." [15]

– The Editors

---

[14] From Letter #7 (written in December of 1861) from Eliphas Levi to his student Baron Spédalieri, available in *The Kabalistic and Occult Philosophy of Eliphas Levi, Volume 1: Letters to Students*
[15] From Ch.3 of Book 1 in the Third Part of *The Key to the Great Mysteries* (1861)

## Description or Meaning given by Lévi for the Hebrew Letters:

|    | Hebrew Letter | From his Book *Key to the Great Mysteries* | From his Correspondence with the Baron Spédalieri |
|----|---|---|---|
| 1  | א - Aleph | Unity, represented in a relative manner | Being; man with universal knowledge; numeral unity; Providence |
| 2  | ב - Beth | Reflection, thought, the moon, the angel Gabriel, prince of the mysteries | The unity which exteriorizes itself while creating; the hieroglyphic image of that divine mother; divine Wisdom |
| 3  | ג - Gimel | Love, willpower, Venus, the angel Anael, prince of life and death | The central point of equilibrium |
| 4  | ד - Daleth | Force, power, Jupiter, Sachiel, Meleck, king of kings | The tetragrammaton, Gedulah (Chesed) or mercy; the master, power |
| 5  | ה - Heh | The passive producing principle, the cteis | A great priest; the great hierophant; the blazing star. |
| 6  | ו - Vau | The union of the two or the lingam | God in nature; the idea in the verb; the number of man; creation, liberty |
| 7  | ז - Zain | [not given] | Netzach, Victory; Triumphant and sacred. Charity, crown of the temple |
| 8  | ח - Cheth | [not given] | Justice; eternal life, which maintains itself by the equilibrium of movement |
| 9  | ט - Teth | [not given] | The number of the initiate; the number of prudence and of initiation |
| 10 | י - Yod | The absolute principle, the productive being | The universe, the law; absolute unity |
| 11 | כ - Caph | Violence, battle, work, Mars, Samael Zebaoth, Prince of Phalanges | Force or Strength |
| 12 | ל - Lamed | [not given] | Perfect movement; sacrifice; consumption by the cross; God and the science of God or his verb |
| 13 | מ - Mem | Spirit, or the Jakin of Solomon | The number of death and of immortality, the most mysterious of the numbers |
| 14 | נ - Nun | [not given] | the equilibrated and absolute triumph of the good |
| 15 | ס - Samech | [not given] | [not given] |
| 16 | ע - Ain | [not given] | the equilibrating law of forces |
| 17 | פ - Peh | Eloquence, intelligence, Mercury, Raphael, prince of the sciences | The complete life; the brilliant star or intelligence of nature |
| 18 | צ - Tzadi | [not given] | The number of initiation and of dogma, the number of hierarchy and mystery |
| 19 | ק - Qoph | [not given] | The number of the sun and of the truth |
| 20 | ר - Resh | Destruction and regeneration, Time, Saturn, Cassiel, king of tombs and of solitude | The perpetuity of life ever renewing itself at the call of the divine verb |
| 21 | ש - Shin | Matter [or the material], or the column Boaz [of Solomon] | Image of the eternal triple fire; material equilibrium or elementary justice injured by the aggressors |
| 22 | ת - Tav | The truth, the light, the Sun, Michael, king of the Elohim | Hierogram of the cross [X or +] |

# Explanation of the Layout and Sources of the Materials

The information on the following pages are taken from the writings of Eliphas Levi about the meaning of each of the Hebrew letters and corresponding Tarot cards.

**1)** Excerpts from the section called "The Sacred Letters or Major Keys" from Levi's manuscript *Clef Majeures et Clavicules de Salomon [Major Keys and Clavicles of Solomon]*. This manuscript of the 'Holy Clavicles' was published in Paris, in 1895, and was an exact reproduction of what was originally drawn and written in 1860, and then copied for the Baron Spedalieri in the Fall of 1861.

**2)** This part is from the second edition of the *Dogme and Rituel de la Haute Magie [Dogma and Ritual of High Magic]* (1861) series:
  a. Chapter headings from *Dogma of High Magic* with definitions (the definitions are from the Editors' research).
  b. Chapter names from *Ritual of High Magic*.
  c. Description from Introduction to *Dogma of High Magic* for the letter.
  d. Description from Ch.10 from *Dogma of High Magic* for the letter.
  e. Description from Ch.22 from *Ritual of High Magic* for the letter.

**3)** Tarot card images drawn by Oswald Wirth, originally published in *Le Tarot des Bohemiens* (1889), but in some cases have been modified by the Editors.

**4)** From *The Magic Ritual of the Sanctum Regnum* (1896) which was a previously unpublished manuscript given to W. Wynn Westcott by Edward Maitland who obtained it from the Baron Spedalieri. Since we do not have the French original, we have to work with Westcott's translation. This manuscript is an explanation of the Great Arcanum in 22 parts or chapters, who's titles are those of the French Tarot cards.

At the end of the last card, there is an additional section called "The Kabalistic Prayer", followed by "The Conclusion" and finally "Occult and Religious Maxims", which we are including here as well.

In the Preface to his translation, Westcott says that "The original MSS., which is in the handwriting of Levi himself, is written upon pages interleaved with the text of a printed copy of a work by Trithemius of Spanheim, entitled *De Septem Secundeis*: the edition was published at Cologne, and is dated 1567." Which means that this manuscript is the 'interposed manuscript' that Levi refers to in his letters to the Baron Spedalieri when he says that he is sending "*The Key of secondary Causes* by Trithemius, with a interposed manuscript which is like an occult commentary on the clavicles of Solomon..." (See Letter #5 in *The Kabalistic and Occult Philosophy of Eliphas Levi, Volume 1: Letters to Students* by the same publishers).

# Explanation

### #1

*The Major Keys and Clavicles of Solomon*
The Sacred Letters
or Major Keys

[words in the pictures]
words below the pictures

### #2

*Dogma of High Magic*
Chapter Headings
with definitions

*Ritual of High Magic* - Chapter Names

*Dogma of High Magic* - Introduction

*Dogma of High Magic* - Chapter 10

*Ritual of High Magic*
Chapter 22

### #3

Oswald Wirth
*Le Tarot des Bohemiens*
Associated Tarot Plate

### #4

*The Magic Ritual of the Sanctum Regnum*
Whole Chapter/Section

Explanation

# The Kabalistic and Occult Tarot of Éliphas Lévi

# 1

## THE LETTER ALEPH

HIEROGLIPHIC — THE JUGGLER / TUMBLER

[the earth]

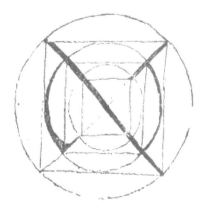

The pentacle of Eden, prototype of the sacred letters

# 1 א A

## THE RECIPIENT.

**DISCIPLINA.** – A Latin noun which refers to education and training, self-control and determination, knowledge in a field of study and an orderly way of life.

**AINSOPH.** – (Hebrew אין סוף), also spelled En Soph, Ein Sof, Ayn Sof, etc., is the Infinite. It is the divine origin of all created existence and can also be translated as "no end", "unending", or "limitless".

**KETHER.** – (Hebrew: כתר), also spelled Keter, is the Crown. It is the uppermost sephiroth [1] of the Kabalistic tree of life.

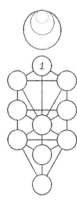

## PREPARATIONS.

א *Aleph.* — He sees God face to face, without dying, and converses familiarly with the seven genii who command the entire celestial army.

1 א Everything announces an intelligent, active cause.

א Being, spirit, man or God; the comprehensible object; the unity who is mother of the numbers, the first substance.

All its ideas are expressed hieroglyphically by the figure of the JUGGLER [or Magician].

His body and arms form the letter א; he carries around his head a nimbus in the form of a ∞, symbol of life and of the universal spirit; in front of him are swords, cups and pentacles, and he raises the miraculous wand towards heaven.

He has a youthful figure and curly hair, like Apollo or Mercury; he has the smile of confidence on his lips and the look of intelligence in his eyes.

# I

# LE BATELEUR – THE JUGGLER / MAGICIAN

Listen to the words of Solomon which he spoke to his son Rehoboam:

> "The fear of God is the beginning of wisdom, but the end of wisdom is the knowledge and love of Him who is the Source of all good, and the supreme Reason, whence all things do proceed."

Adonai had passed an eternity in heaven, and then created Man; so a time on earth is given to man to comprehend Adonai. In other words, the knowledge which man attains concerning the Supreme Being springs from the faculties which have been bestowed upon him at his creation, in order that he might in his turn formulate an image of the Being who has sent him into this world.

By Understanding man conceives of the ideal of God, and by Willpower he should turn to good works. But human will without works is dead, or at any rate is only a vague wish: the same is true of a thought not expressed in language; it is not a word, but only a dream of the understanding. An imagination is not a realised thing, it is only a promised something, while an act is a reality. For the same reason there is no piety without prayer, and no religion without worship.

Words are the formal and social reality of ideals, and ceremonies are religion put into practice; there is no real faith unless it shows itself by actions prompted through faith. A formulated expression in words, confirmed by actions, demonstrates the two powers of a human soul. To work it is necessary to will, and to will it is necessary to formulate the wish. Actions imply ideas even if the ideas are not themselves translated into acts.

Thought is the life of understanding, words show the creative force of thought, while actions are the last effort of words, and the desirable complement of words. Words have been spoken, thought has been translated into action; by the act of creating, speech has taken place.

A word is the requisite formula of a thought, an act is an exhibition of will. This is why prayer is a necessity, and may obtain all that it asks for. A prayer is a perfected act of the will, it is a link connecting human words with the divine Will.

All ceremonies consecrations, ablutions, and sacrifices are prayers in action, and are symbolic formulas; and they are the most potent prayers because they are translations of word into action, showing the power of will and persistence, seeing that they require more constrained attention than silent prayer, or prayer expressed in words; and so they constitute real work, and such work demands a man's whole energy.

# 2

## THE LETTER BETH

### THE GREAT PRIESTESS

[the air; runic; Estranghelo[16]; arab; syriac; latin]

The binary is the first number,
it is the unity multiplied by itself.

---

[16] This refers to Estrangela, the oldest Syriac script, but the associated character is the 1st letter ("Olaph"), not the second.

# 2 ב B

## THE COLUMNS OF THE TEMPLE.

**CHOCMAH.** – (Hebrew: חכמה), also spelled Chockmah, Chokhmah, Hokhmah, Hockmah, etc., is Wisdom. It is the second sephiroth [2] of the Kabalistic tree of life.

**DOMUS.** – A Latin word which means house, home, residence.

**GNOSIS.** – (Greek: γνῶσις) meaning knowledge, although it is often used to refer to spiritual knowledge or insight.

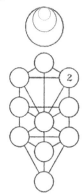

## MAGICAL EQUILIBRIUM.

ב *Beth*. — He is above all griefs and all fears.

2 ב The number serves to prove the living unity.

ב The house of God and of man, the sanctuary, the law, gnosis, kabalah, the occult church, the binary, the wife/woman, the mother.

Hieroglyph of the tarot: THE FEMALE POPE: a woman crowned with a tiara, wearing the horns of the moon or of Isis with her head enveloped in a veil, the solar cross [ ☿ ] upon her bossom, and holding a book on her knees which she conceals with her mantle.

## II

## LA PAPESSE – THE POPESS / PRIESTESS

Depth is equal to height, darkness is contrasted with light, matter is but the garment of the spirit. That which is below is like that which is above. The breath of God is born along over the waters, and the waters remain aloft carried on by the breath of God.

That which we call the Breath of God is the Life Essence spread over the worlds; it is that warm luminous fluid which gives a soul to the planets; the common reservoir of progressive animal life; the universal basis of the sympathies between bodies, and the medium of love between souls; it is the vehicle of the will, and the common basis for all the varied modifications of the Creative Word.

The Breath of the mouth of God leads to the corresponding human breath. God said, "Let us make man," and man answers, "Let us make ourselves into God." When God made creation manifest as a temple, He illumined the planets as light-bearers, He decorated the earth with flowers as an altar, He gave mysterious properties to metals and plants, and He drew with His finger circles, triangles, and the cross, as eternal pantacles, traced in living fire upon the immense vault of the skies. The Magus should imitate his God upon this earth, his dwelling.

Know, Will, and Act; these are the three essentials for sacerdotal and royal high magic. Matter and form are instruments placed in the power of the Magus, his acts should be dependent on the Word, and so shall none of his deeds be lost, and his teachings shall be preserved.

You then who wish to understand the mysteries of this Science and to perform marvels, consider and tremble lest you have as yet failed to attain to knowledge and wisdom; for if so, you stand on the brink of an abyss; stop, before it is too late.

But if you have secured the Lamp and Wand of Initiation, if you are cognisant of the secrets of the Nine, if you never speak of God without the Light which proceeds from Him, if you have received the mystical baptism of the Four Elements, if you have prayed upon the Seven Mountains, if you know the mode of movement of the Double Sphynxed Chariot, if you have grasped the dogma of why Osiris was a black god, if you are free, if you are a king, if you are in truth a priest in the temple of Solomon—act without fear, and speak, for your words will be all-powerful in the spiritual kingdom, and the breath of God will follow the utterances of your mouth, and the powers of the heavens and of the earth will be obedient unto you.

# 3

## THE LETTER GIMEL

THE TERNARY — THE FECONDATED MOTHER — GENERATION

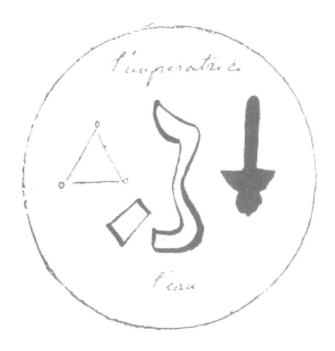

[the empress; the water]

The first great sacred number.

The triangle of Jehovah.

The Mercury of the sages.

# 3 ג C

## THE TRIANGLE OF SOLOMON.

**PLENITUDO VOCIS.** – Latin meaning Perfection of Speech/Voice. It comes from Vox or Vocis meaning voice; word/power, right, authority and Plenitudo meaning fullness, abundance, plentitude; thickness.

**BINAH.** – (Hebrew: בינה) is Understanding. It is the third sephiroth [3] of the Kabalistic tree of life.

**PHYSIS.** – (Greek: φύσις) meaning origin, birth; nature, quality, property, temperment; form, shape; type, kind; creature.

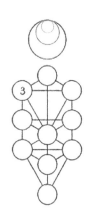

## THE TRIANGE OF THE PENTACLES.

ג *Ghimel*. – He reigns with all of heaven and is served by all of hell.

3 ג Nothing can limit the one who contains everything.

ג The verb, the ternary, plenitude, fecundity, nature, generation in the three worlds..

Symbol, THE EMPRESS: a winged woman, crowned, seated and hold a sceptre with the globe of the world at its end; she has as her sign an eagle, image of the soul and of life.

This woman is the Venus-Urania of the Greeks and has been represented by Saint John, in his *Revelations*, as the woman clothed with the sun, crowned with twelve stars and having the moon beneath her feet.

This is the mystical quintessence of the ternary; it is spirituality, it is immortality, it is the queen of heaven.

## III

## L'IMPERATRICE — THE EMPRESS

You should, before all other things, study and understand the sacred laws of Nature. Discern the Father Spirit and Mother Spirit, and recognise the sex aspect of the two breaths, and the soul of their movements; learn how the black female seeks the caresses of the white male, and why the white male does not disdain the dark woman. The white man is Day, or the Sun; and the black woman refers to Night, and the Moon.

It is necessary to know the names and powers of the twelve precious jewels which are included in the crown of gold referring to the Sun, and the names also which are allotted to the chief of the powers of the Moon. You will then be required to be familiar with the keys of the Fifty Gates, the secret of the Thirty-two Paths, and the characters of the Seven Spirits.

These Seven Spirits are:
1. Michael of the Sun,
2. Gabriel of the Moon,
3. Samael of Mars,
4. Raphael of Mercury,
5. Zachariel of Jupiter,
6. Anael of Venus, and
7. Orifiel of Saturn.

These govern the world in successive order, and the completion of their seven ages of ruling power constitutes a Week of the Time of God.

You must learn also the plants, colors, perfumes, and musical notes which correspond to the seven planetary powers; and it is essential to retain those correspondences with the utmost exactitude. Thus when it is required to do perfect magical work, the procedure of each day is different in many particulars.

On Sunday you must wear a purple robe, a tiara, and golden bracelets; you must arrange about the altar or tripod, garlands of laurel, heliotrope, or sunflower; you must use as a fumigating incense cinnamon, frankincense, saffron, and red sandalwood; you require in your right hand a golden wand set with a ruby or a chrysolite; and your operations must be carried out between one hour past midnight up to eight in the morning, or between three in the afternoon and ten in the evening.

On Monday you should wear a white robe with silver ornaments, with a collar of three rows consisting of pearls, crystals, and selenites; a tiara yellow with the letters of Gabriel in silver. The proper perfumes are those of camphor, white sandalwood, amber, and cucumber seeds; the garlands for the altar should be of armoise (query, mugwort, artemisia), evening primrose, and yellow ranunculus. Avoid with care anything of black color; use no cup or vessel of gold, silver only, or clear white china or pottery. The same hours as before mentioned for the Sun, but use rather the night hours.

On Tuesday the color of the robe should be fiery, or rusty, or of blood colour, with a girdle and bracelets of steel; the wand should be of magnetised steel; a sword may also be used and a consecrated dagger; garlands of absinth and rue; an amethyst and steel ring on the finger should also be worn.

On Wednesday the robe should be green or of shot silk many tinted; the necklace of pearls, or of glass beads containing mercury; the perfumes are benzoin, myrrh, and storax; the flowers for the garlands are the narcissus, lily, the annual or perennial mercurialis, fumitory, or marjoram; the precious stone is the agate.

On Thursday the robe of scarlet, a lamen of tin upon the forehead, bearing the symbol of Jupiter and the three words Giazar of Fire, Bethor of Water, and Samgabiel, also fiery; the perfumes for incense, ambergris, cardamon, grains of paradise, balm, mace, and saffron. The ring should contain an emerald or a sapphire; the garlands of oak, poplar, fig-tree, or pomegranate; the wand of glass or resin. The robe should be made of wool or silk.

On Friday the robe of azure blue, its decorations of green or rose color, the wand of polished copper; the perfumes are musk, civet, and amber; crown of violets; garlands of roses interspersed with boughs of myrtle and olive; the ring ornamented by a turquoise. Lapis lazuli and beryl should decorate the crown or diadem. The operator should hold a fan formed of swan's feathers, and should wear around his loins a circlet, being a copper plate on which is engraved Anael, with its sigil, and on a circle surrounding these the words Ave Evah; Vade Lilith.

On Saturday the robe should be black, or dark brown, with appropriate designs embroidered in orange-colored silk. Around the neck should be worn a chain and lamen formed of lead engraved with the name Saturn and his sigil, with the addition of the words Almalec, Aphiel, and Zarahiel. The proper perfumes for the incense are scammony, aloes, sulphur, and asafoetida. The wand should be ornamented with an onyx stone, and the proper garlands are of ash, Cyprus, and black hellebore. Upon the onyx on the wand there should be engraved with a confederated tool, during the hours of Saturn, a figure of the double-faced Janus.

3 - Gimel

# THE LETTER DALET

THE QUATRINARY — THE QUADRATURE

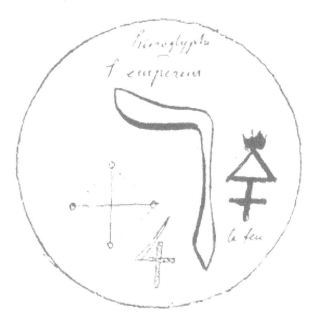

[hieroglyph; the emperor; the fire]

The number of the perfect cycle.

The philosophical cross.

The elemental fire of the sages.

# 4 ד D

## THE TETRAGRAM.

**GEDULAH** – (Hebrew: גדולה), is Greatness or Majesty. It is also sometimes translated as grandeur, grandness; magnitude. It is an alternate name for the fourth [4] sephiroth of the Kabalistic tree of life.

**CHESED.** – (Hebrew: חסד), also spelled Hesed, is Kindness. It is also sometimes translated as loving-kindness or love. It is the fourth sephiroth [4] of the Kabalistic tree of life.

**PORTA LIBRORUM.** – Latin meaning 'Door of [all] Books[17]'. It comes from Porta meaning gate, entrance, door and Libororum meaning books.

**ELEMENTA.** – A Latin word meaning elements (refering to the 4 elements); basic prinicples; the alphabet.

## THE CONJURATION OF THE FOUR.

ד *Daleth.* – He make use of his own health and life and can equally make use of others'.

4 ד Alone, before everything was, he is present everywhere.

ד The door or government of the Easterners, initiation, power, the tetragram, the quaternary, the cubic stone or its foundation.

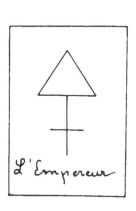

Hieroglyph, THE EMPEROR, a sovereign whose body represents a right-triangle and his legs a cross, being an image of the Athanor[18] of the philosophers.

---

[17] Doubleday/Wilder say that 'Porta Librorum' means "Gate of the Free" which is because they are taking the word 'librorum' as the plural of 'liber' meaning "free", but it can also mean "child; Bacuus (the god) or wine; book, letter or any sort of text". But it is more likely that "Gate of the Free" would have been 'Porta Libererum/Librerum'

[18] Literally 'athanor' means "athanor, a digester furnace with a self-feeding fuel supply contained in a towerlike contrivance, ensuring a constant, durable temperature."

# IV

# L'EMPEREUR — THE EMPEROR

The clothing of a Magician should be new, clean, and woven by a virgin; magical implements should be new, and consecrated by prayers and incense.

The Magician needs to be abstinent, chaste, and devoted to the Work. His spirit and heart must be free from other claims upon them, and his willpower devoted wholly, perseveringly, and with intelligent faith to the success of any great work, and to the results of his scientific occult performances.

Magical operations should commence with Exorcisms of air, earth, and water, and end by Consecrations with fire.

The Exorcism of Air is performed by breathing forth toward the four cardinal points, by the Word, and by repeating this invocation :—

> "The Spirit of God brooded over the waters, and God breathed into Man the breath of life.
> "The Spirit of God filled the universe; in it all things exist, and in it is the Word of Power.
> "May the Word be in my spirit, and so may all things be subservient to me.
> "Be ye exorcised then, ye beings of Air, in the Name of Him whose breath first filled all things with the Holy Spirit. Amen."[19]

The Prayer of the Sylphs should then be recited.

> [Extract from Ch. 4 of *Ritual of High Magic*:
>
> PRAYER OF THE SYLPHS
>
> Spirit of Light, spirit of wisdom, whose breath gives and takes away the form of all things; you before whom the life of every being is a shadow that changes and a vapor that passes away; you who ascends upon the clouds and who walks upon the wings of the wind; you who breaths, and the limitless spaces are populated; you who aspires, and all that came forth from you returns to you: endless movement in the eternal stability, be eternally blessed.

---

[19] Editor's note: The Latin of this Exorcism is given in Ch. 4 of Ritual of High Magic as follows:

"Spiritus Dei ferebatur super aquas, et inspiravit in faciem hominis spiraculum vitoe.

Sit Michael dux meus, et Sabtabiel servus meus, in lute et per lucem.

Fiat verbum halitus meus; et imperabo spiritibus aeris hujus, et refrtenabo equos solis voluntate cordis mei, et cogitatione mentis mea3 et nutu oculi dextri.

Exorciso igitur te, creatura aeris, per Pentagrammaton et in nomine Tetragrammaton, in quibus surit voluntas firma et fides recta.

Amen. Sela, Fiat. So be it."

We praise you, we bless you in the transforming empire of created light, of shadows, of reflections and of images; and we aspire without ceasing to your immutable and imperishable clairity.

Let the ray of your understanding and the heat of your love penetrate into us: so that which is moving can be fixed, so that the shadow will become a body, the spirit of the air will be a soul, and the dream will be a thought.

And we will no long be swept away by the storm, but we will hold the bridle of the winged horses of the morning and direct the course of the evening winds, in order to fly before you.

Oh spirit of spirits, oh eternal soul of souls, oh imperishable breath of life, oh creative sigh, oh mouth that aspires and that breathes the existence of all all beings in the ebb and flow of your eternal speech, which is the divine ocean of movement and of truth.

*Amen.* ]

The Exorcism of Earth is performed by the sprinkling of consecrated water, by the breath, by the Word, and by the burning of incense suitable to the day of the ceremony. Then recite the Prayer of the Gnomes.

[Extract from Ch. 4 of *Ritual of High Magic*:

PRAYER OF THE GNOMES

Invisible king, who has taken the earth as his support and who has dug the abysses in order to fill them with your omnipotence; you whose name makes the vaults of the world tremble, you who makes the seven metals flow through the veins of the stone, monarch of the seven lights, rewarder of the subterranean workmen, bring us the desirable air and to the kingdom of clarity.

We watch and we work without stopping, we seek and we hope, by the twelve stones of the holy city, by the talismans which are buried, by the pole of loadstone which passes through the center of the world.

Lord, Lord, Lord, have pity on those who suffer, enlarge our hearts, detach and elevate our minds, enlarge us.

Oh stability and movement, oh day eveloped in night, oh obscurity veiled by light! oh master who is never held back before labourers! oh silver whiteness, oh golden splendour! oh crown of living and melodious diamonds! you who wears heaven on your finger like a sapphire ring, you who hide under earth the marvellous seed of stars in the stoney kingdom, live, reign and be the eternal dispenser of the riches that you have made us the gardians of!

Amen. ]

The Exorcism of Water is performed by the laying on of hands, by the breath, by the Word, and by sprinkling upon it consecrated salt mixed with a little of the ash taken from the censer, and duly consecrated.

The Water is to be sprinkled around by a brush composed of sprays of vervain, periwinkle, sage, mint, valerian, and basil; these are to be tied with a thread taken from a virgin's distaff, to a handle of the wood of a nut-tree which has not yet borne fruit. Upon this handle you must engrave, with the magical dagger, the characters of the Seven Spirits.

The Salt is consecrated by reciting over it the following Latin prayer :—

"In isto Sale sit sapientia, et ab omni corruptione servet mentes nostras et corpora nostra, per Chokmah, et in virtute Ruach Chokmael; recedant ab isto phantasmata hylae ut sit Sal celestis, Sal terrae et Terra salis, ut nutrietur bos triturans, et addat spei nostrse cornua tauri volantis. Amen."

Then this Latin prayer over the ashes from the censer:—

"Revertatur cinis ad fontem aquarum viveritium, et fiat terra fructificans et germinat arborem jucunditatis, et incensum suavitatis, per tria nomina Binah, Chokmah et Kether, in principio et in fine, per Alpha et Omega, qui sunt in Spiritu Azoth. Amen."

While you sprinkle the mixed salt and ashes into the water, recite :—

"Emittes Spiritum O Tiphereth, et creabuntur omnia nova in his ergo sit semen venturi saeculi. Amen."

## EXORCISM OF WATER.

"All powerful Father, God of Abraham, Isaac, and Jacob, whose voice is heard in the great waters, who didst cleave the waters of the Red Sea to make a passage for the children of Israel, and then didst cause the sea to swallow up the Egyptians who were pursuing them, Mi Kamoka Baalim Jehovah, thou whose altar, composed of the Twelve Jewels, is beneath the waters of the sacred river, deign to bless this water and to banish from it all baneful influences, Shaddai, Shaddai, Shaddai (breathe three times over the water).

By the great names, Araritha, Eloah va Daath, Elohim Tzabaoth and Elohim Gibur, may this water be consecrated for the service of those who are about to invoke the Divine Powers for the benefit of their souls. Amen."

Then the Prayer of the Undines should be recited.

[Extract from Ch. 4 of *Ritual of High Magic*:

## 4 - Dalet

### PRAYER OF THE UNDINES

Terrible king of the sea, you who holds the keys of the floodgates of heaven and encloses the waters of the underworld in the caverns of earth; king of the deluge and of the rains of spring; you who opens the sources of rivers and fountains; you who command the humidity, which is like the blood of earth, to become the sap of plants, we adore you and we invoke you.

We, your moving and changing creatures, speak unto us in the great commotions of the sea, and we will tremble before you; speak to us also in the murmur of the pristine waters, and will desire your love!

Oh immensity into which flow all rivers of being, that are continually reborn in you!

Oh ocean of infinite perfections! height which reflects you in the depth; depth, which exhales you in the height, bring us to true life through understanding and love!

Bring us to immortality through sacrifice, so that we are found worthy to one day to offer you the water, the blood and the tears, for the remission of errors!

Amen. ]

To perform the Exorcism of Fire, cast upon it salt, incense, and sulphur, while you pronounce the names of Anael, Michael, and Samael; the prayer of the Salamanders should then be recited.

[Extract from Ch. 4 of *Ritual of High Magic*:

### PRAYER OF THE SALAMANDERS

Immortal, eternal, ineffable and uncreated, father of all things, who is carried upon the ever-rolling chariot of worlds which are always revolving; dominator of ethereal immensities, where the throne of your power is exalted, from which height your terrible eyes discover all, and your beautiful and holy ears hear all, give to your children, whom you have loved since the birth of the centuries; for your golden and great and eternal majesty shines above the world and the heaven of stars; you are exalted over them, oh sparling fire; there, you spark and commune with yourself through your own splendor, and inexhaustible streams of light pour from your essence which the nourishment your infinite spirit.

This infinite spirit nourishes all things, and makes that inexhaustible treasure of substance ever ready for the generation which appropriates forms which you have impregnated from the beginning.

The three holy kings who surround your throne, and who compose your court, derive also their origin from this spirit, oh universal father! oh unique one! oh father of blessed mortals and immortals.

In particular you have created powers which are marvellously like your eternal thought and your adorable essence; you have established them higher than the angels, who announce your will to the world; finally, you have created us at the third rank within our elementary empire.

There, our continuous exercise is to praise you and adore your wishes; there we burn without end in aspiring to possess you.

Oh father! oh mother, most tender of all mothers! oh admirable archetype of maternity and of pure love! oh son, flower of sons! oh form of all forms, soul, spirit, harmony and number of all things!

Amen!]

You must thoroughly understand that elemental beings are souls of an imperfect type, not yet raised in the scale up to human existence, and that they can only manifest power when called into action by the adept as auxiliaries to his will, by means of that universal astral fluid in which they live.

The kingdom of the Gnomes is assigned to the North, the Salamanders to the South, the Sylphs to the East, and the Undines to the West.

These Elemental beings are related to, and bear an influence over persons, accordingly as they are of one or other of the four Temperaments. The Gnomes are related to the Melancholic type, Salamanders to the Sanguine, Undines to the Phlegmatic, and Sylphs to the Bilious Temperament.

Their symbols are those of Taurus, the Bull, for Gnomes; Leo, the Lion, for Salamanders; the Eagle for Sylphs; and the sign of Aquarius for Undines.

Their Rulers are respectively Ghob, Djin, Paralda, and Nicsa.

The combination of these four types of face and being represents the Created Universe, a complete and eternal entity, Man in fact, the Microcosm; and this is the first formula of the mystical explanation of the enigma of the Sphynx.

# 5

## THE LETTER HEH

### THE NUMBER FIVE OF THE LETTERS AND FIFTEEN OF THE PATHS

[hieroglyph; the great hierophant;
the quintessence]

The number of the science
of good and evil.

The letter of womankind [the wife]
and of religion.

The angelic or diabolic pentagram.

# 5 ה E

## THE PENTAGRAM.

**GEBURAH.** – (Hebrew: גבורה), also spelled Gevurah, Gebrah, etc., is Severity. It is the fifth sephiroth [5] of the Kabalistic tree of life.

**ECCE.** – a Latin word meaning Lo!, Behold!, See!.

## THE BLAZING PENTAGRAM.

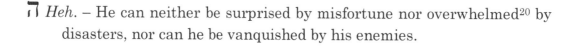

ה *Heh*. – He can neither be surprised by misfortune nor overwhelmed[20] by disasters, nor can he be vanquished by his enemies.

5 ה Because he is the only master, he is the only one worshipped.

ה Indication, demonstration, teaching, law, symbolism, philosophy, religion.

Hieroglyph, THE POPE or great hierophant. In the more modern Tarots, this sign is replaced by the image of Jupiter.

The great hierophant, seated between the two columns of Hermes and of Solomon, makes the sign of esotericism and leans upon a cross with three crossbars of a triangular form.

In front of him, two inferior ministers kneel, in such as way that above him the two heads of the ministers are the tops of the two columns, he is thus the center of the quinary and represents the divine pentagram and he gives its complete meaning. As a fact, the columns are necessity or law; and the heads are liberty or action.

A line may be drawn from each Pillar to each head and two lines from each Pillar to each of the two heads. We obtain then a square cut into four triangles by a cross is, and in the middle of this cross will be the great hierophant, we might say that like the garden spider in the center of his web, if this image image could acknowledge things of truth, of glory and of light.

---

[20] Literally 'accablé' means "overwhelm or overcome (as with force or emotion); overpower; oppress, overburden; condemn"

# V

# LE PAPE — THE POPE / HIEROPHANT

To control the Willpower and make it subservient to the law of Understanding—this is the Great Work of our sacerdotal art.

Ceremonies are made use of in order to educate the Will by means of the Imagination. Ceremonies which are performed without understanding and without faith, in the absence of the higher aspirations of the soul, are but superstitious observances which tend to the degeneration of those who take part in them.

It is an error to attribute Magical Power to ceremonies, for Magical Power exists only in the trained Will of the operator. For this reason the Magical Axiom is true, that the Sanctum Regnum—the Divine Kingdom—the Kingdom of God—is *within* us.

I.N.R.I., Intra Nobis Regnum deI; and hence also is it that great marvels can be shown by the PENTAGRAM, which is the seal of the Microcosm; for the Microcosm is the reflection of the Macrocosm; the Microcosm is Man and his human Will; he is the reflection of the Universe, which is the Macrocosm.

The Man whose Understanding has received culture can by his Willpower, exerted through the Pentagram, control and command the powers and beings of the Elements, and restrain evil elementaries from their perverse works.

The HEXAGRAM is the symbol of the Macrocosm ; it is often called the Seal of Solomon. It consists of two interlaced triangles; the erect triangle is of blazing color, the inverse triangle is colored blue. In the center space there may be drawn a Tau Cross and three Hebrew Yods, or a Crux ansata, or the Triple Tau of the Arch-masons.

He who, with Understanding and Will, is armed with this emblem has need of no other thing, he should be all potent, for this is the perfect sign of the Absolute.

This is the Monogram of Hermetic Truth; it expresses the subject of the Great Work. It is made up of Hebrew, Greek, and Latin letters, and the mode of expressing this ideal in the presence of the uninitiated is through the word Azoth, or by the name Magnes: other Magi have applied to it the titles of the flying dragon of Medea, and the serpent of the mystical Eden.

This is the high and incommunicable Tetragram traced in a Kabalistic and Hermetic design. All initiates, even of the first grade, will at once understand its symbolism.

# 5 - Heh

This emblem is the monogram of the Universal Gnosis; it is formed of Greek and Latin letters; it expresses through symbols the secrets of the Wheel of Ezekiel, and the Book of Saint John the Evangelist; it includes the sign of the Labarum of Constantine.

This emblem naturally shows the word ROTA; but viewed in the light of the Kalabah, the word TAROT.

These Characters, with the Philosophic Cross, include all science *in esse*, and those who are initiates of the Great Arcanum need no further symbols or emblems; nor do those adepts who know the true but concealed meanings and powers of the words JAKIN and BOAZ, which are related to the two Pillars at the Porch of the Temple, one of which was of white marble, and the other of black, while both were decorated with Brazen ornaments.

By these Characters the spirits of evil nature are bound and held in control; by these also, if the operator be just and pure, he makes himself known to angels and may incline them to his aims. For indeed nothing can resist, in the magical arts, the combined powers of the divine Pentagram, Hexagram, and Tetragram.

All other signs, seals, and symbols are but arbitrary, and the keys of their meaning may be found in the Steganographia, or the Polygraphia of the Abbot Trithemius of Spanheim, or else in the magical treatises of Peter of Abano, of Paracelsus, of Arbatel, or of Cornelius Agrippa.

# 6

## THE LETTER VAU

### THE ARROW OF LOVE — THE LINGHAM

[hieroglyph; The lovers]

The number of antagonism
and of liberty.

Coupling.

The work.

The week of creation.

# 6 ו F

## MAGICAL EQUILIBRIUM.

**TIPHERET.** – (Hebrew: תפארת), also spelled Tiferet, Tifaret, Tifereth, Tyfereth, Tyfereth, etc., is Adornment or Beauty. It is the sixth sephiroth [6] of the Kabalistic tree of life.

**UNCUS.** – A Latin word meaning hook or barb; a hook used to drag criminals by the neck; a surgical instrument.

## THE MEDIUM AND THE MEDIATOR.

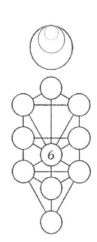

ו *Vau.* – He knows the reason of the past, present and future.

6 ו He reveals his true dogma to the pure hearts.

ו  Enchantment, interlacement, lingam, entanglement, union, embrace, struggle, antagonism, combination, equilibrium.

Hieroglyph, man between Vice and Virtue. Above him is the ray of the sun of truth, and in this sun is Love, bending his bow and threatening Vice with his shaft.

In the order of the ten sephiroth, this symbol corresponds to TIPHERETH, that is to say to idealism and beauty.

The number six represents the antagonism of the two ternaries, that is to say of absolute negation and absolute affirmation.

It is therefore the number of labor and liberty; this is why it also corresponds with moral beauty and with glory.

# VI

## L'AMOUREUX — THE LOVERS

Always keep in mind that Equilibrium results only from the opposition of forces; the active has no existence without the passive; light without darkness produces no form; and affirmation can only triumph over negation. Love again gains accession of strength from hate, and hell is the heated soil of such plants as shall bear root in heaven.

It should be known also that the great Fluidic Agent which is called the "Soul of the World," and which is delineated with the horned head of the Cow of Isis to express animal fecundity, is a blind force.

The power which the Magus wields is composed of two opposing forces, which unite in love and disjoin in discord; love associates contraries, while hate makes similars to be rivals and enemies; hatred succeeds love when the void has become filled by saturation, unless the full cannot become empty; but the usual result is an equilibrated saturation, due to mutual repulsions.

From these considerations the existence and causes of sympathy and antipathy between persons can be deduced, and so the means of becoming loved can be shown to those who are good as well as wise and discreet.

Sexual love is a physical manifestation; repugnance and pain may be forgotten by those who are under its sway. This is a form of inebriation arising from the attraction of two contrary fluids; and at the conjunction of the positive and negative poles there results an ecstasy and orgasm during which the loved one seems the brilliant phantom of a vision. When the conjunction has set up the state of equilibrium anew, attraction is succeeded by repulsion ; and very often an exaggerated love leads to an unjust share of disgust.

All created beings participate either in the positive or negative attitude of the universal sympathetic fluid, and may help to maintain or re-establish a Sympathy; but it is necessary to distrust knowledge while it is imperfect, and not to expose oneself in suggesting remedies to the risk of administering poisons.

Enchantment by means of any object which has belonged to a beloved one is often a magnetic operation leading to useless and yet dangerous results; it is better to establish new currents of force, to produce a void where satiety exists, for the surest means of regaining the affection of man or woman is to bestow some signs of love on another.

Consider the bodily and mental disorders which result from solitude and its accompanying fluidic congestions, due to want of equilibrium;—such are nervous maladies, hysteria, hypochondriasis, megrim, vapours, and insane delusions. It will be possible also to understand the ailments of maidens, and of women of an uncertain age, of widows and of celibates.

Inspired by the natural law now under consideration, you may often predict the future course of a life, and may cure many such ailments, often by distracting the attention when unduly fixed, and so may the Magus become as great a physician as Paracelsus, or as renowned a Diviner as was Cornelius Agrippa.

You will come to understand the diseases of the soul; the fact that learned and chaste persons often hunger after the pleasures of vice will be noticed, and so will it be observed that men and women steeped in vices turn at times to the consolations of virtue; and thus you may predict, without striking a blow, the occurrence of strange conversions and of unexpected sins, and great astonishment will be shown at your facility in discerning the most carefully concealed secrets of the heart and home.

By such means of divination girls and women may be shown in dreams the forms of lover and husband; such confidantes are potent auxiliaries in magic arts; never abuse their position, never neglect their interests, for they are good gifts to the Magus.

In order to possess an assured sway over the heads and hearts of women, it is essential to obtain the favor of both Gabriel the Angel of the Moon, and of Anael the Angel of Venus.

Certain evil female demons must be overcome and cast down; foremost of these are :—

Nahemah, princess of the Succubi of the dreams of men.

Lilith, queen of the Stryges, tempting to debauchery, and destroyer of maternal desire.

Nahemah presides also over illicit and sterile caresses.

Lilith rejoices in strangling in their cradles children whose origin has been soiled by the touch of Nahemah.

The truly wise master of the Kabalah understands the concealed meaning of these names, and of such evil demoniac powers, which are also called the material envelopes or cortices, or shells of the Tree of Life, soiled and blackened by the outer darkness; they are as branches which are dead, having been torn off from the Tree, whence issue light, life, and love.

6 - Vau

## THE LETTER ZAIN

### The Sacred Septenary

[the victor]

The complete number of the Kabalah.

Spirit and form.

The three powers of the ternary
and their four relations.

# 7 ז G

## THE FLAMING SWORD.

**NETZACH.** – (Hebrew: נצח) is Eternity or Victory. It is the seventh sephiroth [7] of the Kabalistic tree of life.

**GLADIUS.** – A Latin word meaning sword.

## THE SEPTENARY OF TALISMANS.

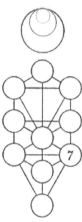

ז *Zain*. – He possesses the secret of the resurrection of the dead and the key of immortality.

7 ז But there must be a single chief for the works of faith,

ז Weapon, sword, flaming sword of the cherub, the sacred septenary, triumph, royalty, priesthood.

Hieroglyph, a cubic chariot, with four columns, with an azure and starry drapery.

In the chariot, between the four columns, is a victor crowned with a circle upon which three golden pentagrams stand and shine.

Upon his breast plate are three superimposed squares; he has on his shoulders the urim and thummim[21] of the sovereign sacrificer, represented by the two crescents of the moon in Gedulah [or Chesed] and Geburah; he holds in his hand a sceptre surmounted by a globe, with a square and a triangle; his attitude is proud and tranquil.

A double sphinx or two sphinxes connected below the waist are harnessed to the chariot; they are pulling the chariot one to one side, the other to the other side; but one of the two turns his head, and they are looking to the same side.

---

[21] Urim and Thummim (האורים והתומים) is a phrase associated with the High Priest's breastplate mentioned in Exodus 28:30. It has traditionally been translated as *lights and perfections*, or, metaphorically, as *revelation and truth*, or *doctrine and truth*.

The sphinx which turns its head is black, and the other is white.

On the square which forms the front of the chariot, one sees the indian lingam surmounted by the flying sphere of the Egyptians.

This hieroglyph, which we give here the exact figure, is perhaps the most beautiful and the most complete of all those that make up in the clavicle of the Tarot.

LE CHARIOT D'HERMÈS

## VII

## LE CHARIOT — THE CHARIOT OF HERMES

The Chariot of Hermes has a white and also a black Sphynx attached to its car; each of these symbolic animals propounds an enigma to the neophyte. The word of the White Sphynx is Jachin. The word of the Black Sphynx is Boaz. The former word here signifies Love; the latter word here signifies Power.

Samael guides the White Sphynx, Anael guides the Black Sphynx; because attraction is set up by contraries. Hermes, seated in the Chariot, touches the Black Sphynx with the point of a sword of steel, but the White Sphynx with a sceptre of gold.

It is after the type founded by the Thrice Great Hermes that the Magus learns how to use the Magical Wand and the Sword in order to control good and evil powers and beings.

Evil beings fear the sword because their astral forms are subject to wounds and to being severed by such a weapon.

White spirits obey the consecrated magical wand because of its correspondence to the type of the Wand of the God-sent magician Moses.

### FORMATION AND CONSECRATION OF A MAGICAL SWORD.

The sword-blade of steel should be forged in the hour of Mars, and new smith's tools should be used.

The pommel should be of silver, made hollow, and containing a little quicksilver; the symbols of Mercury and the Moon, with the monograms of Gabriel and Samael, should be engraved upon its surface.

The hilt should be encased with tin, and should have the symbol of Jupiter and the monogram of Michael engraved upon it; see Cornelius Agrippa, *De occulta Philosoiphia*, liber iii., cap. 30.

There should be a small triangular copper plate extending from the hilt up the blade of the sword a short distance on each side; on these should be engraved the symbols of Venus and Mercury.

The guard should end in two curved plates on each side; on these, the words Gedulah, Netzach upon one side, and Geburah, Hod upon the other, should be engraved; and in the middle between them engrave the Sephirotic name, Tiphereth.

Upon the blade itself engrave upon one side Malkuth, and upon the other side the words *Quis ut Deus*.

The Consecration of the Magical Sword must be performed on a Sunday during the Solar hour and under the invoked power of Michael.

Drape the Altar, prepare the Tripod, and burn therein the wood of laurel and cypress, consecrate the fire, and then thrust the blade of the sword into it, saying, "Elohim Tzabaoth, by the power of the Tetragrammaton, in the name of Adonai and of Mikael, may this sword become a weapon of might to scatter the beings of the unseen world, may its use in war bring peace, may it be brilliant as Tiphereth, terrible as Geburah, and merciful as Chesed."

Withdraw the sword from the fire, and quench it in a liquid composed of the blood of a reptile mixed with the sap to be obtained from a green laurel: then polish the blade with the ashes of vervain carefully burned.

### FORMATION AND CONSECRATION OF THE MAGIC WAND.

Choose the wood of an almond or nut tree which has just flowered for the first time; the bough should be cut off at one blow by the magical sickle. It must be bored evenly from end to end without any crack or injury, and a magnetised steel needle of the same length must be introduced.

One end must be closed by a clear transparent glass bead, and the other end by a similar bead of resin : cover up these two ends with sachets of silk. Fit two rings near the middle of the wand, one of copper and one of zinc, and supply two portions of fine chain of the same metals; roll them round the wand, and fix the ends into the wand close to the ends.

Upon the wand should then be written the names of the Twelve Spirits of the Zodiacal Cycle; their sigils should also be added.

| | |
|---|---|
| Aries | Sarahiel |
| Taurus | Araziel |
| Gemini | Saraiel |
| Cancer | Phakiel |
| Leo | Seratiel |
| Virgo | Schaltiel |
| Libra | Chadakiel |
| Scorpio | Sartziel |
| Sagittarius | Saritiel |
| Capricornus | Semaqiel |
| Aquarius | Tzakmaqiel |
| Pisces | Vacabiel |

Upon the Copper Ring engrave in Hebrew letters from right to left the words "The Holy Jerusalem," H QDShH JRUShLIM [ ה קדשה ירושלים ]; and upon the Zinc Ring engrave in Hebrew letters from right to left the words "The King Solomon," H MLK ShLMH, Heh Melek Shelomoh [ ה מלך שלמה ].

When the wand is complete, it must be consecrated through invocations of spirits of the Four Elements and the Seven Planets by ceremonies lasting over the seven days of a week, using the special incense and prayers as already described for each day.

The consecrated Wand, and indeed all magical implements, should be kept wrapped in silk, and never allowed in contact with any color but black; and it is well to keep them in a cedar or ebony box.

With this Wand duly made and fully consecrated, the Magus can cure unknown diseases, he may enchant a person, or cause him to fall asleep at will, can wield the forces of the elements and cause the oracles to speak.

# 8

## THE LETTER CHETH

### Universal Equilibrium

[hieroglyph; justice]

The tetragram with its reflection.

The double Stauros.

The quaternairy multiplied by the binary.

# 8 ח H

## REALIZATION.

**HOD.** – (Hebrew: הוד) is Majesty or Splendor. It is the eighth sephiroth [8] of the Kabalistic tree of life.

**VIVENS.** – A Latin word meaning living; being alive, surviving; residing in.

## ADVICE TO THE IMPRUDENT.

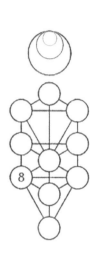

ח *Cheth.* – To find the philosophical stone.

8 ח  This is why we have but one altar, [and] but one law;

ח  Balance, attraction and repulsion, life, terror, promise and threat.

Hieroglyph, JUSTICE with its sword and its scale.

## VIII

## LA JUSTICE — JUSTICE

You must never forget that the priest is a king, and the wise man is a judge. There are in this world both the weak and the strong, the poor and the rich, there are both the ignorant and the learned. The former are always the servitors of the latter; but if the former do their works worthily they thereby become worthy of admission to the concourse of masters, while the useless servants are to be cast away.

It is well, therefore, to teach men how to serve well, so that they may come forward into a place of power.

All things upon this world, and all below the surface, belong to the domain of man. Created beings roar, groan, hiss, coo, and weave around man as a center; man alone speaks to his fellows and to God; and the voice of God upon earth is spoken through man.

The science of life is written in the Book of Nature, but man alone can read it. The wise and powerful translate the words of this book into creeds and symbols for the instruction of the feeble and ignorant. When you speak to such as are like children, speak as to children. Do not sell the secrets of wisdom, and do not divulge them in order to pander to curiosity.

A man should form his opinions in freedom, and thus he may resemble the ideal of divinity.

Cast not the pearls of mystic science before those of low and evil mind who have no knowledge, those whom the Testament calls swine. To such persons, whether you speak the truth, or veil the truth, there is but misunderstanding; deception haunts them, they estimate all things by a faulty conscience. You may dazzle them by the glancing of the sword, but do not let them approach the wand or clavicule.

If you wish to have no need to fear an evil person, make him fear you. Remember the conduct of Moses before the Pharaoh. Do not put faith in the benevolence of a priest of idols, nor in the sincerity of a pretender to wisdom, for these men will hate you as a destroyer of their livelihood and domination.

Keep a steady watch against being placed in danger by accepting the caresses of a woman; remember how Samson was decoyed by Delilah. Do not be familiar with any woman when alone with her, or in the dark; remember Orpheus and Eurydice. Make yourself beloved of women, that they be made happier; but never love any woman so much that you cannot be happy without her.

As to the beings of the elements, the love which they have for a Magus immortalises them, whether Sylphs, Gnomes, Undines, or fiery Salamandrines, but the love of such beings by a Magus is insensate and may destroy him. Be ever intelligent and just to such elemental beings, and you will be rewarded with happiness because of your good actions.

# 9

## THE LETTER TETH

THE NUMBER OF THE HIERARCHY

[hieroglyph; Prudence or the sage]

Nine

The number of the initiate.

The great magic number.

# 9 ט I

## INITIATION.

**YESOD.** – (Hebrew: יסוד), also spelled Jesod and Iesod, is Foundation. It is the ninth sephiroth [9] of the Kabalistic tree of life.

**BONUM.** – A Latin word meaning good, honest, brave, noble, kind, pleasant; right; useful; valid; healthy.

## THE CEREMONY OF THE INITIATES.

ט *Teth*. – To have the universal medicine.

9 ט And never will the Eternal change the foundation.

ט The good, the horror of evil, morality, wisdom.

Hieroglyph, a sage leaning on his staff, and holding a lamp in front of himself; he is completely enveloped in his cloak.

Its inscription is THE HERMIT OR THE CAPUCHIN, because of the hood of his oriental cloak; but his true name is PRUDENCE, and he thus completes the four cardinal virtues[22], which seemed incomplete to Count de Gebelin and Etteilla.

---

[22] In the Old Testament the four cardinal virtues are listed in the Book of Wisdom (8:7) "Or if one loves justice the fruits of her works are virtues; For she teaches *moderation [or restraint / temperance]* and *prudence*, *justice* and *fortitude [or courage]*, and nothing in life is more useful for men than these."

# IX

## L'ERMITE — THE HERMIT

When the adept has provided himself with the Magical Sword and Wand, he yet needs a Magical Lamp whose beams will chase away all the phantoms of darkness.

Four metals should enter into its composition: gold, silver, brass, iron. The foot of iron, the knot of brass, the reservoir of silver, and a golden triangle above this, and erect in the middle; from each side springs an arm composed of three tubes of gold, silver, and brass, twisted together; there are nine wick burners, three on each side arm, and three above the triangle over the reservoir; upon the iron foot is engraved a Hermetic triangle, with the symbols of Mercury above, Sol and Luna below; around the rim of the semiglobular base is fixed a brazen serpent; and above the globular part, between it and the brazen knot, there should be an androgyne figure with male and female heads, whose arms are stretched over the globe.

Engrave diverse forms on the brass knot; and upon the silver cup must be placed the Hexagram with the letters of the Tetragrammaton in its center. Upon the golden triangle above engrave a God surrounded by rays, as a symbol of the fecundity of the infinite and eternal. On each side of the reservoir for oil, fix a ring, and hang chains to these rings— one of silver, one of iron; by these chains the lamp may be suspended, or carried by the magician. The wicks for the burners should be of new linen threads, but dyed, the three on the right blue, the three on the left red, and the three middle wicks gold coloured.

The Lamp should be lit from a consecrated fire, but the greatest effect arises when the Lamp burns without wicks and without oil; lighted only by the Lux of the Universal Fluidic Agent, or by one of the material elementals of Water.

The light of this Magical Lamp should work marvels, it should illuminate the consciences of men and women so that you may read them, and should enable you to recognise each type of spiritual being.

The magician should not attempt any serious ceremonial until he has grasped the Wand, and illumined the Lamp; just as in common life, if you want to walk safely in the dark, you must carry a candle and try the ground before you with a staff.

# 10

## THE LETTER YOD

THE NUMBER OF CREATION
AND OF THE KINGDOM

[hieroglyph; The wheel of fortune]

Malkuth.

The kingdom of God.

The visible universe.

The natural principle
of supernatural things.

# 10 י K

## THE KABBALAH.

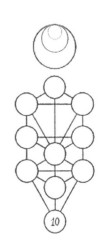

**MALKUTH.** – (Hebrew: תמלכו), also spelled Malchuth and Malkut, is Kingdom. It is the tenth sephiroth [10] of the Kabalistic tree of life.

**PRINCIPIUM.** – A Latin word meaning a beginning, an origin; a groundwork; the elements, the first principles; the front ranks, camp headquarters.

**PHALLUS.** – A Latin word meaning a penis, especially when erect; a representation of an erect penis symbolising fertility or potency.

## THE KEY OF OCCULTISM.

י *Yod.* – To know the laws of perpetual motion and to be able to demonstrate the quadrature of the circle.

10 י By heaven and by day he rules each phase.

י Principle, manifestation, praise, virile honor, phallus, virile fertility, paternal sceptre.

Hieroglyph, THE WHEEL OF FORTUNE, that is to say the cosmogonic wheel of Ezekiel, with a Hermanubis ascending on the right, a Typhon descending on the left, and a sphinx above, in equilibrium and holding a sword between his lion's claws.

An admirable symbol, disfigured by Etteilla, who replaced Typhon by a man, Hermanubis by a mouse, and the sphinx by an ape, a very crazy allegory of Etteilla's kabalah.

# X

## LA ROUE DE FORTUNE — THE WHEEL OF FORTUNE

The Wheel of Ezekiel is the type upon which all the Pantacles of the Higher Magic are designed.

When the adept is in the blessed possession of a full knowledge of the powers of the Seal of Solomon, and of the virtues of the Wheel of Ezekiel, which is indeed correspondent, in its entire symbolism, with that of Pythagoras, he has sufficient experience to design talismans and pantacles for any special magical purpose.

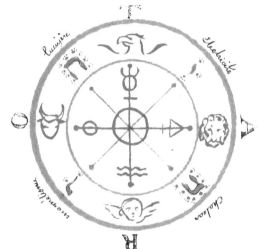

The Wheel of Ezekiel contains the solution of the problem of the quadrature of the circle, and demonstrates the correspondences between words and figures, letters and emblems; it exhibits the tetragram of characters analogous to that of the elements and elemental forms. It is a glyph of perpetual motion.

The triple ternary is shown; the central point is the first Unity; three circles are added, each with four attributions, and the dodekad is thus seen. The state of universal equilibrium is suggested by the counterpoised emblems, and the pairs of symbols. The flying Eagle balances the man; the roaring Lion counterpoises the laborious Bull.

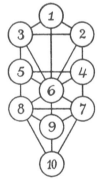

Kether [1], the Crown; Tiphereth [6], Beauty; and Yesod [9], Foundation, form a central axis; while Wisdom, Chokmah [2], equilibrates with Understanding, Binah [3]; and the Severity of Justice, Geburah [5], makes a counterpoise with the Mercy of Justice, Chesed [4]; similar conceptions are the contests between Eros and Anteros, between Jacob and the Angel, Samael and Anael, Mars and Venus.

The Philosophic Cross and the Greek monogram of Christos are comparable also to this magical wheel.

In order that a consecrated talisman shall give real help to you, it must be well understood, and the correspondences realized; for a pantacle is an ideal materialized, made visible, made portable, and may contain as much knowledge as a book. It is an image of some part of God and His works, it is as a card of the eternal kingdom.

Consider well the aim to be accomplished, and the powers to be invoked; select the symbols, emblems, and letters with the greatest care, seeking Chokmah and Binah from that spark of the Divine which overshadows you, and then trace, mark, or engrave your chosen design upon a plate of gold, silver, or of Corinth brass, or cut it on precious stones, or draw it upon virgin parchment.

When the work has been skilfully and accurately finished, then submit it to consecration with prayers and invocations of the Four and of the Seven, using suitable perfumes in the incense; after which wrap up the talisman in clean silk and place it in a cedar casket, and it will be effectual to carry it always about with you.

La dixième clé du Tarot.

## THE LETTER KAPH

THE NUMBER OF FORCE / STRENGTH

[hieroglyph; force/strength]

Synthetic unity.

Grown/made man.

Virility.

The age of reason.

# 11 כ L

## THE MAGIC CHAIN.

**MANUS.** – A Latin word meaning a hand; figuratively meaning bravery, valor, violence, fighting; labor; power, might.

**LA FORCE.** – French term meaning literally "the force", where force means strength, force, power; potency; manpower, might.

## THE TRIPLE CHAIN.

כף *Caph.* – To change not only all metals into gold but also the earth itself, and even the trash of the earth.

11 כ Rich in mercy and strong in order to punish,

כ The hand in the act of taking and holding.

Hieroglyph, STRENGTH, a woman crowned with the vital ∞ and who calmly, and without effort, closes the jaws of a furious lion.

## XI

## LA FORCE — FORCE / FORTITUDE / STRENGTH

Listen now to the secret of strength. A constant drip will wear away a stone and, in the end, will perforate it. The aim to which you constantly devote your willpower will, in the end, be attained; you begin to succeed as soon as you begin to will success.

Real willpower is not a privilege in the hands of the multitude. To exercise true willpower you must be free; no one of the multitude is free; to be free is to be the master of your life, and over others. To learn how to will is to learn how to exercise dominion. But to be able to exert willpower you must first know; for willpower applied to folly is lunacy, death, and hell.

To mistake the means for the end is an absurdity.

To mistake for the end that which is not even a means is the peak of absurdity.

You are the master of all the events you can overcome. Things for which you have an imperious need are masters over you.

Things you possess the right to desire, you have the power to obtain.

You must be ever watchful in the exercise of your will, and be heedful that you do not fall into a position of dependence from want of exertion, from simple idleness.

Men who are to contend together in a race must go through a long and severe training.

Magical ceremonies may be regarded as a sort of gymnastic exercise of the power of will, and for this reason all the great teachers of the world have recommended them as proper and efficacious. In any religious sect only those who carry out the external observances are reckoned as real supporters of the cause.

The more one does, the more one can do in the future.

To live a life guided by the caprice of the moment is to lead the life of an animal; this may conceivably be a life of innocence, but it is a life of submission.

Those who watch, those who fast, those who pray, those who refrain from pleasure, those who place body at the command of mind, can bring all the powers of nature into subjection for their purposes.

Men such as these are the world's masters; such men alone do works which survive them.

Never confuse the slaves of superstition and fear with such masters of nature.

To abstain from pleasant things through fear is to enslave the will; such conduct tends to lower rather than to raise your position.

To live like an anchorite, without the superstitious ignorance which leads him to such a course of life, this is wisdom indeed, and power is the reward.

11 - Kaph

ל

# 12

## THE LETTER LAMED

THE NUMBER OF THE PERFECT CYCLE

[the sign of the perfection of the great work;
hieroglyph; The hanged man]


Accomplishment.

The sacrifice.

The consummation.

The crucifixion.

The spirit that gets itself out of matter.

# 12 ל M

## THE GREAT WORK.

**DISCITE.** – A Latin word meaning learn, study, practice.

**CRUX.** – A Latin word meaning a wooden frame upon which criminals were crucified, especially a cross.

## THE GREAT WORK.

ל *Lamed*. – To tame the most ferocious animals, and to know how to say words which which paralyse and charm serpents.

12 ל He promises his people a king in the future.

ל Example, instruction, public teaching.

Symbol, a man hanging who is hung by one foot and who's hands are bound behind his back, in such a way that his body makes a triangle with the point aiming down, and his legs make a cross above the triangle.

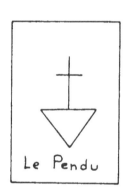

The gallows has in the form of a Hebrew tav [ ת ]; the two trees which hold him each have six cut branches on them.

We have explained elsewhere this symbol of sacrifice and the accomplished work; we will therefore not return to it.

"This hanged man is therefore the adept, bound by his engagements, spiritualized or having his feet turned towards heaven; it is also the ancient Prometheus, suffering in an immortal torture which is the penalty of his glorious theft."[23]

---

[23] From Ch.12 of *Dogma of High Magic* (1861)

# XII

## LE PENDU — THE HANGED MAN

The number Twelve completes a cycle, and this highly mystical Trump represents the Completion of the Great Work.

This startling design might be also represented by a cross above a triangle within a Tav [ ת ], that is, by four multiplied by three and enshrined in a Universe.

The pack of Tarot Cards, otherwise the Book of Taro —a word which is an anagram of Rota, a wheel or cycle— consists in truth of a magical, hieroglyphic and kabalistic alphabet, to which are added four decades, and four quaternions, which enshrine the mystic significance of the Wheel of Ezekiel.

The true aim of the Great Work is to volatilize the fixed after having accomplished the fixation of the volatile.

By a mystical rectification and a subsequent sublimation the Universal Medicine is obtained, and so is also the art of the Transmutation of metals; by which art indeed, even the most gross and impure substances, may be at once changed into pure and living gold. But no one will succeed in this magical transmutation until he has learned to despise earthly riches, and is content with the holy poverty of the true adept.

So, then, if any one attains to this sublime secret, he will treasure it with almost superhuman care, and it will so never be divulged to any other human being; it must be self-attained.

The secret matter of the Philosopher is composed of volatilised Salt, of Mercury which has been fixed, and of purified Sulphur; this perfected Matter is the Azoth of the philosophers. The Salt is only to be volatilized by condensation from the Seven rays of Sol, which are the respective soul essences of the seven metals. The Mercury is fixed by saturation with the Solar essence. The Sulphur is purified by the heat of the Seven luminous rays.

When a man is fully initiated he has a knowledge of all those processes, and he knows that he holds these secrets under the penalty of death. The Taro can preserve you from the danger of such punishment, by rendering you incapable of the commission of such a crime.

Remember the histories of Prometheus and of Tantalus. The former stole the sacred fire from heaven and transferred it to the earth. The latter violated the privacy of nature to seize the secrets of divinity. Remember also the fate of Ixion, who attempted to ravish the Queen of the Sky. Remember also the Cross and the Stake. Ponder over the long martyrdom of Raymond Lully, the inconceivable sufferings of Paracelsus, the madness of William Postel, the wandering life and miserable end of Cornelius Agrippa.

Love God, gain wisdom, and preserve unutterable silence.

# 13

## THE LETTER MEM

DEATH

[(the rose from the mouth of a skull)]

The renaissance.

Immortality through change.

Transmutation.

# 13 מ N

## NECROMANCY.

**EX IPSIS.** – Latin meaning 'out of themselves' or 'from themselves'. It comes from Ex meaning out of, from; as well as the name of the letter X; and Ipsis which is the plural of Ipse meaning himself; herself; itself.

**MORS.** – A Latin word meaning death; corpse; annihilation.

## NECROMANCY.

מם *Mem.* – To have the notable art which gives the universal science.

13 מ   The tomb is the passage to the new earth,

    Death alone ends; life is immortal.

מ   The heaven of Jupiter and Mars, domination and strength, new birth, creation and destruction.

Hieroglyph, DEATH which reaps crowned heads in a prairie where men are seen growing.

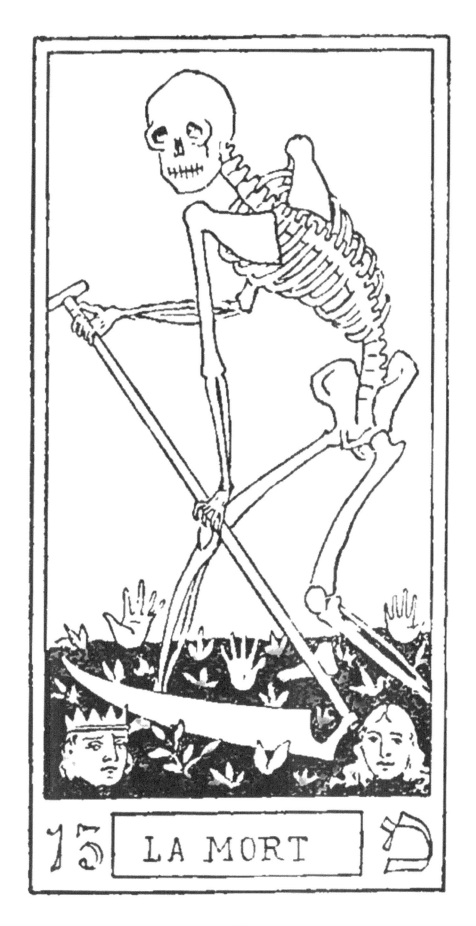

## XIII

## LA MORT — DEATH

An effort must now be made to learn the truth concerning the greatest and most consoling, yet also the most formidable of the Major Arcana —concerning Death. Now, in truth, Death is but a phantom of your ignorance and fear. Death has no existence in the Sanctum Regnum of existence.

A change, however awful, demonstrates movement, and movement is life; only those who have attempted to check the disrobing of the spirit have tried to create a real death. We are all dying and being renewed every day, because every day our bodies have changed to some extent. Be troubled lest you soil and tear your bodily raiment, your coat of skin, but fear not to leave it aside when the time has come for a period of repose from the work of this world.

Leave not your material garment for ever, until the time for your departure has come; that is, destroy not your own life, for it may be that you would awake to find yourself naked, chill, and ashamed: it may be too that such a corpse feels its own necropsy. Do not attempt to preserve the bodies of the dead, let nature do her work at once; let there be no worship of a dead body, for it represents but the ragged old clothes of a life.

Do not grieve for the beloved dead, for they are even more alive than you. If you regret the loss of their affection and support, you may still love their memory, and waft messages to them, and perchance may receive an answer; for by the aid of the Keys of Solomon the barriers of the thither world, the plane of disembodied beings, and even of the heaven, may be raised for a moment.

Understand well that the life-current of the progress of souls is regulated by a law of development, which carries the individual ever upward, and there is no tendency to a natural fall. Souls shall only fall who elect to descend and choose the evil rather than the good. The material plane on which you live is a prison to you, and if souls fall and come back to it, they become again imprisoned.

If you desire to communicate with those who have passed on, you must. But be warned in time against many deceptions, for your fancied souls in heaven may be but phantoms of the air; elementaries, shadows of humanity energised by elemental beings; mere senseless astral forms, and of no more value than the mirage of dreams.

Necromancy, and Goetia, which is Evil Magic, do produce such shells and demons, apparitions of deceit. If, however, you are an adept of the True White Higher school, you will at all times condemn and challenge the practice of such fatal science.

The only possible mode of communion with souls of a higher sphere, who have passed beyond the terrestrial aura by reason of the change called Death, is by dream or ecstasy; but on waking to common consciousness there will be no recollection present in the mind of what has passed, because, owing to the change of plane, each idea necessarily suffers a change of form—a recurrence of the dream, or a return to the ecstasy, recalls what has gone before.

It is a curious fact that most persons fail to remember anything of good and happy dreams, even although they do often recall dreams of sin and folly and absurdity; the reason being that these latter are more closely, and good ideals are less closely, related to our very materially minded lives on earth.

Now if the purely minded adept and pupil of the Higher Magic does seriously aspire to communion with a soul on the plane above him, the true way is as follows. But again you must take warning that unless the aspirant is pure, and strong with health, and wise in procedure, there will be grave risk of disordering the mind, or of catalepsy, or even of death.

Every childish and commonplace thought must be banished from the mind, for if this be not done, and if a ceremony of such awful solemnity be entered upon lightly, frivolously, or from a vain curiosity, there will come a moment when the dread "King of Earth" will appear and punish. The mind and emotions must then be raised to a pitch of sublime exaltation proceeding from a pure and disinterested love.

Bring to remembrance all the sweet sayings of the departed one, formulate her aims and good efforts, collect around you all that belonged to her and reminds you of her face, form, and personality. Observe the dates of her birth and death (and of any special events which have drawn you two together) ; choose such a day.

Prepare for this date by daily retiring to a quiet room, if possible where she has lived, or where she has been, and pass an hour there in darkness, or at least with the eyes shut, pondering over her words and ideas, conversing in imagination with her as listening to her conceived answers. When the day comes near you must for seven days, and should for even fourteen days, abstain rigorously from useless communications with other persons, from follies, from demonstrations of affection to all others, and from every form of physical and mental excess; take but one meal a day, and drink no stimulant nor narcotic liquids.

When the fateful day has come, take a portrait of the beloved one, a sun picture is the best (photograph), or if a painting, it should be one executed with the greatest care and detail.

With great care and delicacy prepare the room and the collected objects which have belonged to the deceased, make them all spotlessly clean, and give especial care to the portrait; place it in a good position, and decorate the frame with the flowers she loved.

During the day you should pass several hours in the chamber alone, seated in contemplation of the portrait and the ideas and reminiscences of the dead friend.

When the evening has come you must bathe, and clothe yourself in clean linen, and put on a white mantle.

## 13 - Mem

Enter the sacred chamber, fasten the door and perform the Conjuration of the Four Elements.

Upon a chafing-dish you then burn wood of the laurel, with aloes and incense. There must be no other light in the room.

When the wood and incense have burned down and the fire is at the point of extinction, then in a deep and solemn voice call three times in succession upon the name of the beloved dead one. This you must do with all your force of heart and of spirit, with intense will power; close the eyes, cover them with the hands, sink on your knees and pray.

Then at last, after a solemn pause, call softly and with sweet voice the name of the loved one three times; and open your eyes, and see ------------- .

# 14

## THE LETTER NUN

THE EFFUSIONS — THE MIXTURES

[hieroglyph; temperance]

Forms tempered by equilibrium.

The harmony of the mixed [or mixture].

# 14 נ O

## TRANSMUTATIONS.

**SPHERA LUNÆ.** – Latin meaning 'Sphere of the Moon'. It comes from Sphera meaning ball, globe, sphere; a globe of the heavens; a ball for playing; and Lunae meaning the Moon; (figuratively) a month or a night; a crescent shape.

**SEMPITERNUM.** – A Latin word meaning everlasting, perpetual, eternal.

**AUXILIUM.** – A Latin word meaning help, aid; antidote, remedy.

## TRANSMUTATIONS.

נ *Nun*. – To speak learnedly on all subjects, without preparation and without study.

14 נ The good angel is he who calms and who tempers.

נ The heaven of the Sun, temperatures, seasons, movement, changes of life which are always new and yet always the same.

Hieroglyph, TEMPERANCE, an angel with the sign of the sun upon her forehead, and upon her breast the square and triangle of the septenary, pours from one goblet into another the two essences which compose the elixir of life.

## XIV

## LA TEMPERANCE — TEMPERANCE

If you desire long life and health then avoid all excesses, and carry nothing to extremes. Once more preserve the equilibrium; you must neither abandon yourself to the benignities of Chesed, nor restrict yourself to the rigors of Geburah.

So when you have passed beyond the mortal sphere by the allurements of ecstasy, return to yourself, seek repose and enjoy the pleasures which life supplies for the wise, but do not indulge too freely.

If you feel fatigued by the tempting fascination of a prolonged fast, then take food and drink; but if you have loss of appetite from generous diet, then fast by all means. If you are feeling the seductiveness of womankind, seek relief from women.

You must learn to overcome all passions, and conquer all tendencies to folly. But let there be no misunderstanding. To vanquish an enemy there must be no running away: true victory can only follow meeting him face to face, joining in a struggle, and so showing your command over him.

It is related of Paracelsus that he became intoxicated daily, and sobered himself by violent exercise; thus he was found strong as a man with sangfroid, and yet possessing all the animation of alcoholic stimulation.

You should repose for as long a period as is expended in the preparations for and in the actual operations of magic; spend the hours of rest upon the bosom of Mother Nature, and in the chaste embrace of Nature's sweet restorer, Sleep.

Pass alternately from the triangle to the circle, and from the circle to the triangle.

Temperate the wine with water, and rectify the water with wine. Wine is the emblem of Truth; yet it is not well to pour out either, in pure form, to ordinary men and women; some dilution with water is very desirable. Know that the Luminous Septenary has as its enemies, and as obstacles, but acting also in some ways as auxiliaries, a Dark Septenary of averse forces.

If a man abuses the high forces of the Septenary of Powers, his errors form the Seven Capital Sins.

Give but little wine to one who easily gets intoxicated; and, in like manner, give but little occult instruction to those who make light of it, who abuse instead of use, and so change truth into error.

# 15

## THE LETTER SAMECH

THE NUMBER FIFTEEN — THE ASTRAL SERPENT

[hieroglyph; The devil]

The physical and fatal life.

Perpetual movement.

The great magical agent.

# 15 ס P

## BLACK MAGIC.

**SAMAEL.** – "The just and terrible force … was named by the Hebrews, Samael; by the Orientals, Satan; and by the Latin people, Lucifer. The Lucifer of the kabalah is not an cursed and blasted angel, he is the angel who illuminates and who regenerates while burning…"[24]

**AUXILIATOR.** – A Latin word which means helper, aide, assistant.

## THE SABBATH OF THE SORCERERS.

ס *Samech*. – To know at a glance the depth of the souls of men and the mysteries of the hearts of women.

15 ס  The evil angel is the spirit of pride and rage.

ס  The heaven of Mercury, occult science, magic, commerce, eloquence, mystery, moral strength.

Hieroglyph, THE DEVIL, the goat of Mendes or the Baphomet of the temple with all his pantheistic attributes.

This is the only hieroglyph which was perfectly comprehended and properly interpreted by Etteilla.

---

[24] From the Introduction to *Ritual of High Magic* (1861)

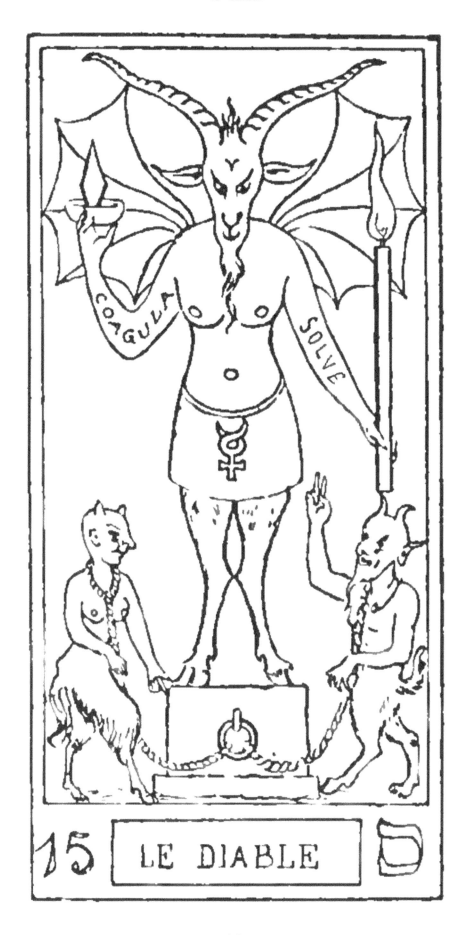

# XV

## LE DIABLE — THE DEVIL

Come close now and let us consider without fear this great one, the bugbear of the Christian creed, this ghost of Ahriman, the monstrous androgynous sphynx of Mendes; it is the synthesis of unbalanced forces—a Demon.

The Devil is truly Blind Force/Strength.  If you help the blind, you may be served by him; if you let the blind lead, you are lost.

Each element and every number has its demon, because each element and every number enshrines a force which ignorance may put to evil purposes.  The same sword by which you defend your father, may also slay him.  Know then that the demonic force of each entity must be conquered by knowledge and good purpose.  Avoid darkness where demonic power prefers to manifest; fight it in broad daylight, and fearlessly.

The Devil, one day, desiring to stop the progress of an adept, broke one wheel of his chariot; but this true adept compelled the Devil to curl himself up on the wheel and act for the time as its tire, and so drove on, reaching his destination even sooner than he would have done if the Devil had let him alone.

Meditate deeply on this old allegorical epigram, *Aude*[25] *et Tace*[26], and when you have seized its occult sense, tell no other of your success.

The symbolic representation of the Devil shows a multiple, disharmonious and anarchic sort of sphynx, typical of confusion and disorder.  Note this maxim: —A devil is a magnetic current consisting of a concourse of blind and perverse wills.

When certain superstitious mystics relegated intelligence and reason to the Devil, they reversed the Absolute.  That is to say, they chose as their God him who was truly the Devil, and they attributed the malice of Satan to the True God.

There is no child with even ordinary sense who is not more learned than the Devil.  The Devil is even of lower grade than the beings of the Elements.  He is doubtless more powerful, but he is as blind as poor Samson became.  But to enable the Devil to pull down the pillars of a temple, you would have to lead him to the pillars and say to him, There they are.

No true Magician ever made any attempt to evoke the Devil, for he knows where the Devil is always to be found; but he may order the Devil to work – and the Devil obeys.

In Black Magic, the Devil means the employment of the Great Magical Agent for a wicked purpose by a perverted Will.

---

[25] Latin meaning "to venture, dare, be bold, dare to do, risk", so this could be 'dare'
[26] Latin meaning "to be silent, not speak, say nothing, hold one's peace", so this could be 'keep quiet'

# 16

## THE LETTER AYIN

THE NUMBER SIXTEEN — THE GREAT EQUILIBRIUM

[hieroglyph; The tower of Babel]

Destruction by antagonism.

Balance of the great powers.

# 16 ע Q

## EFFIGYISM.

**FONS.** – A Latin word meaning a spring, fountain; fresh water, spring water; (by extension) origin, source of something.

**OCULUS.** – A Latin word meaning an eye; (by extension) the power of sight; a spot resembling an eye, such as on a peacock feather.

**FULGUR.** – A Latin word meaning lightning, a flash of lightning; thunderbolt.

## EFFIGYISMS AND SPELLS.

ע *ayin*. – To force nature to submit, when it pleases him.

16 ע God commands the lightning and governs the fire.

ע The heaven of the Moon, alterations, subversions, changes, weaknesses.

Hieroglyph, a tower struck by lightning, probably that of Babel.

Two persons, no doubt Nimrod and his false prophet or his minister, are precipitated from the heights to the bottom of the ruins.

One of the personages, in falling, perfectly represents the letter ayin ע.

# XVI

## LA MAISON DE DIEU — THE TOWER OF GOD / TOWER OF BABEL

Do you know why the Fiery Sword of Samael is stretched over the Garden of Delight, which was the cradle of our race?

Do you know why the Deluge was ordered to erase from the earth every vestige of the race of the giants?

Do you know why the Temple of Solomon was destroyed?

These events have been necessary because the Great Arcanum of the Knowledge of Good and of Evil has been revealed.

Angels have fallen because they have attempted to divulge this Great Secret. It is the secret of Life, and when its first word is betrayed, that word becomes fatal. If the Devil himself were to utter that Word, he would die.

This Word will destroy each one who speaks it, and every one who hears it spoken. If it were spoken aloud in the hearing of the people of a town, that town would be given over to Anathema. If that Word were to be whispered beneath the dome of a Temple, then within three days the Temple doors would fly open, a Voice would utter a cry, the divine indweller would depart, and the building would fall in ruins. No refuge could be found for one who revealed it; if he mounted to the topmost part of a tower the lightning-flash would strike him, if he tried to hide himself in the caverns of the earth, a torrent would whirl him away; if he sought refuge in the house of a friend he would be betrayed; if in the arms of the wife of his bosom, she would desert him in affright.

In his passion of despair he would renounce his science and knowledge, and, condemning himself to the same blindness as did Oedipus, would shriek out —"I have profaned the bed of my mother."

Happy is the man who solves the Enigma of the Sphynx, but wretched is he who retails the answer to another.

He who has solved the secret and guards its secrecy is as the "King of Earth"; he disdains mere riches, is inaccessible to any suffering or fear from destiny, he could await with a smile the crash of worlds. This secret is, moreover, profaned and falsified by its mere revelation, and never yet has a just or true idea come from its betrayal. Those who possess it have found it. Those who pronounce it for others to hear have lost it—already.

# THE LETTER PEH

## The number seventeen

[hieroglyph; Nature]

Nature immortal
and one in its diversity.

The eternal fecundity.

# 17 פ R

## ASTROLOGY.

**STELLA.** – A Latin word meaning a star or planet.

**OS.** – A Latin word meaning mouth; face, appearance, head; opening, entrance; as well as bone; heartwood; the hard or innermost part of trees or fruits; framework of discourse.

**INFLEXUS.** – A Latin word meaning bent, curved, bowed.

## THE WRITING OF THE STARS.

פה *Pe.* – To foresee all those future events which do not depend on a superior free will, or on an imperceptible cause.

17 פ Vesper [or Venus, the Morning Star] and her dew obey God.

פ Heaven of the Soul, outpourings of thought, the moral influence of the idea upon form, immortality.

Hieroglyph, the blazing star and eternal youth. We have given the description of this symbol elsewhere.

"We also see on the seventeenth page of the Tarot an admirable allegory: A naked woman, who represents simultaneously Truth, Nature and Wisdom, without a veil, she turns two urns towards the earth, and pours out fire and water; above her head shines the seven stars around a star of eight rays, that of Venus, symbol of peace and love; around the woman grow the plants of earth, and upon one of these plants the butterfly of Psyche lands (emblem of the soul) which is replaced in some copies of the sacred book by a bird, a more egyptian and probably more ancient symbol. This figure (which, in the modern Tarot, carries the title of "the brilliant Star") is analogous to many hermetic symbols, and is not without analogy with the blazing Star of the initiates of free-masonry, expressing the greater part of the mysteries of the secret doctrine of the rose-cross."[27]

---
[27] From the Ch.17 of *Dogma of High Magic* (1861)

# XVII

## L'ETOILE — THE STAR

You must become thoroughly acquainted with the planets and also with the fixed stars. When their names are mastered, their influences must be learned; you must discover the particular hours and in what sign the Psyche of the World pours forth from her two goblets the waters of life like two rivers.

Learn both day and night hours, in order that you may select such as are most suitable for the work you wish to perform.

The midnight hour is marked by the special tendency toward the appearance of phantoms. The first and second hours, which follow, are solemn and sad for those who are ill or are sleepless. During the third hour the sufferer from insomnia falls asleep; the fourth, fifth, and sixth are calm, and lead to a healthy repose in sleep.

The seventh and eighth hours of morning are of a voluptuous nature; the ninth, tenth, and eleventh are very suitable for works of friendship; the mid-day hour is a time of heedlessness and languor in summer, and of a sense of well-being in winter.

You should find your own particular Planet in the sky; your intuition should guide you in discovering it; and when found you should salute it with reverence every night that you see it shining down upon you. The genius of this star must be invoked in your conjurations, and the allotted name of the star may be worked out by means of the learned tables and Kabalistic permutations designed by Trithemius and Agrippa.

You should then make a talisman of sympathy to connect the planetary forces with yourself; make it of the metal of the planet which presided at your birth (the lord of the ascendant of your natus); engrave upon this plate of metal the sign of the Microcosm with the numbers of your name, the numbers related to the planet or star, and the name of the genius.

When you are seeking divine inspiration gaze at your star, holding the talisman with your left hand pressing it against your heart; if it be daytime, or the star be invisible, gaze upon the talisman itself, and recite the name of the genius or spirit of the star, three times.

When you see the star become brilliant and glitter in response to your aspiration, be of good hope for success; but should it be seen to pale at your glance, then be very prudent and take the greatest care of yourself.

# 18

## THE LETTER TZADIK

### THE NUMBER EIGHTEEN

[hieroglyph; The moon]

Hierachical distribution of the light.

Occultism.

Dogma.

The mysteries.

Esotericism.

# 18 צ S

## LOVE POTIONS AND SPELLS.

**JUSTITIA.** – A Latin word meaning justice.

**MYSTERIUM.** – A Latin word meaning mystery (secret rite or worship); secret.

**CANES.** – A Latin word meaning dog or dogs.

## LOVE POTIONS AND MAGNETISM.

צק *Tsade.* – To give all-at-one and to everyone the most effective comforts and the most wholesome counsels.

18 צ He places in our turn the moon as watchman.

צ The elements, the visible world, reflected light, material forms, symbolism.

Hieroglyph, the moon, dew, a crab in the water rising towards land, a dog and wolf barking at the moon and chained to the foot of two towers, a path which is lost in the horizon and sprinkled with drops of blood.

# XVIII

## LA LUNE — THE MOON

The Moon exercises a very considerable amount of influence upon the magnetic fluid of the earth, as is shown by the ebb and flow of the waters of the seas; you should then examine carefully the effects of the influences of the Moon in her several phases, and take note of the days and hours of the Moon's course.

The quarter of the New Moon is favourable for the commencement of all magical enterprises; the first quarter gives an influence of heat, the full moon an influence of dryness, and the last quarter a cold influence.

These are the special characters of the days of the Moon, distinguished by the twenty-two Tarot Keys and the signs of the Seven Planets.

I. The Juggler, or the Magus. The first day of the Lunar course: the Moon was created, says Rabbi Moses, on the fourth day.

II. The Gnosis, or The Priestess. The second day, whose genius is named Enodiel, the fish and birds were created; it is propitious for the works of occult science.

III. The Mother, or Empress. The third day saw the creation of humanity. The Kabalists often call the Moon by the name Mother, and allot the number three to her: this day is propitious for generation.

IV. The Despot, or Emperor. The fourth day is baneful, for on this day Cain was born; but it is a powerful day for unjust and tyrannical acts.

V. The Pope, or Priest. The fifth is a day of happiness; it was the birthday of Abel.

VI. The Lovers, or the Struggle. Birth of Lamech, a day marked by contest and anger; suitable for conspirators and for revolt.

VII. The Chariot. Birth of Hebron; a day very propitious for religious ceremonies.

VIII. Justice. Death of Abel; the day of expiation.

IX. The Hermit. Birth of Methuselah; a day of joy for children.

X. The Wheel of Fortune. Birth of Nebuchadnezzar; a day for conjurations of plagues; a baneful day: reign of brute force.

XI. Strength. Birth of Noah. The visions of the day are deceitful; but children born this day are healthy and long lived.

XII. The Hanged Man, the Tav [ ת ]. Birth of Samael; a day favorable for Kabalah and prophecy, and for the accomplishment of the Great Work.

XIII. Death. Birth of Canaan, the cursed son of Ham; an evil day and an evil number.

XIV. Temperance. Benediction of Noah. On this day Cassiel of the hierarchy of Auriel presides.

XV. The Devil, or Typhon. Birth of Ishmael; a day of reproof and exile.

XVI. The Tower. Birth of Esau and Jacob; the latter is predestined to ruin Esau.

XVII. The Star. The Ruin of Sodom and Gomorrah; this day is under the rule of Scorpio. Health for the good, ruin for evil persons; dangerous when it falls on a Saturday.

XVIII. The Moon. Birth of Isaac; a day of good augury.

XIX. The Sun. Birth of Pharaoh; a day of danger.

XX. The Judgment. Birth of Judah; a day propitious for divine revelations.

XXI. The World or the Sphynx. Birth of Saul; a day for physical force and material prosperity.

XXII. Saturn. The birth of Job.

XXIII. Venus. The birth of Benjamin.

XXIV. Jupiter. The birth of Japhet.

XXV. Mercury. The Tenth plague of Egypt.

XXVI. Mars. The passage of the Red Sea by the Israelites.

XXVII. Luna. The victory of Judas Maccabeus.

XXVIII. Sol. Samson carries off the gates of Gaza.

XXIX. The Tarot Trump called The Lunatic / Fool, the unwise man; a day of abortion.

# 19

## THE LETTER QOPH

### THE NUMBER NINETEEN

[hieroglyph; The Sun]

The true light.

The truth.

The holy city.

The philosophic gold.

# 19 ק P

## THE STONE OF THE PHILOSOPHERS. – ELAGABALUS.

**VOCATIO.** – A Latin word meaning summons; invitation, bidding; calling, vocation.

**SOL.** – A Latin word meaning the Sun.

**AURUM.** – A Latin word meaning gold.

## THE MAGISTER OF THE SUN.

ק *Koph.* – To triumph over adversities.

19 ק His sun is the source where everything renews itself.

ק Mixtures, the head, the summit, the prince of heaven..

Hieroglyph, a radiant sun and two naked children who hold hands within a fortified enclosure.

In other Tarots, substitute a spinner unwinding people's destinies; and in others a naked child mounted upon a white horse and displaying a scarlet banner.

## XIX

## LE SOLEIL — THE SUN

The Sun is the center and source of all high Magical force, and this force nourishes and renews without pause that latent Light which is the grand agent manifested in magnetism and vital energy.

The Sun is the central and yet universal magnet of the stars. It has two poles, one possessing attractive force and the other repulsive force; it is only by the balance of these two energies that it maintains cosmic equilibrium and universal motion.

The Sun it is which bestows radiance upon the planets and meteors, it is of the principle of Fire, and in this world it is the source of the phosphorescence of the sea and even of the scintillation of the glow-worm. It is the heat of the Sun which constitutes the stimulant essence of the generous wine from the fruit of the grape, and which brings to perfection the luscious sweetness of all fruits.

It is the Sun which awakens the dormant energies of all beings in spring time, and which prompts to the enjoyment of all the sweet mysteries of sexual love.

It is the Sun's force which courses in our veins and palpitates in our hearts, and it is the light of the Sun which empurples our blood and makes it resemble the purple redness of wine.

The Sun is the sanctuary of spiritual beings who have been loosed from the ties of earthly life, and there is the blazing tabernacle in which resides the Soul of the Messiah. You place your altars where the Sun's rays fall upon them, and renew the sacred fire upon them from its rays. When you consecrate a talisman or pantacle you open up a path along which a solar ray may pass thence into it during the ceremony.

When the adept seeks to heal the sick or relieve any pain he raises his hands towards the Light and Heat of the Sun, and then lowering them he touches the sick man, saying, "Be thou healed if thou hast faith and will." The perfumed flowers and leaves to be used as incense should be dried in the Sun's rays, notwithstanding the fact that flowers and leaves gathered in darkness have more potency than those plucked by daylight; because plants exhale their aroma in sunlight, and close up their pores to preserve it during the absence of the creating rays.

Gold is the special metal of Sol, and it tends to augment the solar force in all with which it is brought into contact. A golden lamen applied to the forehead renders the mind more open to and receptive of divine influences.

A golden talisman worn on the breast over the heart increases the force of emotions which are good and benevolent, while it tends to banish impure passions.

# 20

## THE LETTER RESH

THE NUMBER TWENTY

[hieroglyph; the angel[28] of the tomb]

The rememberance of everything
or the great arcanum of eternal life.

---

[28] This French word 'ange' or "angel", might also be 'auge' meaning "trough, long and narrow receptacle (e.g. for holding food and water for animals)"

# 20 ר U

## THE UNIVERSAL MEDICINE.

**CAPUT.** – A Latin word meaning head.

**RESURRECTIO.** – A Latin word meaning resurrection.

**CIRCULUS.** – A Latin word meaning circle; an orbit; a ring, hoop; a necklace, chain; a company, social gathering, group; a calendrical cycle.

## THAUMATEURGY.

ר *Resh*. – To tame love and hate.

20 ר His breath makes the dust of the tombs germinate

ר The growing, generative virtue of the earth, eternal life.

Hieroglyph, JUDGEMENT.

A genius sounds the trumphet and the dead come out of their tombs; these dead people become living ones, they are a man, woman and child: the ternary of human life.

# XX

## LE JUGEMENT — JUDGMENT

These are the Privileges and the Powers of a Magus[29]; and first are recited the Seven Grand Privileges :—

[ א ] Aleph. 1. He sees God and is able to commune with the Seven Genii around the throne.

[ ב ] Beth. 2. He is above the influence of all pains and fears.

[ ג ] Ghimel. 3. He has authority over High Spiritual Powers, and can command Infernal forces.

[ ד ] Daleth. 4. He is the master over his own life, and can influence the lives of other men.

[ ה ] Heh. 5. He can never be taken unaware, nor weakened, nor overcome.

[ ו ] Vau. 6. He understands the reasons for the Present, the Past, and the Future.

[ ז ] Zain. 7. He holds the secret of what is meant by the Resurrection from the dead.

The Seven Major Powers are :—

[ ח ] Cheth. 1. The power of making the Philosopher's Stone.

[ ט ] Teth. 2. The possession of the Universal Medicine.

[ י ] Yod. 3. The knowledge of the mode of Perpetual Motion, and of the Quadrature of the Circle.

[ כ ] Kaph. 4. The power of changing any base matter into gold.

[ ל ] Lamed. 5. The ability to coerce wild beasts, and to charm serpents.

[ מ ] Mem. 6. To possess the Notorial Art and to have universal knowledge.

[ נ ] Nun. 7. The power of discoursing with knowledge and learning upon any subject, even without previous study.

The Seven Minor Powers are :—

---

[29] Editor's note: Compare these with the descriptions given in the Introduction to *Dogma of High Magic*

## 20 - Resh

[ ס ] Samech. 1. To know in a moment the hidden thoughts of any man or woman.

[ ע ] Ayin. 2. To compel any one to act with sincerity.

[ פ ] Peh. 3. To foresee any future events which do not depend upon the will of a superior being.

[ צ ] Tzaddi. 4. To give instantly wise counsel and acceptable consolation.

[ ק ] Qoph. 5. To be always calm and content in the most grievous adversity.

[ ר ] Resh. 6. Never to feel love or hatred unless it is designed.

[ ש ] Shin. 7. To possess the secret of constant wealth, and never to fall into destitution or misery.

These Privileges are the final degree of Human Perfectibility; these are open to attainment by the elect, by those who can dare, by those who would never abuse them, and who know when to be silent.

[ ת ] Tav. In conclusion, Magi can control the elemental forces, calm tempests, heal the sick, and raise the dead. But these things are sealed with the triple Seal of Solomon: initiates know of them, this is sufficient; as to other persons, whether they deride you, or whether they are overcome with fear at your audacity, what does it matter to you?

20 - Resh

# 0 or 21

## THE LETTER SHIN

NO NUMBER

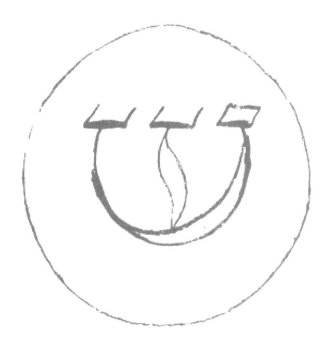

Fatality.

Blindness.

The Lunatic [or Fool].

Matter left to itself.

# 21 ש X

## DIVINATION.

**DENTES.** – A Latin word meaning teeth.

**FURCA.** – A Latin word meaning a two-pronged fork, pitchfork; a fork-shaped prop, pole or stake; an instrument of punishment, a frame in the form of a fork, which was placed on a culprit's neck, while his hands were fastened to the two ends; yoke.

**AMENS.** – The plural form of the Latin word Amen meaning 'so be it'. From Ancient Greek ἀμήν (āmēn), from Classical Hebrew אמן (amén, "certainly, truly").

## THE SCIENCE OF THE PROPHETS.

ש *Shin.* – To have the secret of riches, to be always its master and never its slave. To know how to enjoy even poverty and never fall into humiliation nor into misery.

0 or 21 } ש Where the mortals who lack a brake descend in herds.

ש The sensitive principle, the flesh, eternal life.

Hieroglyph, THE LUNATIC: a man dressed as a lunatic, walking aimlessly, burdened with a satchel which he carries behind him, and which is no doubt full of his follies and vices; his disordered clothes allow the discovery of what should be concealed, and a tiger who follows him also bites him without him wondering how to escape or defend himself.

21 - Shin

121

## XXI

## LE MAT[30] — THE UNWISE MAN

Do not ally yourself either in affection or interest with any one who is not an earnest student of the higher life, unless you can completely dominate him, and even then be sure that you either recompense or chastise him according to his deserts; for the profane person hears many truths, but understands none; his ears are large but have no discretion.

The profane passes his life in giddy risks, deluded with vain desires, listening to imaginary promptings, and with his eyes fixed on fancied sights. You may think he is pleased with your aims, but the truth is that he is absorbed by his own follies; the profane has no appreciation of the truth, and feels no real affection. The profane is imprudent and shameless; he discloses things which should be kept concealed, and attracts to himself brute forces which may devour him. That which he most neglects is himself; he wears his vices as a blazon, but they are an ever-present burden to him, yet he does not recognise that they are a constant source of weakness. Make it a definite rule of life always to avoid:—

1. Such as are ever judging and condemning their parents, who despise their fathers and have no true affection for their mothers.

2. All men who show no courage, and all women who have not modesty.

3. Those who do not maintain their friendships.

4. Those who ask for advice, and then do not take it.

5. Those who are never in the wrong.

6. Those who are always seeking the impossible, and who are obstinately unjust to others.

7. Those who, when danger is present, seek only their own safety.

All such persons are neither worthy of your confidence nor of your love. Fear contamination from them; avoid them.

Yet even as you yourself must also avoid the follies of life, be careful not to put yourself in an attitude of superiority to the conditions of existence merely from a false pride, and never stoop to debase yourself to the level of the brute creation; rise above the common ways of life, and never become the slave of custom and conventionality. Treat the habits of ordinary life as others treat the weaknesses of childhood. Amuse the crowd to prevent personal injury, but never address it except in parables and enigmas; such has been the mode of conduct of all the great Masters of Magic, and in such an attitude there is wisdom.

---

[30] Literally 'mat' means "dull, matt, unpolished; checkmate"

# 21 or 22

## THE LETTER TAV

### THE NUMBER TWENTY ONE

[hieroglyph; the key of the Tarot]

Three times seven.

The absolute.

The summary of everything.

The universal science.

## 22 ת Z

## SUMMARY AND GENERAL KEY OF THE FOUR OCCULT SCIENCES.

**SIGNA.** – A Latin word meaning mark, sign; seal, stamp.

**THOT.** – "…the hieroglyphic book of Hermes, which is also named the book of Thot"[31]. Hermes or Thot (also spelled Thoth) was the ancient Egyptian god of wisdom, learning, and magic.

**PAN.** – "The devil is the personification of atheism and idolatry. For the initiates, this is not a person, it is a force created for good, and which can serve for evil; it is the instrument of liberty. They represented this force, which presides over physical generation under the mythological form of the horned god Pan…"[32]

## THE BOOK OF HERMES.

ת *Tav*. – Let us add to these three septenaries that the sage governs the elements, that he appeases storms, cures diseases by touching them, and resurrects the dead!

21 or 22 } ת His crown illuminates the reconcilation,

And, upon the cherubims he spreads out his glory.

ת The microcosm, the summary of all in all.

Hieroglyph, the kether, or the kabalistic crown between four mysterious animals; in the middle of the crown, one sees Truth holding a magic wand in each hand.

---
[31] From the Ch.2 of *Dogma of High Magic* (1861)
[32] From the Ch.3 of Book 3 in *History of Magic* (1860)

## XXII

## LE MONDE — THE WORLD

Do you now understand the Enigma of the Sphynx?

Do you know the thought which exists in its human head? the love which pervades its woman's bosom? the labor denoted by the loins of the bull? the struggle which the lion's claws can wage? the beliefs and the poetry of its eagle's wings? Yes, you know that the Sphynx refers to Man.

But do you know that the Sphynx is one and alone, and remains unchanged, while as to man, —is not each one a Sphynx of a different synthesis? In some there is the head of a Lion, such as is drawn on talismans of Fire; these are descendants of the Salamanders. Others have the head of a Bull, or of an Eagle or Ibis. Each of these has its divine counterpart, and this it is which the wise men of Egypt depicted in those hieroglyphic figures which the profane scholars of our time find so ridiculous and misleading. May they be forgiven from the recesses of the Tomb of the divine Hermes.

It is by reason of this diversity of divine inspiration, and its influence over the human will, that the wise have formed such diversified pantacles and talismans. All initiates have had faith in the efficacy of symbols and emblems. How else could the Word be expressed without letters and characters, and why should not letters and characters express the power of the Word they represent.

Write the words "I love" upon a golden jewel and wear it upon the breast; then every time you feel its touch, will not the idea of your love arise in the mind? and I tell you that this jewel, magnetised by your will and your faith, will deflect from you and will extinguish all the attacks directed against you. If you pass through the heat of fire, this will be as a breeze of fresh air to you. If you are in danger of drowning, this will bear you up amid the waters. Never then condemn the use of amulets, pantacles, talismans, and phylacteries. Unfortunate is the man who is not impressed by the appearance of any image, and who does not bow his head before any symbol.

But each wise man should have his phylactery or talisman, as every Master has his clavicule. Such are the talismans of Hermes; there are others of Solomon, of Rabbi Chael, and of Thetel; there are other signs used by Paracelsus, by Agrippa, and Albertus Magnus.

The symbols of Abraham the Jew gave rise to the emblematic designs of Nicholas Flamel, which again differ from those of Basil Valentine and Bernard of Treves.

All embody the same ideas, but according to the special form of consecration speak another idiom of the language of the hieroglyphics.

If you become initiated you will at length make and vary your own talismans and pantacles; you will choose the proper hours, select your perfumes and compose your own invocations, upon the models you may find among the various clavicules of Solomon.

Ponder carefully over this axiom: "The man who addresses himself to a Power unknown to him words and which he does not fully comprehend, makes a tenebrous prayer to the spirit of darkness"; in other words, he invokes the devil. All that happens in the world, that is devoid of justice and right, and has the devil for its author. Remember also that he who consults the oracles abdicates, in some part, his liberty and makes an appeal to fateful forces.

The true sage directs or corrects the oracle but he never consults it. Saul was already conquered and lost when he consulted the Witch of Endor. In the difficulties of life consult, in preference, the Sphynx.

Is it a decision that is needed, ask it from the human head.

Is it affection that you desire, ask it of the woman's breast.

Is it help and protection that you need, ask the Lion's claws to afford it.

Are you poor and ignorant, invoke the power of the Bull, and work yourself.

Do the struggles of life weary you, take the Eagle's wings and raise yourself on high above the earth.

The Sphynx only devours those who fail to comprehend her; she will obey any one who has learned the answer to her riddle.

All the forces of Nature correspond to human forces, and are dependent on the will in its sphere of action: constant use of willpower extends the sphere of its action.

Man (and by man I do not intend either fools or profane persons) —man is worth whatever he believes himself to be worth; he can do whatever he believes himself capable of doing; he does whatever he really desires to do; he may at length become all that he wills to be.

He, who was not mad, and yet could say, "I am the only Son of God," was the only Son of God. Examples of the past may be re-acted at any time: the types are still existent, and can be brought again into action.

Would you become a Moses, or an Elias?

Would you re-live the career of Paracelsus or of Raymond Lullius? Then learned all that they knew, put your faith in the doctrines they believed, do the acts they did; while awaiting the result, be sober in body, calm in mind, work and pray.

# THE KABALISTIC PRAYER[33]

Be favourable to me, oh ye Powers of the Kingdom Divine.
May Glory and Eternity be in my left and right hands, so that I may attain Victory.
May Mercy and Justice restore my soul to its original purity.
May Understanding and Wisdom Divine conduct me to the imperishable Crown.
Spirit of Malkuth, Thou who hast laboured and hast overcome; set me in the Path of Good.
Lead me to the two pillars of the Temple, to Jakin and Boaz, that I may rest upon them.
Angels of Netzach and of Hod, make ye my feet to stand firmly on Yesod.
Angel of Gedulah, console me. Angel of Geburah, strike, if it must be so, but make me stronger, so that I may become worthy of the influence of Tiphereth.
Oh Angel of Binah, give me Light.
Oh Angel of Chokmah, give me Love.
Oh Angel of Kether, confer upon me Faith and Hope.
Spirits of the Yetziratic World, withdraw me from the darkness of Assiah.
Oh luminous triangle of the World of Briah, cause me to see and understand the mysteries of Yetzirah and of Atziluth.
Oh Holy Letter ש, Shin.
Oh ye Ishim, assist me by the name Shadai.
Oh ye Kerubim, give me strength through Adonai.
Oh Beni Elohim, be brothers unto me in the name of Tzabaoth.
Oh Elohim, fight for me by the Holy Tetragrammaton.
Oh Melakim, protect me through Jehovah.
Oh Seraphim, give me holy love in the name Eloah.
Oh Chashmalim, enlighten me by the torches of Eloi and the Shekinah.
Oh Aralim, angels of power, sustain me by Adonai.
Oh Ophanim, Ophanim, Ophanim, forget me not, and cast me not out of the Sanctuary.
Oh Chaioth ha Kadosh, cry aloud as an eagle, speak as a man, roar and bellow.
Kadosh, Kadosh, Kadosh, Shadai.
Adonai, Jehovah, Ehyeh asher Ehyeh.
Hallelu-Jah.    Hallelu-Jah.    Hallelu-Jah. !

Amen.    Amen.    Amen.

This prayer should be made use of every morning and evening, and it should be recited as a preliminary to all grand magical and Kabalistic ceremonies; it should be recited when facing the orient with the eyes raised to the heavens, or fixed on the Kabalistic emblem of the sublime Tetragrammaton, which you will find drawn for your instruction on an accompanying page.

---

[33] This seems to be a version of the Kabalistic prayer 'The Invocation of Solomon'

So soon as you apply both body and soul to the Higher Magic you will have to defend yourself against all the blind forces of the world and of Hades. Earth will send the Bacchantes of Orpheus and the temptresses who assailed Samson and Solomon, even the stones will rise up and hurl themselves at you; Hades will send its Larvae and Phantoms to attack you. As a defence you will possess the Divine Word, the aura, the magical sword, the magnetic wand, the consecrated water, and the sacred fire, but above all the vigilant power of your invocation.

If you are Royal you may rely upon revolts and counterplots to force the spiritual powers to obey you. Perform the conjuration of the Four by means of the Pantacle of Ezekiel, and proceed by the Septenary and the Triadic method, and by the Pantacle of the Hexagram of Solomon, which latter is the Symbol of the Macrocosm.

For the conjuration of the Tetrad —the Four, you bring into action the powers of the four elements duly consecrated, and you must trace in the air and upon the earth the pentagrams of fire and of water; then make four expirations of the breath, and recite— making the cross—Nicksa, Ghob, Paralda, Djin.

*Fluat udor per Spiritum Elohim.*

Let the waters flow on, through the spiritual energy from Elohim, or ye Undines must roll back through the influence of this consecrated water.

*Maneat terra per Adam.*

Let the earth remain solid through Adam. Work, ye Gnomes, as I will, or return to the earth in which I can imprison you by this Pantacle.

*Fiat firmamentum per Elohim.*

The firmament must persist through the Elohim. Submit, ye Sylphs, or pass away by the current of my breathing.

*Fiat judicium per ignem.*

Let the decree be carried out by the Fire. Ye Salamanders, be calm, or be coerced by the sacred fire.

You may formulate the Undine as an angelic form with the eyes of death; the Gnome as a winged bull, the Sylph as an eagle chained, and the Salamander as a gliding serpent.

## LATIN INVOCATION.

O caput mortuum impero tibi per vivium Serpentem
Kerub impero tibi per Adam
Aquila impero tibi per alas Tauri.

Serpens impero tibi per Angelum et Leonem.

The Conjuration of the Heptad —the Seven, is made with the Magical Wand and fumigations by means of the Seven Planetary Spirits.

### PLANETARY CONJURATION.[34]

In the name of Michael, whom Jehovah decrees to command Satan!
In the name of Gabriel, whom Adonai decrees to command Beelzebub!
In the name of Raphael obey Elohim, thou Sachabiel.
By Samael Tzabaoth, and by the name of Elohim Gibur, lay down thy weapons, thou Adramelek.
By Zachariel and Sachiel Melek, submit to the power of Eloah, thou Samgabiel.
In the divine and human name of Shadai, and by the power of Anael, of Adam and of Chavah, thou Lilith retire, leave us in peace, thou Nahemah.
By the holy Elohim, and by the power of Orifiel, in the names of the spirits Cassiel, Schaltiel, Aphiel, and Zarahiel, turn back, thou Moloch, there are no children here for thee to devour.

———

You must then trace in the air and upon the earth, with the Magical Wand, the famous and powerful Hexagram, the Seal of Solomon.

———

The Conjuration of the Three is performed with the Tetragrammaton, pronouncing three times in a deep sonorous voice the Three letters of the Great Name, tracing in the air and upon the earth the signs of the four radii of the Wheel of Ezekiel's Vision, with the words Yod, Heh, Vau, Heh, and then make the sign of the Cross.

———

You should well understand that the names Satan, Beelzebub, and others like them, do not mean spiritual personalities, but rather legions of impure spirits.

My name is Legion, said the Spirit of darkness, because we are numberless; in hell, the kingdom of anarchy, it is number which makes law, and progress is inverse; for there the most degraded are the least intelligent and most weak. Thus the law of fatality compels the demons to descend when they believe and wish to rise; and so those whom I call the Chiefs are the most powerless and the most contemptible of them all.

---

[34] As previously suggested, this seems to be a version of the 'Conjuration of the Seven'

Those evil spirits which form the crowd, tremble before a Chief who is unknown, implacable, and deaf, never speaking, and whose arm is always raised to strike. To this phantom are given the names of Lucifer, Adramelek, and Belial; but this phantom is but the shadow of God disfigured by their perversity, and remains among them to torment and terrify them for ever.

Be guarded in the words you speak. Speak not of God, unless you are illuminated. All the images which you create, whether of God or of other ideals, remain imprinted on that luminous medium —the Astral Light of the soul, and of the world; and there is that Book of the Conscience which shall be opened and its records revealed in the Last Day.

Know that the Human Brain, although it receives, does not make any visible record of impressions; otherwise they would be engraved upon the grey matter of the Brain and anatomists would see them there. The nerve substance does but perceive and collect, by reason of this essence (the Astral Light), the living and ineffaceable pictures of the spiritual atmosphere which you evoke.

You may even by sympathy, present or past, with the desires, evoke the impressions of other persons ; and thus it is that you can communicate with those who are dead and even perceive the bodily form they have thrown aside, and which they must retake when the grand Consummation arrives and the world is transfigured.

To those who ask you where Paradise and Hell are situated, you should answer: Paradise exists whereever you speak the truth, and do the right; Hell is present wherever you speak that which is false, or do that which is evil.

Paradise and Hell are not localities, they are states, and the contrasted states will remain to eternity; even as good must ever remain in opposition to evil; as the essential of a personality is opposed to that of Intelligent Existence, which is Liberty.

The plastic universal medium, the unsubstantial substance, which is light, motion, and life, this androgyne magnetic force, receives, preserves, and communicates all the forms and images which are the impressions of the Word: this it is which gives form and color to plants; it is this which stamps upon the fruit of a mother's womb the impression of her thoughts and desires.

It is this which produces apparitions and the sensible visions of exaltation and ecstasy when Superior Spiritual Powers communicate to us by the correspondences of the Word, or when Inferior spirits seek to mount to our plane by sympathy with our grosser passions.

There is no real isolation in this world, there is no point of form and no variety of thought which has not its correspondence, item by item, through analogy, with that which is above, as well as that which is below, in the infinite and finite worlds. This is the true ideal of the mystical Ladder of Jacob whose rungs are bound together by the two Pillars of Light, and which provide for the unbroken circulation of Intelligence and Love through the vast areas of the Universe.

Nothing entirely new happens under the Sun; causes lead to new causes and effects precede these. Prophetic intuitions are but the result of a consideration of the analogies between the past and the future, read in that luminous volume composed of such mobile yet incorruptible characters as are the waves of the sea.

Hence it follows, that to divine —is to see.

Each man bears his earthly future in his natural character, and he has his character imprinted on his face and in his hands, in his natural movements, in his glances and his voice.

Each personal will has at its disposal three modes of force —moral power, instinctive power, and physical energy. Moral power is that solidarity which exists between all truly spiritual souls; instinctive power is the solidarity given by the sympathies and antipathies existing in the magnetic aura; while physical energy is the solidarity subsisting between the impulses and resistances of material substances. To each of these forces there is a corresponding form of life.

The middle or Instinctive force acts upon us without our active participation when our Moral force is in abeyance, and when one desires to give it free play one must slumber, or at least sleep more or less.

There is a voluntary slumber, as there is an involuntary or physiological sleep. Voluntary slumber is somewhat lucid, because it does not absolutely break away from reminiscence.

---

Prophecy and Thaumaturgy are Natural faculties.

The Re-animation of the Dead in the case of certain men and under certain circumstances is not a thing naturally impossible. At the moment of death the soul finds itself free from, yet near, the earthy tenement it has just left, and if the really vital organs have not been destroyed, it can be recalled by one whose will has tremendous force. Death is only absolute when the vital organs have lost their integrity.

Examples of re-animation are not infrequent, but when they occur the occurrence of death is denied, and the facts observed are explained by saying that the person was only in a trance or lethargy.

To deny that death has occurred in these cases may be permissible, but public opinion should have the courage of its convictions and should always deny it.

Oh thou who art now wise, thou hast been an infant; what has become of that infant? it has passed away, but you still live.

You have been a youth, he has passed away, but you are still with us. You were once a young man; what has become of that young man? you still live. You are now a man of full years, or perhaps even an old man; what will become of you, old man? You will die, but you will exist for ever. Is it the corpse which impresses you with terror? Yet each of your stages of development has left its corpse, only you do not happen to have seen it. Only believe then that your last corpse will not be appreciable by you, and so you may rest in a peaceful immortality.

You have but to undergo one more transformation before you remount to that source of life from which you once sprang.

Transformation results from eternal motion, which is the essential law of vitality; check this and enforce a stability at any stage of evolution, and you create a real death.

---

Behold thyself then, by natural law, immortal. Would you then be for ever the slave of secondary causes, or will you become their controller?

Will you submit to them, or will you choose the high alternative of directing them?

If you will become a Master, set free your spirit by relying on the Hermetic Stone, and exercise your Will Power through the Word transmuted into action. Join to an Intelligence, really set free, an all-powerful Will, and you will find yourself Master of the powers of the Elements. L. P. D.

Liberty, Power, Despotism. Power is the correct equilibrium between Despotism and Liberty. This is the solution of the Enigma of three letters which Cagliostro the Initiate formulated to represent the Kabalah of political and social stability.

Liberty is Chokmah [2].
Despotism is Binah [3].
Beneficent Power is Kether [1].

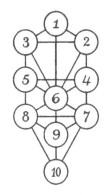

Liberty is Gedulah [or Chesed 4].
Despotism is Geburah [5].
Beneficent Power is Tiphereth [6].

Liberty is Netzach [7].
Despotism is Hod [8].
Beneficent Power is in Yesod [9].

In the essence of the First Cause, Liberty has Necessity as a counterpoise; this Necessity is the despotism of Supreme Reason, and resulting from this equilbrium is a Wise and Absolute Power.

If you seek to be absolute, be first wise; and if you are wise, be then absolute. To be a Master you must be free; to be free you must have attained the mastery of yourself.

Liberty is Jakin.
Despotism is Boaz.
Power is represented by the Temple Gate which was between them.

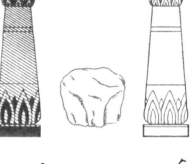

Four phrases constitute and include all that is required for the possession of High Magical Power.

To know.
To dare.
To will.
To be quiet.

Knowledge is represented by the Human head of the Sphynx.
Courage, by its Eagle's wings.
Will, by the Lion's claws, and the loins of the Bull.
Secrecy, by its stony silence and by the hidden answer to its enigma.

When the pupil has grasped the meaning of, and can carry into practice, these four requirements, he may then receive permission to Love.

---

Every force corresponds to all forces, and may become all powerful in the hands of one who knows how to direct and use it.

Each form of weakness has a similarity to all weaknesses, and may become a slave to one who is strong and knows how to avail himself of it. Through the knowledge of this secret, the Magus commands the forces alike of heaven and hell, and they can but be submissive to his Will.

Realize clearly that an intelligence which is Free is of necessity both just and wise. Nero and Caligula were possessed of despotic will, but their intelligence was not free; intoxicated with absolute power, they were attacked by vertigo. Absolute will power unguided by a right Reason is the quintessence of the Devil; and here is the explanation of the secrets of Black Magic, which lead to madness of mind and poisoning of body. Hence the sorcerer is said to give himself to the Devil, and in the end the Devil will wring his neck.

---

You will now need to learn the last secret of magical force and the final degree of human will power.

It is Resistance to Universal Attraction; this is the conquest of nature, it is the Royal Authority of Soul over Body—it is Continence. To have the power and opportunity to do what gives pleasure, yet to abstain because one wills it; this shows the Royal power of the Soul over the body.

Happy is the man who can be so placed, and yet so act: thus it is that the most sublime use of liberty is absolute obedience. Without obedience no society can continue to exist. This is why the Magi worshipped the Christ in the stable at Bethlehem. Christ, that son of God, greatest of initiates, and the last initiator.

But Christ had, as all great teachers have had, one teaching for the people and also an esoteric doctrine. To John, the beloved disciple, he confided the deepest mysteries of the Holy Kabalah; and John after years revealed or reveiled them in his Apocalypse, which is indeed a synthesis of all earlier magical, prophetic, and Kabalistic works.

The Apocalypse requires as its key or Clavicula the Wheel of Ezekiel, which is itself explained by the hieroglyphs of the Tarot.

## THE CONCLUSION

One last word remains to be said. When the Temple is rebuilt, there will be no more sacrifice upon its High places. Centuries have passed since Hermes and Zoroaster lived and taught. A voice greater than that of the Soul of the World has imposed silence upon the Oracles.

The Word has been made Flesh; a new symbol of salvation by holy water has replaced the magical ceremonies of the day of Luna.

The sacrifices to Samael on the day of Mars are surpassed by the heroic severities of penitence.

The sign of the Gift of Tongues and the Christian code have replaced the sacrifices to Mercury.

The day once sacred to Jupiter is now devoted to the sign of the Kingdom of God in man by the transubstantiation of love under the forms of the bread and the wine.

Anael has vanquished Venus: Lilith and Nahemah are consigned to Hades, and the sacred rite of marriage gives divine approval to the alliances of men and women.

Lastly, the extreme unction, which prepares a man for a death of peace, has replaced the sad offerings of Saturn; and the priesthood of light gives forth illumination on the day sacred to the Sun.

Glory be to the Christ, who has brought to their completion the symbols of the Ancient Mysteries, and who has prepared the reign of knowledge by faith. Will you now be greater than all Magi? Hide away your science in the recesses of your mind.

Become a Christian, simple and docile; be a faithful servant of the Church, believe, mortify yourself, and obey.

## OCCULT AND RELIGIOUS MAXIMS

Every idle word is a fault.

Show your learning by your actions.

The Word is Life, and the First Principle of Life.

The quality of a life is shown by its actions.

An idle word is either without meaning or is of the nature of a lie.

An idle word in religious matters is a sin.

He who is content with idle words is as if he were dead.

He who does not make his worship manifest has no religion.

Better is superstition than impiety.

God judges actions rather than vain thoughts.

He who is religious will do works which accord with the Word of his religion; he who has no religion and believes not in any word, yet he also must be judged by his actions, for to every man shall it be according to his works.

True religion is that which shows a form of worship which is pure and living; the perfection of worship, however, lies in self-sacrifice, which is complete and enduring.

The beauty of self-sacrifice is taught in the Church of Christ, Catholic and Roman; and it is an article of faith, that any one who denies himself and takes up this cross, and follows the Mediator to the Altar, assumes at once the offices both of Priest and Victim.

No man ever saw GOD at any time.

Before the dawn of the Microcosm, Azoth was the Flying Eagle and the Royal Lion; it was the Mastodon of the Earth and the Leviathan of the Sea. When the human-headed Sphynx appeared —Azoth became Man among men, and Spirits among Elementals. Every substance can and should become Azoth by adaptation.

In Azoth is the Principle of the Light, which is the Quintessence of Splendor and Gold. This is the grand Secret of universal Transmutation.

No man has ever seen the Light; but we see by reason of it those objects which reflect the light.

There is nothing occult which shall not be known: there is nothing concealed which shall not be revealed.

The Kingdom of God is within us.

Initiation passes from East to West.

Intelligence passes from South to North.

Power passes from North to South.

The Word is the garment of the Truth.

God wields not absolute, but regulated power.

To tell the Truth to those who cannot understand it, is to lie to them.  To unveil the Truth to such persons is to profane it.

**THE END**

# THE KEY OF SECONDARY CAUSES

## De Septem Secundeis

id est, intelligentiis, sive Spiritibus Orbes post Deum moventibus.

## IOHN TRITEMIVS,

Abbot of Spanheim, [Seven Secondary Causes] of the heavenly INTELLIGENCIES, governing the Orbes under GOD.

1508

**Dedication, to the Emperor Maximilian**

Renowned Caesar, it is the opinion of very many of the Aunceints, that this inferious World by ordination of the first *Intellect* (which is God) is directed and ordered by *Secundarian Intelligences*, to which opinion *Conciliator Medicorum* assents, saying, that from the Originall or first beginning of heaven and earth, there were 7. Spirits appointed as Presidents to the 7. Planets.

Of which number every one of those ruleth the world 354. years, and four months in order.

To this Position, many, and they most learned men, have afforded their consent; which opinion of theirs *my self* not affirming, but delivering, do make manifest to your most sacred Majesty.

**De septem secundeis**

The first Angell or Spirit of *Saturn* is called *Orifiel*, to whom God committed the government of the World from the beginning of its Creation; who began his government the 15, day of the moneth of *March*, in the first year of the World, and it endured 354 years and 4 moneths.

*Orifiel* notwithstanding is a name appertaining to his Office, not Nature. Attributed to the Spirit in regard of his action: under his dominion men were rude, and did cohabite together in desert and uncouth places, after the homely manner of Beasts. This needs not any manner of proof from me, sith its so manifest out of the Text of Genesis.

The second Governour of the World is *Anael* the Spirit of *Venus*, who after *Orifiel* began to rule according to the influence of this Planet, in the year of the world 354. the fourth moneth, that is, the 24 day of the moneth of June, and he ruled the world 354 years, and 4 moneths, untill the year from the Creation of the world 708. as appears to any that shall Calculate the Age thereof.

Under the Regiment of this Angell, men began to be more Civilized, built Houses, erected Cities, found out Arts *Manuall (viz. Monifactury)* the Art of Weaving, Spinning, and Cloathing, and many such like as these, did indulge themselves plentifully with the pleasures of the flesh, took unto themselves faire women for their wives, neglected God, Receded in many things from their naturall simplicity; they found out Sports, and Songs, sang to the Harp, and did excogitate whatsoever did belong to the worship and purpose of Venus. And this wantonness of life in men did continue untill the flood, receiving the Arguments of its pravity from hence.

*Zachariel* the Angell of *Jupiter*, began to govern the world in the year of the Creation of Heaven and Earth 708. the eighth moneth, that is, the 25 day of the moneth of *October*, and he did regulate the World 354 years, 4 moneths, untill the year of the worlds Creation 1063 inclusively. Under whose moderation, men first of all began to usurp Dominion over one another, to exercise Hunting, to make Tents, to adorn their bodies with severall garments: and there arose a great Division betwixt the good and evill men; the Pious invocating God, such as *Enoch*, whom the Lord translated to Heaven' the wicked running after the snares and pleasant allurements of the Flesh.

Men also under the Dominion of this *Zachariel* began to live more civilly, to undergo the Laws and Commands of their Elders, and were reclaimed from their former fierceness. Under his rule *Adam* the first man died, leaving to all posterity an assured Testimony, that necessarily once we must dye.

Various Arts and Inventions of men did about this time first appear & manifest themselves, as Historians have more clearly expressed.

The fourth Rector of the World was *Raphael*, the Spirit of *Mercury* which began in the year of the Creation of Heaven and Earth 1063 the 24 day of *February*, and he reigned 354 years 4 months, and his Government continued untill the year of the World 1417 and fourth moneth. In these times writing was first found out, and letters excogitated of Trees and Plants, which notwithstanding afterwards and in process of time received a more gracefull shape, and the Nations varied or changed the Face of their Characters according to their own fancy. The use of Musicall Instruments, under the time and rule of this *Raphael*, began to be multiplied, and Commerce or Exchange betwixt man and man was now first invented: A presumptuous, rude and simple Audacity in these times begot Navigation or the manner of Sayling from one place to another, and many such like things in one kinde or other, &c.

The fifth *Gubernator* of the World was *Samuel* the Angell of *Mars*, who began the 26 day of the moneth of June in the year of the World 1417. and swayed the rule of this World 354 years 4 moneths, untill the year of the World 1771. and eighth moneth, under whose Empire and Government men imitated the nature of *Mars*, also under the Dominion of this Angell, the Universall deluge of waters happened *Anno Mundi* 1656. as evidently it appears by History out of *Genesis*. And its to be observed, what the aunceint Philosophers have delivered, that so oft as *Samuel* the Angell of *Mars* is ruler of the World, so often there ariseth notable alterations of Monarchy. Religions and sects do vary, Laws are changed, Principalities and Kingdomes are transferred to Strangers, which we may easily finde out in order by perusall of Histories.

Notwithstanding *Samuel* doth not immediately in the very beginning or entrance of his Dominion manifest the disposition of his behaviour or custome: but when he hath exceeded the middle time of his *Gubernation* which very thing is likewise to be understood concerning the Angels of the other Planets, (as it may be manifested from Histories) all which do send down their influence according to the Proprieties of the natures of their Stars, and operate upon the inferiour bodies of this World.

The sixth Governour of the World is *Gabriel* the Angell of the *Moon*, who began after *Samuel* the Angel of *Mars* had finished his course: the 28 day of the moneth of *October* in the yeare of the World 1771 and eighth moneth: and he ordered the affaires of the World 354 years and 4 monaths, untill the year of the World 2126. Again in these times men were multiplyed, and builded many Cities: and we must note: that the Hebrews do affirme that the Generall deluge, was *Anno Mundi* 1656. under the moderation of *Mars*: But the Septuagint interpreters, *Isidorus* and *Beda* confirme the Deluge to be in the year of the World 2242. under the Regiment of Gabriel, the Angel of the Moon, which seems unto me by Multiplication to be rather constenteaneous unto truth, but to express my further conception hereof, is not the work of this present discourse.

*Michael* the Angel of the Sun was the 7. Ruler of the World, who began the 24. of *February*, in the year of the World according to common computation 2126. and he governed the world 354. years and four moneths, untill the year of the age of the world 2480. and four moneths.

Under the Dominion of the Angel of the Sun even as Histories consent with truth, Kings began first to be amongst Mortall men, of whom *Nimrod* was the first, that with an ambitious desire of Soveraignty, did Tyrannize over his Companions.

The worship of several Gods by the foolishness of men, was now instituted, and they began to adore their petty Princes as Gods.

Sundry Arts also about this time were invented by men; to wit, the Mathematicks, Astronomy, Magique, and that worship which formerly was attributed to one onely God began now to be given to divers Creatures: the knowledge of the true God, by little and little, and the superstition of men became forgotten.

About these times Architecture was found out, and men began to use more policy both in their civill institutions, and manners, or customs of living.

From henceforth the eighth time in order, again *Orifiel* the Angel of *Saturn* began to govern the World the 26. day of the moneth of *June*, in the year from the beginning of the world 2480. and four moneth; and he continued his government of the world this second return, 354. years and four moneths, untill the year of the world 2834. and eight moneths.

Under the regulation of this Angel, the Nations were multiplied, and the earth was divided into Regions; many Kingdoms instituted; the Towel of *Babel* was built, the confusion of Tongues then fell out, men were dispersed into every part of the earth, and men began to Till, and Manure the earth more acurately, to ordain Fields, sow Corn, plant Vineyards, to dig up Trees, and to provide with greater diligence, what ever was more convenient for their food, and rainment.

From that time forward, first of all, amongst men, the discerning of Nobility begun to be taken notice of; which was, when men in their manner of living, and in wisdom did excell the rest of men, undertaking Trophies of glory from the great ones of the earth, as rewards for their merits: From hence first of all, the whole world began to come into the knowledge of men, whilest every where the Nations being multiplied, many Kingdoms did arise, and various differences of tongues did follow.

The ninth time in order and course, *Anael*, the Angel of *Venus* began again to sway the world the 29. day of *October*, and in the year of the Creation of Heaven and earth 2834. and 8. moneths: and he presided 354. years, four moneths, untill the year of the World 3189.

In these times men forgetting the true God, began to honour the dead, and to worship their Statues for God, which Errour hath infected the World more then two thousand years: Men did now devise curious and costly Ornaments, for better trimming, and adorning their bodies: found out divers kindes of Musicall Instruments; again, men prosecuted too much the lust and pleasures of the flesh, instituting, and dedicating Statuas and Temples to their Gods. Witchcraft, and Incantations in these times were first excogitated by *Zoroaster* King of the *Bactrians* (and divers others as well as he) whom Ninus King of Assyria overcame in War.

In order the tenth time *Zachariel* the Angel of *Jupiter*, again began to ruler the world the last day of *February*, in the year of the building, or framing the heaven and earth, 3189. and he moderated according to his custom, and manner 354. years, and four moneths, untill the year of the world 3543. and four moneth.

These were joyfull times, and might truly be called golden, wherein there was plenty of all manner of usefull things, which much conduced for the increase of mankinde, giving thereby exceeding beauty and adornment to the things of this World.

In like manner about this time, God gave to *Abraham* the *Law* of *Circumcision*; and first of all promised the *Redemption* of *Mankinde* by the *Incarnation* of his onely begotten Son.

Under the Government of this Angel, the Patriarchs first *Founders* of *Justice*, were famous, and the righteous were divided from the ungodly, by their own proper indeavour and consent.

About these times in *Arcadia*, *Iupiter* grew famous, who was stiled also *Lisania*, the Son of Heaven and God, a King, who first of all gave Laws to the Arcadians, made them very civill in their manners and behaviour, taught them the worship of God, erected them

Temples, instituted Priests, procured many advantagious benefits for mankinde, for which his so great benefits, he was by them termed *Jupiter*, and after his death accounted for a *Deity* or God.

He had his Original from the sons of *Heber*, viz. *Gerar*, as ancient Histories do record to posterity.

*Prometheus* also the son of *Atlas* is reported under the Government of this Angel to have made Men; onely, because of rude and ignorant, he made them wise and knowing, humane, courteous, accomplished in learning and manners: he made Images by Art to move of themselves.

He first found out the use of the Ring, Scepter, Diadem, and all kingly ornaments.

In or about these times other joviall men did excell; *men* most *wise*, and *women* also, who by their own understanding delivered many profitable inventions to mankinde; who being dead, for the greatness of their wisdom, were reputed as Gods: viz. *Photoneus*, who first of all instituted amongst the Greeks, Laws, and judgements, as also, *Sol, Minerva, Ceres, Serapis* amongst the *Aegyptians*, and very many besides.

In order the 11. time *Raphael* the Angel of *Mercury* again undertook the ordering of the world the first day of the moneth of *Iuly*, in the year of the world 3543. and fourth moneth; he continued in his Commands 354. years, and four moneths, untill the year of the Creation of heaven and earth 3897. and 8. moneth.

Verily in these times, as it evidently appears from the Histories of the Ancients, men more earnestly applied themselves to the study of wisdom, amongst whom the last learned and most eminent men, were *Mercurius, Bacchus, Omogyius, Isis, Inachus, Argus, Apollo, Cecrops*, and many more, who by their admirable inventions, both profited the world then, and posterity since.

Severall Superstitions also about these times, concerning the worship of their Idols were instituted by men.

Sorceries, Incantations, and Arts of framing Diabolical Images, were now in a marvellous manner increased, and whatsoever either of subtilty, or wit, that could possibly be attributed to the invention, or cunning of *Mercury* about these times, did exceedingly increase.

*Moses* the wisest Commander of the Hebrews, expert in the knowledge of many things and Arts, a Worshipper of one onely true God, did deliver the people of Israel from the slavery of the *Aegyptians*, and procured their liberty.

About this time *Janus* first of all reigned in *Italy*, after him *Saturnus*, who instructed his people to fat their grounds with soile or dung, and was accounted or esteemed for a God. Near these times Cadmus found out the Greek Letters, or Characters, and *Carmentis*, the daughter of *Evander*, the Latine.

God Omnipotent, under the Government of this *Raphael*, the Angel of *Mercury*, delivered by the hands of *Moses*, to his people a Law in writing, which giveth a manifest testimony of our Saviour *Iesus Christ*, his future birth and nativity to be born in the flesh.

Here arose in the World a wonderful diversity of Religions: During these times, here flourished many *Sybills, Prophets, Diviners, Soothsayers*, or such as used inspection into the entrals of Beasts, *Magitians*, or *Wise-men, Poets*, as *Sybilla, Erythraea*, she of the Isle of *Delphos*, she whom we call the Phrygian, because she lived in *Phrygia* with the rest.

Again in order the twelfth time *Samuel* the Angel of *Mars*, began to exercise his Dominion upon the world, the second day of the moneth of October, in the year of the world 3897. and eighth moneth, and his time of ruling, was 354. years, and four monveths from thence, untill the year 4252. under whose Empire and rule, was that great and most famous Destruction of *Troy* in *Asia* the less: as also an admirable mutation, and alteration of *Monarchy*, and many Kingdoms together with new institutions, or moldings of many Cities, as *Paris, Monunce, Carthage, Naples*, and very many besides these.

Many new Kingdoms were newly erected, or now had their first beginning, as that of the Lacedemonians, Corinthians, Hebrews, and divers more.

Here in these times all over the whole world, there was very great wars, and Battels of Kings and Nations, and several alterations of Empires.

The Venetians from this time, do compute and reckon the originall both of their people and City from the Trojans.

And its observable that very many other Nations, as well in Europe as in Asia, pretend to have taken their originall from the Trojans, to whom I thought good to give so much credit, as they themselves were able to perswade me was truth, upon sufficient testimony and proof.

The Arguments they produce concerning their Nobility and Antiquity are frivolous, being desirous to magnifie themselves openly, as if there were no People, or Nation in Europe, before the Destruction of Troy, or as if there had been no Pesant, or Clown amongst the Trojans.

Under the moderation also of this Planet, Saul was made first King of the Jews, after him David, whose son King Salomon, built in Ierusalem the Temple of the true God, the most famous and glorious of the whole world: from hence the Spirit of God illustrating, and enlightening his Prophets with a more ample illumination of his grace, they did not only foretell of the future incarnation of our Lord and Saviour, but also many other things, as holy Scriptures do testifie, amongst whom were Nathan son of King David, Gad, Asaph, Achias, Semeias, Asarias, Anan, and many others.

Homer the Greek Poet, VVriter of Troys Destruction, Dares, Phrygius, Dyctis Cretensis, who were themselves at the rasing, and sacking thereof, and have likewise described it, are supported to have been alive near about these times.

The thirteenth time in order, Gabriel the Spirit of the Moon, again undertook the ordering of this world the 30. day of Ianuary in the year from the beginning of the Universe 4252. and he presided in his Government 354 years, 4 moneths, untill the year of the World 4606. and fourth moneth.

In this time many Prophets were famous and excelled amongst the Jews, viz. Helias, Heliseus, Micheas, Abdias, with many others: There were many alterations of the Kingdom of the Jews: Lycurgus gave Laws and Ordinances to the Lacedemonians, Capetus, Sylvius. Lyberius Sylvius, Romulus Sylvius, Procas Sylvius, Numitor, Kings of Italy flourished, during the moderation of this spirit: more Kingdomes also had their Originall or foundation under him, as those of the Lydians, Medes, Macedonians, Spartans, and others: the Monarchy of Assyrians under Sardanapalus now ended. And in like manner the Kingdome of the Macedonians was consumed, or worn out.

Sundry lawes are imposed on men, the worship of the true God is neglected, and the Religion of false Gods too much propagated: the City of Rome is built under the Dominion of this Spirit, in the year 1484. which yeare in order, was the 239 of the Angell Gabriel, the Kingdome of the Sylvans in Italy now ended, and that of Rome began in these times, Thales, Chilon, Periander, Cleobulus, Bias, and Pittacus, the seaven wise men of Greece florished, and from thence Philosophers and Poets came into request. At Rome, Romulus the first founder of the City reigned 37. years being a Fratricide and a stirrer up of Sedition. After whom Numa Pompilius continued that Kingdome in peace full 42 years: he amplified the worship of the Gods, and lived in the time of Hezekiah King of Iudea. About the expiration of this Angell of the Moon his government: Nebuchadonozor King of Babylon, took Hierusalem, and destroyed Zedechiah the King and carried away all the people Captive.

Hieremiah the Prophet was now famous, who fore-told this destruction, as also their future delivery from Babylon.

When Gabriel had finished his course, againe Michael Angell of the Sun did assume the 14. government of the World, who began the first day of the moneth of May, in the year of the World 4606. the fourth moneth, and did rule the World according to his own order 354. years, untill the year of the Worlds Creation 4960. and eighth moneth.

In the time of this Angels moderation Evill Merodach King of Babylon, did restore both their Liberty and King to the people of the Jews, according to the direction of the Angell Michael, who as Daniel wrote, stood for the Nation of the Jews, unto whom they were committed by God.

In these times likewise the Monarchy of the Kingdome of the Persians began, whose first King Darius: and the second Cyrus did bring to nothing or utterly ruine, that most powerfull Kingdome of Babylon in the dayes of Balthazar, (as Daniel and the Prophets had predicted.)

In these times Sybilla Cumana was much spoken of, and grew famous; who brought 9 books to Tarquinius Priscus the King to be bought for a certain price; in which were contained the reason, order, and succession of future Avisements, of the whole commonwealth of the Romans. But when the King refused to give her the price demanded, Sybilla (the King seeing it) burnt the three first books, demanding the same price for the other six; which when again he had denyed to give her, she committed to be burnt three of those remaining, and would have done so by the rest; unless the King by perswasion and Councell of others, had not redeemed them from consuming, giving the same price for the three last, for which he might have had the whole nine.

Moreover the Romans having abrogated Government by Kings constituted two Consuls to reign every year.

Phalaris the Tyrant in these times occupied Sicilia: Magique or naturall Philosophy was also in these times highly esteemed amongst the Kings of Persia.

Pythagoras the Philosopher, and very many others flourished amongst the Greeks; the Temple and City of Hierusalem are a new reedified.

Esdras the Prophet repaired the books of Moses, burned by the Chaldeans; who were also called Babylonians, and committed them to memory for example. Xerxes King of the Persians brought his Army against the Greeks, but had no success therein. The City of Rome is taken, burned, and destroyed, by the Gaules; the Capitoll only preserved by a Goose, stirring up the weary Champions. The Athenians had eminent wars in these times: Socrates & Plato Philosophers lived now.

The Romans lessened the power of their Consuls, instituted Tribunes & Aedils, and were also about these times involved in many calamities: Alexander the great after the expiration of the rule of Michael, reigned in Macedonia, destroyed the Monarchy of the Persians in Darius: conquered all Asia, and annexed it with part of Europe to his own Empire.

He lived 33 years, reigned 12 after whose death infinite wars and many mischiefs followed, and his Monarchy became divided amongst four.

Now amongst the Jews, first of all, they began to contend for the Priesthood: the Kingdome of Syria began.

After the Spirit of Michael had finished his course, then the 15 time in order, Orifiel the Angell of Saturn, the third time assumed the regulating of this World, the last day of the moneth of September, in the year from the building of the Universe 4960. and eighth moneth: and he did rule in Chief 354 years, 4 moneths, untill the year of the World 5315. Under whose moderation, the Punick war began betwixt the Romans and Carthaginians: the City of Rome was almost wholly consumed by fire and water. The Brazen Molten

Image called Colossus, in length one hundred and twenty six foot fell down, being shaken by an earthquake. At, or near this time the City of Rome enjoyed peace one year after the Punick War: which Common-wealth had never been without War in 440 years before.

Hierusalem together with the Temple is burnt and destroyed by Antiochus and Epiphanes, the History of the Machabees and their Wars were now acted.

In these times Carthage 606 years after its first foundation is destroyed, and burned continually by the space of 17 whole dayes. In Sicilia seaventy thousand slaves made a Conspiracy against their Masters.

Many Prodigies in these times were beheld in Europe; tame domesticall cattle fled to the Woods, it raigned blood, a fiery Ball shined, appeared, and glistered out of heaven with great noyse and crackling. Mithridates King of Pontus, and Armenia held Wars with the Romans 40 years. The Kingdome of the Jews is restored, which had interruption 575 years from the time of Zedechia untill Aristobalus. The people also of Germany called the Theutines, invaded the Romans and after many fights are overcome and one hundred and threescore thousand of them slain, besides innumerable others of them, who slew themselves and familiars under Cajus and Mantius the Consuls: notwithstanding this, many of the Romans were before this cut off by them: after which time, Civill Wars did much shake the Romane Common-wealth, which endured full 40 years. Three Suns appeared and were seen in Rome, but not long ere they were reduced into one.

A very few years succeeding, Julius Cajus Caesar usurped the government of the Romans, which Octavius Augustus after him amplified, and joyned Asia, Africk and Europe into one Monarchy he reigned 36 years by whom, or whose means God gave peace to the whole World: In the year from the building of the City 751. and of Caesar Octavius Augustus 42. and in the 245 year and eighth moneth, the 25 of December, of the government of the aforesaid Orifiel the Angell of Saturne: Iesus Christ the Son of God is born in Bethelem of Iudea, of Mary the Virgin. Note, how faire and wonderfull the Ordination of Divine providence is; for the World at first was created under the rule of Saturn his Angell Orifiel: and mercifully redeemed, instaurated, and made new again under his third government; so that the great number and agreement of concurring Actions, may seem to administer no small beliefe to this manner of description, or setting forth, that this World is governed by the seaven Angels of the Planets: for in the first Gubernation of Orifiel, there was one only Monarchy of the whole World, under his second (as we mentioned before) it was divided amongst many.

Again, during his third, (as is manifest) it was reduced into one, although, if we consider or measure time aright, it is manifest also that in the second government of Orifiel, there was but one only Monarchy, when the Tower of Babel was built. From this time forward the Kingdome of the Jews was quite taken away, and the sacrifice of meat-offerings ceased, nor shall liberty be restored to the Jews before the third Revolution of the Angell Michael, and this shall be after the Nativity of Christ, in the year 1880. the eighth moneth, viz. In the year of the World 7170. and eighth moneth. Many of the Jews in those times, and of the Gentiles also, shall embrace Christian Religion, most plain and simple men preaching the word of God, whom no humane institution, but a divine spirit hath inspired. The World shall then be brought to its first innocency of its simplicity, the Angell of Saturne Orifiel governing the World every where.

Coelestiall things are mixed with earthly, many of the Christians for that faith which they did Preach, shall be slaughtered by the rulers of this World. About the ending of the Moderation of Orifiel, Hierusalem is destroyed by the Romans, and the Jews are dispersed into every Nation, there being massacred of them eleven hundred thousand, and four score thousand sold for slaves, the residue of them fled; and so the Romans wholy destroyed Judea.

After that Orifiel had finished his government, Anael the Angell of Venus, the sixteenth in order, the third time reassumed his Regiment of the World: the last day of Ianuary, in the year of creating the Heaven & Earth 5315. but from the year of the birth of Christ 109. and he regulated the affaires of the World 354 years, 4 moneths, untill the years of the World 5669. 4 moneths, but of the Nativity of our Saviour Iesus Christ in the flesh 463. And its remarkable, that almost during the whole rule of this Anael the Angel of Venus, the Church of Christians did flourish in her persecutions, and prevailed; many thousands, of men being Butchered for the Faith of Christ. Moreover in these times very many Heresies began to be broached in the Church, which were not extinguished, but after some time, and with labour & the blood of good men.

Many men were eminent about these times in all manner of learning, and such as were learned and Eloquent Divines, Astronomers, Physitians, Orators, Historiographers, and men of like quality, not only amongst the Gentiles, but Christians. At length the persecution of Infidels ceased, after that Constantine Caesar the great, had assumed the Christian faith, in the year of the World 5539. after the middle of the Government of the aforesaid Anael the Angell of Venus. Although those professing the Religion and faith of Iesus Christ in some measure were now and then disturbed and molested by the Ungodly; Yet notwithstanding the peace of the Church did remain free from molestation a long time.

From this time forward, Mankinde which from the time of Ninus the King, for almost the space of two thousand and three hundred years, had most miserably gone astray about the worship of Idols, was now revoked mercifully to the knowledge of one only God.
Various Arts of Subtilty in these times were augmented, and had increase and reputation according to their convenience to the nature of Venus.

For the manners of men are changed with the time, and the inferiour bodies are disposed according to the influence of the superiors.

The mind of man (verily) is free, and receives not the influence of the Stars, unless it doth too much commaculate his affection, by inclining its self with the commerce which it hath with the body. For the Angels who are the movers of the Orbs, do neither destroy nor subvert any thing, which nature it self hath constituted or framed.

A Comet of unwonted and unusuall greatness did precede the death of Constantine.

The Arrian Heresie in many Countreys disturbed the holy Church.

Toward the end of this Angels Government, in the time of Iulianus Caesar, Crosses appeared in lines, and Crosses in the garments of men.

In Asia and Palaestina wars followed, Pestilences and Famine in those places where the Crosses appeared.

In these times also about the year of our Lord 360. the Franks or Franconians in Germany had their Originall; who afterwards wasting Gallia, gave the name unto it of France, having first overcome and conquered the people thereof. The description of Francia in greatness is long and wide, or of great circuit, whose Metropolis Moguntia sometimes was; now truly and only Herbipolis.

The Bavarians, Suevians, the people of Rhine, Saxons, Thuringers, this day do occupie a great part of France in Germany, under jurisdiction of the Papacy in some places. Moreover in the 280 year of the Gubernation of this Angell Anael, the Roman Empire began to decline, whilst the City was taken and burned by the Goths the Imperial seat being first translated into Greece under Constantine, which was very mischievously done, and the only cause of the declining of that whole Monarchy: for neer the determination of this Angell Anael his Regiment, there did arise Radigifus, Alaricus, Atholfus, Kings of the Gothes: Also after this Genserick of the Vandals and Attilas of the Hunns who runing all over Europe, did most miserably teare the Empire in sunder, as is evident in these Histories.

When Anael the Angell of Venus had finished his Regiment, then Zachariel the Spirit of Jupiter did reassume the Universall Government of this World the seaventh time, the first day of June, in the year of the World 5669. the fourth moneth, but in the year of our Lord and Saviour Iesus Christ 463. four moneths; and governed in his turne years and four moneths untill the year of the World 6023. and eighth moneth: but of our Lord God 817.

Many men in these times out of their affection to Christian Philosophy, betook themselves to live in the Wilderness: many Prodigies appeared, Comets, Earthquakes, it raigned blood.

Merlin born in Tumbe, predicted wonderfull things in the beginning or entrance of this Angels Government.

Arthurus who commonly is called Arthur, the most glorious King of great Britain, who overcame the Barbarians, restored peace to the Church, went away conquerour in many battels: propagated the Faith of Christ, subdued to his dominion all Gallia, Norway, Denmark, and many other Provinces. He was the most glorious of all Kings that lived in his time, who after many famous actions performed, did never more appear, being expected to return by the Britains for many years, of whom in times past many praise-worthy songs were published by the Bardes of that people of wonderfull Poesie; for whilest he raigned, England was in its most flourishing condition, unto whom thirteen kingdoms were subject.

In or near these times the severall Orders of Monks began to multiply in the Church of God: Theodoric King of Gothes being an Arrian did possess all Italy, slue Boetius their Consull.

All manner of Estates were full of perturbation, as well the Empire as Church affairs, or Church and Common-wealth were now in great distress.

Zenon and Anastasius, Arrian Emperours in the East, Theodoric and his successors in Italy, Honorius King of the Vandalls in Affrica did excercise no small Tyranny.

Clodoucus King of France at length in Gallia being turned Christian, both overcame the Gothes, and restored peace in many places, though not in every Country and Kingdom.

In the time of St. Benedict, and year of Christ 500. or thereabouts, in the beginning of the government of this Angel Zachariel the Spirit of Iupiter, whose spirits property it is, to change Empires and Kingdoms, which was done in this Revolution, histories do manifoldly declare; and what himself could not perform, he ordained Raphael the Angel of Mercury, his successor, to perfect in Charles King of French-men.

Many Kingdoms came to their periods under these 350. years both of the Gothes, Vandalls, Burgundians, Lumbards, Thuringers, Almains, Bavarians, and very many besides.

Iustinianus the Emperour first of all about these times beautified the Common-wealth very deservedly with his Lawes.

Many gallant and most admirable men flourished under Zachariel.

Iustinianus built the Temple of St. Sophia in Constantinople consisting of 400. Towers. The Empire is divided and made Bi-partite, and ever and anon is more and more oppressed with mischiefs.

Many signs in heaven appeared about these times, as is easily collected from Histories.

Cosdroes king of the Persians took Hierusalem, whom Heraclius the Emperour afterward slue.

Mahomet the Arabian in these times about the year of Christ 600. introduced the Sect of Sarazens, by which Sect the Roman Empire in Asia is now quite extinguished.

Dagobert King of France slue the English, at that time called Saxons (whom in battell he overcame). Its remarkable, that by little and little Christianity about these times began to fail in Asia and Affrick, upon entrance of the Sect of the Sarasins therein, which now had almost poysoned the whole world.

About the years of our Lord God 774. Crosses appeared in the garments of men, and not long after the Roman Empire is divided, a translation of the Monarchy being made to Charles who was of the Frankes Nation in Germany, who preserved the Empire and Church from perishing, and fought many famous battels.

The name of Western Galls, or Westphalians in Saxony after his victory first had its beginning.

In the 18. place after finishing the rule of Zachariel, the Angel of Iupiter, Raphael the spirit of Mercury undertook the disposing of this worlds affaires, the third time, the second day of November in the year of the Creation of the World, 6023. eighth moneth, and he swayed the scepter of the World 354. years, four moneths, untill the years of the world 6378. and of our Lord God 1171.

In the first beginning of this revolution of Raphael the Angel of Mercury, the Monarchy of the Roman Empire (as we mentioned before) was translated to Charles the great.

After Charles his son Lodowick ruled 25. years, who being dead, his sons contending amongst themselves, did again extenuate the strength of the Empire.

The Normans harrowed France: Rome is twice scourged by the Saracens: under Lodowick the second it raigned blood from Heaven in Italy, by the space of three whole dayes.

In Saxony, a certain village with all its buildings, and inhabitants was in a moment swept away by an horrible gaping or opening of the earth.

About the year of our Lord God 910. there were many great motions in Italy, and Italy fell from the Empire of the Franks or Franconians, and ordained proper kings for themselves of their own election; the first whereof was Berengarius the Duke of Fonolivium, after whom seven in order succeeded, near upon fifty years, untill the translation of the Empire unto the Germans: The first Emperour that was thereof was Otho, from which time the Empire began to be reformed; unto whom Otho his son, and hos Nephew Otho after succeeded in the Empire: under whose Government the Hungarians are converted to the Christian Faith. But the third Otho dying without children, instituted after his death Electors of the Empire in the year of Christianity 1002. even as they remain to this present day.

Ierusalem is again taken by the Saracens: many strange sights are seen in the air, in the Heavens, in the Earth and sea, and in waters: But Otho the third being dead, Henry the first by election of the Princes succeeded, raigned 20. years, who founded the Church of Bamburg, and dying a Virgin, together with his wife Kunigunda he shone gloriously in miracles; after whom Conrade, first Duke of the Francks is chosen, and ruled 20. years. Godfrey Earl of Bullen also recovered the holy Land, and City of Jerusalem from the hands of the Infidels.

Before the end of this Revolution many signs and Prodigies were seen, and a little time after the Nation of the Tartars exceeded the bounds of their own Country, and did many mischiefs to the Empire of Rome.

There was Famine, Pestilence, Earthquakes in the Empire: Three suns were seen in the East, and as many Moons. In the year of our Lord God 1153. Frederick first called Barbarossa began to reign, and ruled 33. years, the beginning of whose Government was in the 336. year of Raphael: He did many noble exploits, and enlarged the strength of that Empire, performed sundry wars with great success, in whose ninth year the Egians and Lituotrians were converted to the Faith of Christ.

Samael the Angel of Mars in order, the nineteenth time came to accept the Gubernation of the universall world, it being now his third returne, and this he did the third day of March, Anno Mundi, 6378. and he regulated mundane affaires 354. years four moneths, untill the years of the World 6732. four moneth; and of our Lord God 1525. under whose predominancy many wars were all over the whole world, by which means infinite thousands of men perished, and sundry Kingdoms lost their former bounds: betwixt Frederick the first Emperour and the Romane Nobility, many controversies arose, sundry great battels were fought, and many thousands of Romans perished.

The aforesaid Frederick did wholy subvert Mediolanum: Leige is destroyed, Hierusalem is again taken by the Saracens, the Empire of the Tartarians the greatest in the whole World about these times took its beginning, occasioned a very great plague in the World, nor yet do they cease.

After Frederick, Henrie his Son is elected Emperour. Who being dead, Schism confounds that Empire; under Philip and Otho many battels followed in the confines of Germany, Argentine, Cullen, Liege, Wormes, Spires, and all over the Kingdome. The sect of begging or Mendicant Friars began in these times, in the 40 year year, or thereabouts of Samael: from whence it is most apparent, that all things are done by providence. The Sarazens fought many battels against the Christians in Asia and Africk. Constantinople is taken by the Germans: Baldwin Earl of Flanders is instituted Emperour. In Almain more then twenty thousand young men are drowned in the Sea by Pyrats, who seduced by a vain spirit, did give forth they would recover the holy land.

From Spain many shepheards or keepers of cattle united themselves together, coming to Paris dispoiling the clergy of their livelyhoods, the common people taking part with them, or being well pleased with it.

But when they extended their hands to take away the goods of the Layity, they were quite cut off and destroyed.

In the year of Christ 1212. Frederick the second is elected, he reigned 33. years, and did many acts against the Church. In the yeare 1238. an Eclipse and a continual Earthquake undid many thousands of men.

Frisia also by continuall incursions of the sea, was almost wholly drowned, and there did perish more then one hundred thousand of men and women.

The Tartars waste Hungaria and Polonia, Armenia the greater being first subdued, and many regions besides.

In the year of Christ 1244. a certain Jew digging in the ground at Toledo in Spain, found a book, in which it was written, In the third World Christ shall be born of the Virgin Mary, and shall suffer for the salvation of man, not long after the third World believing, shall be baptized.

It was the third Revolution of the Angell of Saturn, concerning which, what is spoken is intended: in the beginning of whose reign, Christ was born of a Virgin.

The Popes of Rome deposing Frederick, it is said the Empire was vacant 28 years, untill the Election of Rodolph Count of Habspurg, constituting Kings by turns in the Intervals or vacancy. First Henry Count of Schuvartzenburg at Thuring by election of the Princes; then William Earle of Holland, Conrade the Son of Frederick, Alfonsus King of Castile, Richard Earl of Cornwall, brother to the King of England, many evils were multiplied upon the face of the Earth.

At or neer this time about the year of our Lord God 1260. the Confederacy of the Switzers began, a small people in number, but have increased with the time, who have slain many of their Nobility, and being a Warlike people have banished and frighted away many others of their Nobles from their proper habitations, whose Common wealth is now known to all the people of Germany.

In the year of Christians 1273. Rudolphus of Habspurg is constituted Emperour by Election of the Princes he raigned 18 years, the best of men, prudent in all manner of affaires, from whom afterwards descended all the Dukes of Austria. The Tartarians invading the Lands of Christians, Constantinpole and Greece, brought infinite damage to the Christians.

The Saracens do occupie many Cities in Asia, kill and destroy more than four hundred thousand Christians: Rudolphus being dead, Adolph of Nassaw is elected King, he governed six years, whom Albert the son of Rudolph, afterwards overcame and slew in fight neer Wormes and was chosen Imperator in the yeare of Christ 1298. he governed ten years and was slain by his brothers son. The Order of the Knights Templars by command of Pope Clement the fifth is destroyed, the Isle of Rhodes is recovered by Christians out of the hands of the Sarazens, after the War and siege thereof had continued four whole years. Albertus being slain by his Nephew; Henry is constituted the eighth Emperour, being Count of Luxenburg, who reigned 5 years; he being dead Lodowick the fourth of Bavaria reigned 32 years, beginning in the year 1315. unto whom the Popes of Rome gave a Crown.

Frederick Duke of Austria opposeth himself against Lodowick, but is overcome by him.

After Lodowick, Charles the fourth King of Bohemia is constituted Emperour; who converted the Bishoprick of Prague into an Archbishoprick; he reigned 31 years: there were most fearfull Earthquakes. This Charles did institute many things in favour of the Princes Electors, concerning their Customes and Tallayes, which were not in use formerly. Gunther Count of Schuartzenburg stiled himself King, opposed Charles the Emperour, but prevailed nought at all against him.

After Charles, his Son Winceslaus governed 22 years: after whom Jodocus Marques of Moravia succeeded, Sigismund Cozen German of Winceslaus.

Winceslaus was disposed, Leopold Duke of Austria, 8 Earls, and more then 4000 souldiers fighting against the Switzers, were all by them slain.

During the government of Winceslaus King of Bohemia Emperour: the Tenets of Iohn Huss had their beginning. Winceslaus being deposed, Rupert Count Palatine of Rhine, and Duke of Bavaria was elected, and ruled 10. years. In the year of our Lord God 1369. the Christians did ingage themselves in a war against the Sarazens, which succeeded ill by reason of the French mens Arrogancy: because more then one hundred thousand of our men did dye in that war; besides such as were made Captives, amongst whom was Iohn Duke of Burgundy, many were the wars of those times.

In the year of the World 1407 Sigismund is made Emperour, and governed 27 years: he indeavoured to wast and destroy the kingdome of Bohemia thereby to extinguish Heresie, but it little availed him. The Kingdome of France is most grievously wasted and consumed by the English and Burgundians: Sigismund being departed this life, Albert Duke of Austria, Sigismunds son in Law, succeeded in the year of Christians 1438. and only raigned two years, an admirable man and worthy of the Empire. He being deceased, Frederick the third Duke of Austria, the Son of Ernestus, by election of the Princes, is chosen Emperour: and reigned 56 years, a man of a Divine soul and peaceable conversation, who began to rule Anno Dom. 1440.

In the year of Christians 1453. Constantinople is taken of the Turks by Treachery of a certain Genoway, and a little after by degrees all Greece fell from their Christian faith. For a litle time after many Kingdoms and Provinces of the Christians were harrowed, wasted, and taken by the Turks. Many and most grievous wars the Christians had amongst themselves about this time, in France, England, Saxony, Westphalia, Prusia, Flanders, Sweden, and other places. In these times the Art of Printing was newly found out, and invented at Mogunce the Metropolis of Almain, by a wonderfull industry, and not without the speciall gift of the Deity.

In the year of Christ 1456. the Turks were overthrown in Hungaria by the faithfull Christians, whereof many of them perished. The Pilgrimage of young men to Saint Michael was wonderfull. There were Earthquakes in the Kingdome of Naples, and more then fourty thousand people perished thereby.

In the year of the World 1462 Moruntia is taken and spoiled being the Metropolis of the Franconians or Francks in Germany.

Charles Duke of Burgundy overcame the Franconians in Anno 1465. after that in 1467 he destroyed the cities Dinant & Liege, An. 1473. he entered Gelderland, and with much valour obtained it, & in like manner all the whole Dukedome of Loraigne.

A Comet during all the moneth of Ianuary 1472 appeared. Charles Duke of Burgundy not long besieged the Towne of Nussicum one whole years space, viz. in or about 1474. which Magnanimous Prince was afterwards slain in war 1467. The Turks took away from the Christians about these times, many of their cities, Nigropont in Euboia, the Kingdome of Bosnia, Dukedome of Speta, Achaia, Mysia, and more Kingdomes besides these in the East.

Anno 1476 a convocation of fools was in Franconia of Germany neer Niclaushausen, full of errours.

Anno 1480 the Turks besieged the Rhodians with a powerfull Armie but prevailed not; departing the same year from Rhodes, they took the city Hydruntum, more then twelve thousand Christians being slain there, only 22 souldiers escaping. The next year Mahomet Emperour of the Turks died; to whom Bajazet his first born succeeded in the Kingdome, having reigned now at this present 27 years. In the year of Christ 1486. Maximilian the Son of Frederick was instituted King of Romans at Franckford, and saluted Caesar by Iulius the Pope 1508. who instituted the Order of warfare of Saint George purposely against Hereticks and Turks: he brought the Switzers low by war, and even to this day makes war against the Rebellious Sicambrians; he will be fortunate against all such as break their Leagues or Covenants with him.

The King of France after his wonted manner, a constant persecutor of the Empire, is discovered to plot new devices against it. The Omnipotent protects those assigned to the Government of Samael: Anno 1508. the Venetians Rebels to the Empire of Caesar, are threatned with War and Banishment. Punishment of stubbornness will be the reward of an advised satisfaction. About the end of this third Revolution of Samael, the Image of alteration shall pass to the first and shall be the Perdition of many men for unless Aries be reduced again, (God assisting) (ad algos) there will be translation of one Monarchy, or of some great Kingdome.

A strong sect of Religion shall arise, and be the overthrow of the Ancient Religion.

It's to be feared least the fourth beast lose one head.

Mars first of all in the Government of Samael foretold the Flood, in his second returne, the siege and destruction of Troy: in his third toward the end thereof will be found great want of Vnity: from matters preceding may be Judged what will or ought to succeed. This third Revolution of Mars shall not be consummated without Prophecie, and the institution of some new Religion, from this year of our Lord 1508. here yet remains untill the end of the Government of Samael 17. years wherein signes and figures shall be given, foreshewing the beginnings of evill. For in Anno. 1525. Crosses were seen in the garments of men by the space of ten years before, what is past already shall shew their effects: but 13 years from hence being justly summoned away, thou shalt surrender thy place to the (non Intelligent) thou shalt revive again far greater to me, after the Fates in the third; unless it be lawfull thou obscure thy self in a cloud.

The twentieth time in order, Gabriel Angell of the Moon received the moderation of the World, in the year of the World 6732. the fourth moneth, and fourth day of Iune: in the year of Christ 1525. and he shall regulate the world 354. years, and four monenths, untill the year of the world 7086. eighth moneth, but of our Lord Christ 1879. and 11. moneth. The future Series of this Revolution requireth Prophecy.

Most sacred Caesar, I have not wrote these things assertively, or that we must believe it by any means whatever with the injury of Orthodox Divinity.

There are some that in these things have supputed Lunar moneths, which if thou holdest fit to consent unto, then those things I have wrote must be varied.

I protest with my own proper hand, and confess with my own mouth, that in all these things delivered, I beleeve nothing, or admit of anything, unless what the Catholick Church doth hold: the rest, I refute and contemn as vain, faigned and superstitious.
Finis Joh. Trit.

Englished 1647, by William Lilly, student in Astrologie.

# Editor's Appendix

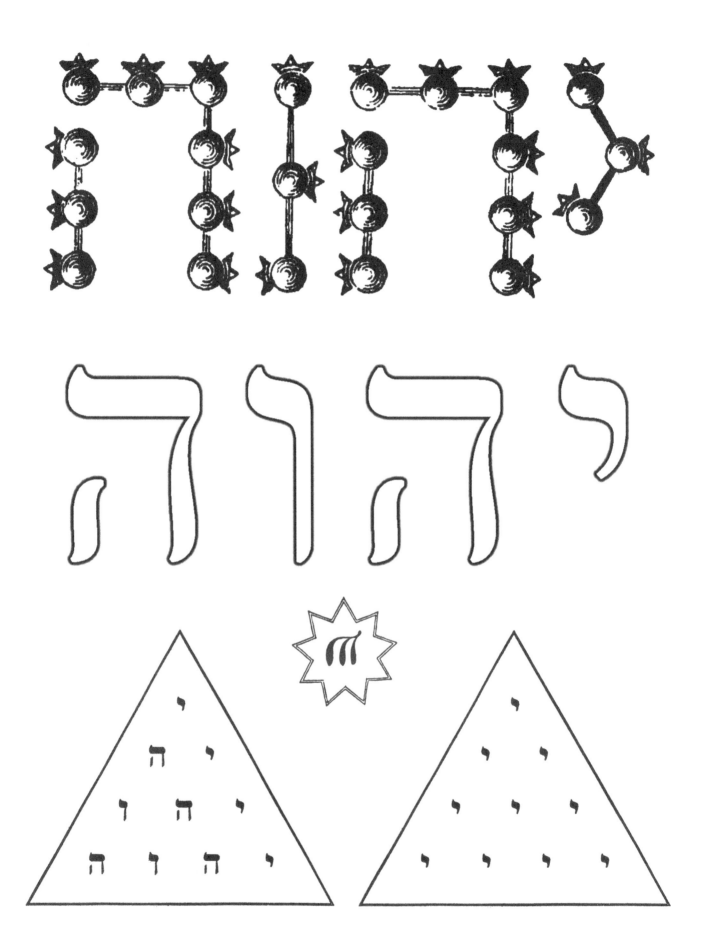

# Some Drawings by Eliphas Levi from *Dogma of High Magic (1854)*

3rd FIG. The Triangle of Solomon.

4th FIG. The four great kabalistic names.

5th FIG. The Pentagram of Faust.

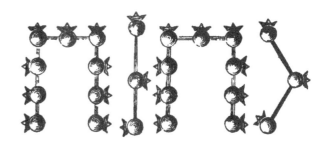

6th FIG. The Tetragram of the Zohar.

**FIRST FIGURE. The great Symbol of Solomon.**

The double triangle of Solomon, figured by the two old persons of the kabalah; the macroprosope and the microprosope; the God of light and the God of reflection; the merciful[1] and the vengeful[2]; the white Jehovah [יהוה] and the black Jehovah [ יהוה ].[3]

The little figures which are on the two sides are analogous to the principle subject.

---

[1] Literally 'miséricordieux' means "merciful, compassionate, forgiving"
[2] Literally 'vengeur' means "retributive, vengeful, vindictive, desiring vengeance"
[3] Editor's note: Both the black and the white יהוה are spelled the same, but are pronounced differently and refer to different entities. The black יהוה is a fallen master. These two have been intentionally confused by some groups in order to deceive unsuspecting people.

**2nd FIG. The Esoteric sacerdotal[4] formula of reprobation[5].**

A sacerdotal hand doing the sign of esotericism and projecting the figure of the demon in its shadow.

Above we see the ace of pentacles from the chinese Tarot and two superimposed triangles, one white and one black.

This is a new allegory explaining the same mysteries; it is the origin of good and evil; it is the creation of the demon by the mystery.

---

[4] Literally 'sacerdotale' means "priestly, sacerdotal"
[5] Literally 'réprobation' means "disapproval, disapprobation, reprobation"

**7th FIG. The Pentacles of Ezekiel and of Pythagoras.**

The cherubim with four heads from the prophesy of Ezekiel, explained by the double triangle of Solomon.

Below, [we have] the wheel of Ezekiel, [which is the] key of all the pentacles, and the pentacle of Pythagoras.

The cherub of Ezekiel is represented here such as the prophet described it.

Its four heads are the quaternary Merkabah; its six wings are the senary[6] of Bereshith [בראשית].

The human figure who is in the middle represents reason, the head of the eagle is belief, the cow is resignation and work; the lion is struggle and conquest.

This symbol is analogous to that of the sphinx of the Egyptians, but it is more appropriate to the kabalah of the Hebrews.

---

[6] Literally 'senaire' means "senary: prepared six by six."

**8th Fig. Addha-Nari, great indian Pentacle.**

This pantheistic image represents Religion or the Truth, [it is] terrible for the profane and sweet for the initiates.

This figure has more than an analogy with the cherub of Ezekiel.

The human figure is placed between a bridled[7] calf and a tiger, which form the triangle of Kether, of Geburah and of Gedulah or Chesed.

In the indian symbol, one finds the four magical signs of the Tarot in the four hands of Addha-Nari: on the side of the initiate and of mercy, [one finds] the scepter and the cup; on the side of the profane, represented by the tiger, [one finds] the sword and the circle, which can become either the ring of a chain, or the necklace of fire.

On the side of the initiate, the goddess is dressed only in tiger skins; [but] on the side of the tiger, she carries a long dress of stars, and [her whole head] including her hair is covered by a veil.

A source of milk flows[8] from her brow[9], running from the side of the initiate, and forms a magic circle around Addha-Nari and her two animals that encloses them in an island, [a] representation of the world.

The goddess carries around her neck a magic chain of iron rings on the profane side, and of thinking heads on the side of the initiates; she carries upon her forehead the figure of the lingam, and on each side [there are] three lines superimposed which represent the equilibrium of the ternary and reminds [us of] the triagrams of Fu-Xi.

---

[7] Literally 'bridé' means "bridle, restrain, clamp, flange, rein, ribbon, tag"
[8] Literally 'jaillit' means "rear up; spurt out, gush forth, spout up; jet, fly out, spray out; squirt, flow; burst out"
[9] Literally 'front' means "forehead, brow; face, front; facade"

Editor's Appendix

# Some Drawings by Eliphas Levi from *Ritual of High Magic (1856)*

5th FIG. Magic Instruments: the Lamp, — the Wand, — the Sword, — the Hook.

6th FIG. [The] Key of Thoth.

10th FIG. Kabalistic signs of Orion.

14th FIG. The Ark [of the Covenant].

**1st Fig. Goat of the Sabbath. — Baphomet and Mendes... Frontispiece.**

Pantheistic and magical figure of the absolute.

The torch placed between the two horns represents the equilibrating[10] intelligence[11] of the triad; the goat's head, which is synthetic, [and] unites some characteristics of the dog, bull, and ass, represents the exclusive responsibility of matter and the expiation[12] of corporal[13] sins in the body.

The hands are human, to exhibit the sanctity of labor ; they make the sign of esotericism above and below, to impress mystery on initiates, and they point at two lunar crescents, the upper being white and the lower black, to explain the correspondences of good and evil, mercy and justice.

The lower part of the body is veiled, portraying the mysteries of universal generation, which is expressed solely by the symbol of the caduceus.

The belly of the goat is scaled, and should be colored green ; the semi-circle above should be blue ; the plumage, reaching to the breast, should be of various hues.

The goat has female breasts, and thus its only human characteristics are those of maternity and toil, otherwise the signs of redemption.

On its forehead, between the horns and beneath the torch, is the sign of the microcosm, or the pentagram with one beam in the ascendant, symbol of intelligent human understanding[14], which, placed thus below the torch, makes the flame of the latter an image of divine revelation.

This Pantheos should be seated on a cube, and its footstool should be a single ball, or a ball and a triangular stool.

In our design we have given the former only to avoid complicating the figure.

---

[10] Literally 'équilibrante' means "balancing, equilibrating, equilibrant"
[11] Literally 'intelligence' means "intelligence, cleverness, intellect; wit, brilliance, cunning; understanding, mind, mentality"
[12] Literally 'expiation' means "expiation, atonement"
[13] Literally 'corporels' means "corporal (of the human body; bodily; physical)"
[14] Literally 'l'intelligence humaine' means "human intelligence", but the word 'intelligence' in French means more that just intellect, it also implies a certain understanding

## 3rd Fig. Trident of Paracelsus.

This trident, figure of the ternary, is formed from three pyramidic teeth superimposed upon a greek or latin tau [ T ].

Upon one of its teeth one sees a yod [ ׳ ] crossing a crescent on one part, and on the other [part] an intersecting line, [a] figure which hieroglyphically reminds [us of] the zodical sign of the crab [ ♋ ].

Upon the opposite tooth is a mixed sign reminding [us of] that of the twins [ ♊ ] and that of the lion [ ♌ ].

Between the claws of the crab one sees the sun [ ☉ ], and next to the lion [one sees] the astronomic cross [ + or × ].

Upon the teeth of the middle is hieroglyphically traced the figure of the celestial serpent, having the sign of Jupiter [ ♃ ] for [its] head.

On the side of the crab one reads the word OBITO, [meaning] "go away, back up"; and on the side of the lion one reads IMO, [meaning] "come on, persist".

In the center, and near the symbolic serpent, one reads AP DO SEL, [which is a] word composed of an abbreviation, a word composed kabalistically and hebraically, and finally [a word] of a complete and vulgar root: AP, which must be read AR, because they are the two first greek letters of the word ARK; DO, which must be read OD and SEL [a French word meaning: SALT].

They are the three primary substances, and the occult names of Ark and Od express the same as the sulphur and the mercury of the philosophers.

Upon the rod of iron, which must serve as the trident's handle, one sees three times the letter P. P. P., [which is a] phalloid and lingamic hieroglyphic; then the words VLI DOX FATO, which must be read by taking the first letter as the number of the pentagram in roman numerals, and completing [it] thus PENTAGRAMMATICA LIBERTATE DOXA FATO, [a] character [which is] equivalent to the three letters of Cagliostro's L.P.D.: liberty, power, duty.

On one side, absolute liberty; upon the other, necessity or invincible fatality; in the middle REASON, [the] kabalistic absolute which creates[15] universal equilibrium.

This admirable magical summary by Paracelsus can serve as [a] key to the obscure works of the kabalist Wronski, [a] remarkable scholar who has been led (more than once) away from his ABSOLUTE REASON by the mysticism of his nation and by the shameful financial speculations of a very distinguished thinker.

Every time, we render him the honor and glory of having discovered, before us, the secret of the trident of Paracelsus.

Thus Paracelsus represents the passive with the crab [ ♋ ], the active with the lion [ ♌ ], [and] intelligence or equilibrated reason with Jupiter [ ♃ ] or the king-man [who] dominates the serpent; then he equilibrates the forces by giving the fecundity of the active figure to the passive with the sun [ ☉ ], and [by giving] the space and the night to the active in order to be conquered, and to be illuminated under the symbol of the cross [ + or × ].

He says to the passive: "Obey the impulse of the active, and walk with him through equilibrium as well as [through] resistance." He says to the active: "Resist the immobility of the obstacle; persist and advance."

Then he explains these alternating forces with the great central ternary: LIBERTY, NECESSITY, REASON. REASON in the center; LIBERTY AND NECESSITY as counter-weights.

Here is the force of the trident: within it is the shank and the base; it is the universal law of nature; it is the essence itself of the verb, realized and demonstrated by the ternary of human life, the ark or spirit, the 'od' or the plastic[16] [or flexible] mediator, and the salt or visible matter.

We have wanted to give [something] outside of [just] the explanation of this figure, because it is of the highest importance, and gives the measure of the highest genius to the occult sciences.

One must comprehend after this explanation why, in the flow of our work, we have always inclined ourselves, with traditional veneration for the true adepts, before the divine Paracelsus.

---

[15] Literally 'fait' means "make, build, draw up; play, take; do, work; cook; prepare, perform; handle, transact"
[16] Literally 'plastique' means "plastic, flexible"

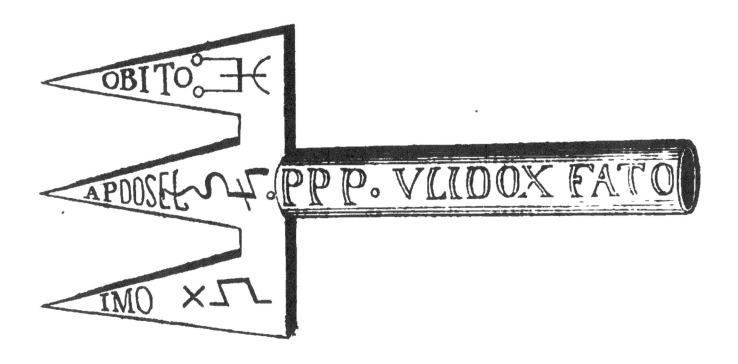

12ᵗʰ Fɪɢ. **Chariot of Hermes, seventh key of the Tarot.**

**LE CHARIOT D'HERMÈS**

Septième clef du Tarot (page 332).

15th Fig. Apocalyptic key. – The seven seals of saint John.

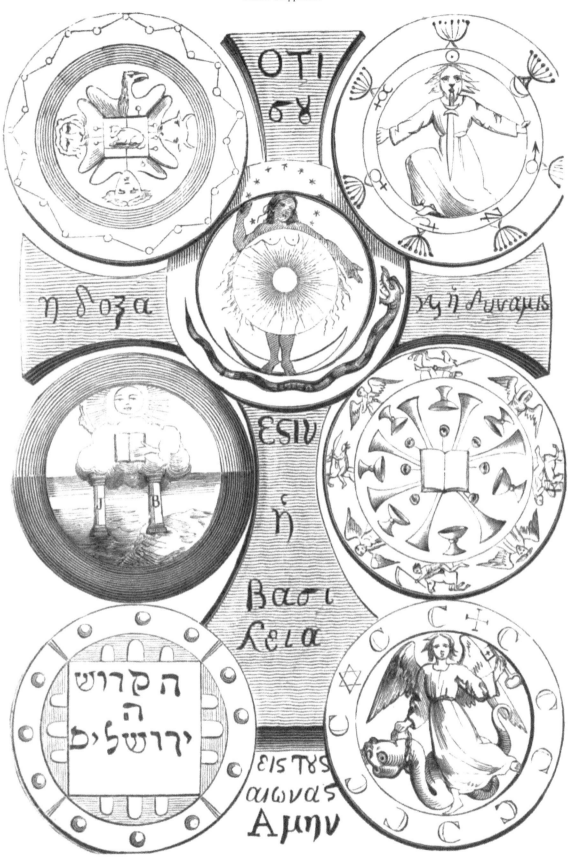

CLEF APOCALPYTIQUE

Les sept Sceaux de saint Jean (page 364).

# Some Drawings by Eliphas Levi from *History of Magic (1860)*

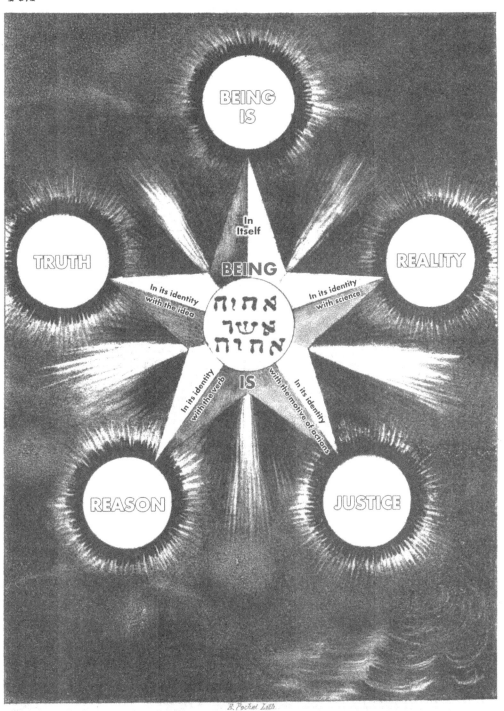

THE PENTAGRAM OF THE ABSOLUTE

## The Magic Head of the Zohar

LA TÊTE MAGIQUE
du Sohar.

## The Great Kabalistic Symbol
of the Zohar

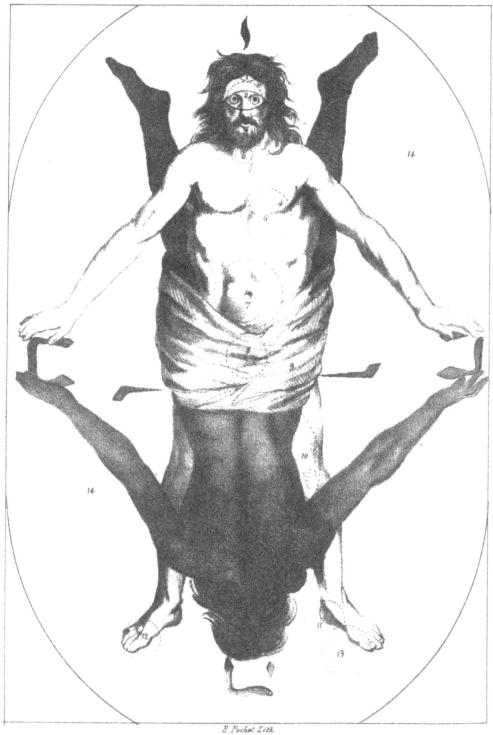

LE GRAND SYMBOLE KABBALISTIQUE
du Sohar.

## Mystery of Universal Equilibrium
According to Indian and Japanese Mythologies

**MYSTÈRE DE L'ÉQUILIBRE UNIVERSEL**
Suivant les Mythologies Indienne et Japonnaise

Editor's Appendix

## Yinx Pantamorphe.

Twenty First Key of the primitive Egyptian Tarot[17]

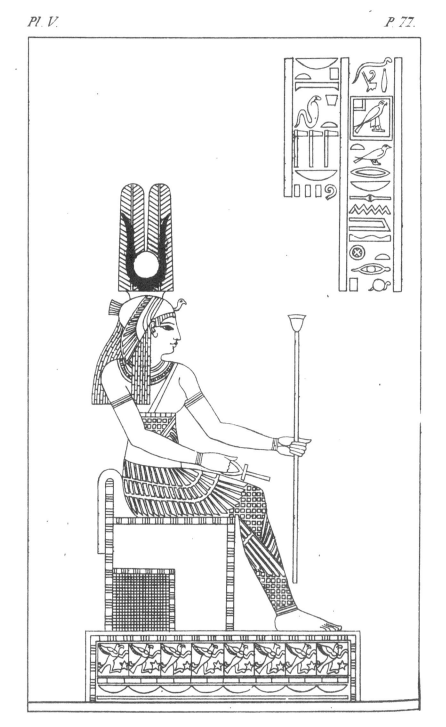

**YINX PANTOMORPHE.**
Vingt et unième Clé du Tarot Égyptien primitif.

---

[17] Editor's note: This would correspond to the final card (#22) in this study guide.

## Explanatory chart of the astronomical and alphabetical table of Bembo;
(*See the Aedipe of Kircher*)

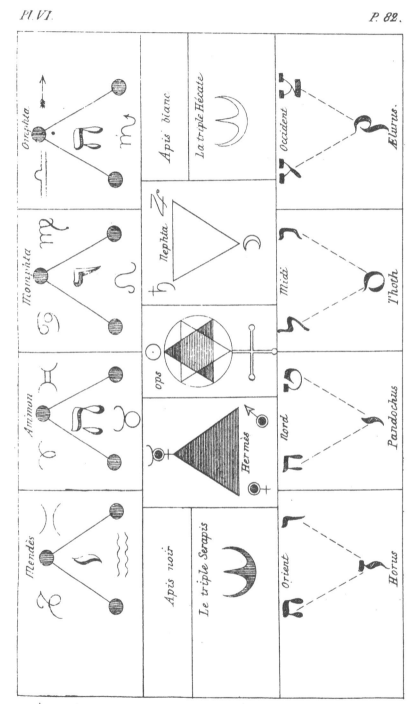

# Pentacle of Kabalistic letters [and] Key of the Tarot, from the Sepher Yetzirah and the Zohar

*Pl. VII.*            *P. 105.*

## LE SEPHER JEZIRAH

Pantacle des lettres Kabbalistiques Clé du Tarot, du Sepher Jezirah et du Sohar.

## The Seal of Cagliostro, the Seal of Junon Samienne, the Apocalyptic Seal and the twelve Seals of the cubic stone, around the Key of the Tarot

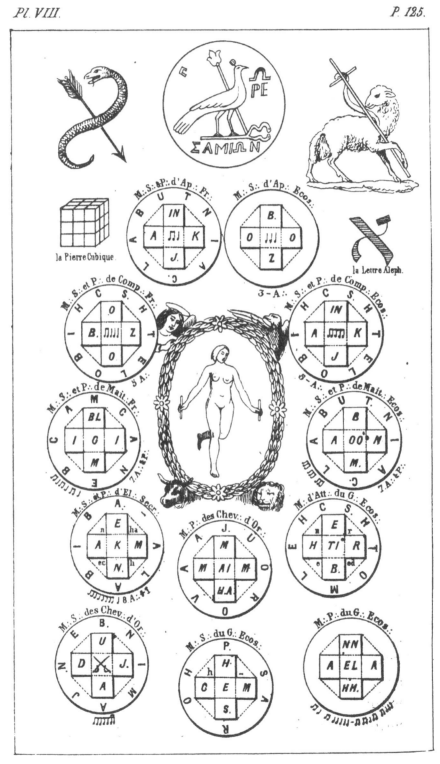

Le Sceau de Cagliostro, le Sceau de la Junon Samienne, le Sceau Apocalyptique et les douze Sceaux de la pierre cubique, autour de la Clé du Tarot.

## Typhonic Symbols

Egyptian Types from the Goethia and Necromacy

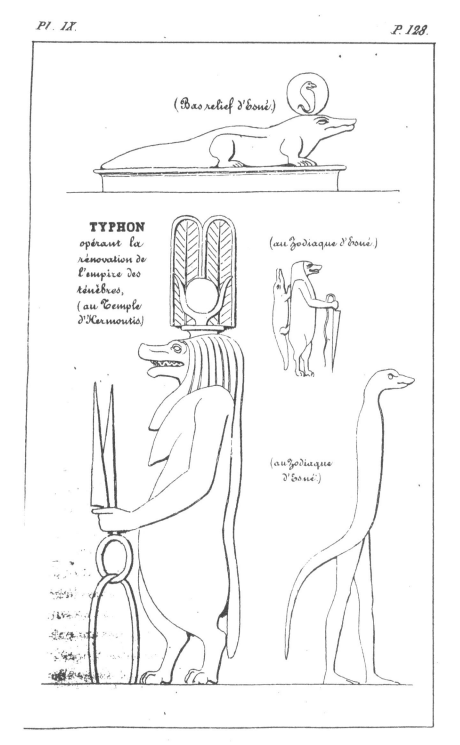

**SYMBOLES TYPHONIENS**
Types Égyptiens de la Goëtie
et de la Négromancie.

## The Seven Marvels of the World

LES SEPT MERVEILLES DU MONDE

## Public Dispute
between St. Peter and St. Paul on one side and Simon the Magician on the other,
Ascension and fall of Simon.
after a 15th Century etching.

### DISPUTE PUBLIQUE
entre S.t Pierre et S.t Paul d'une part et Simon le Magicien de l'autre,
Ascension et chute de Simon.
d'après une gravure du 15.e Siècle.

Editor's Appendix

**Hermetic Magic**
pulled from an ancient manuscript

Pl. XII.    P. 228.

R. Pochet Lith.

## LA MAGIE HERMÉTIQUE
tirée d'un ancien manuscrit.

## The Philosophic Cross
or the plan of the third temple,
prophesied by Ezekiel and that the Templars wanted to build.

**LA CROIX PHILOSOPHIQUE**
ou le plan du troisième temple,
prophétisé par Ezéchiel, et que voulaient bâtir les Templiers.

## The Philosophical Cross [Modified]

[Editor's Note: this image has been edited in order to translate as much as possible. This appears to be an exact replica of part of a Plate given in *Le Soleil Mystique: Journal de la Maçonnerie universelle* (1853) which was a magazine of the "Egyptian" Masonic Rite of Memphis.]

**THE PHILOSOPHICAL CROSS**
or the plan of the third temple,
prophesied by Ezekiel, and that the Templars wanted to build

# Editor's Appendix

**Two Occult Seals,** one of the great work [VISIBLE יהוה INVISIBLE], the other of black magic; after the grimoire of Horonius [OBEY YOUR SUPERIORS AND BE SUBMISSIVE TO THEM BECAUSE THEY TAKE HEED[18]]

**DEUX SCEAUX OCCULTES,**
l'un du grand œuvre, l'autre de la magie noire;
d'apres le grimoire d'Honorius

---

[18] Editor's note: The last part of this phrase 'parce qu'ils y prennent garde', is difficult to translate, but literally it would be "because they take heed [of] it" or "because they are careful [of] it" or "because they are watchful [of] it", where "it" implies an unknown, which (in this case) is probably unknown dangers.

## Primitive Egyptian Tarots
The two and the ace of cups

**TAROTS ÉGYPTIENS PRIMITIFS**
Le deux et l'as de coupe.

## The Seven Planets And Their Genii
(Magic of Paracelsus)

LES SEPT PLANÈTES ET LEURS GÉNIES
(Magie de Paracelse.)

# The Great Hermetic Arcanum
according to Basil Valentine

**LE GRAND ARCANE HERMÉTIQUE**
suivant Basile Valentin.

## General Plan of the Doctrine of the Kabalists

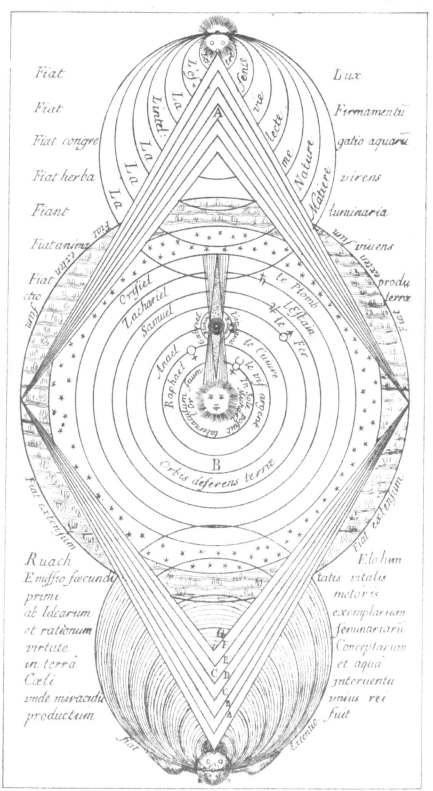

Plan général de la doctrine des Kabbalistes.

Editor's Appendix

# Some Drawings by Eliphas Levi from *Key to the Great Mysteries (1861)*

**Absolute Key of Occult Sciences**

*given by Guillaume Postel and completed by Eliphas Lévi*

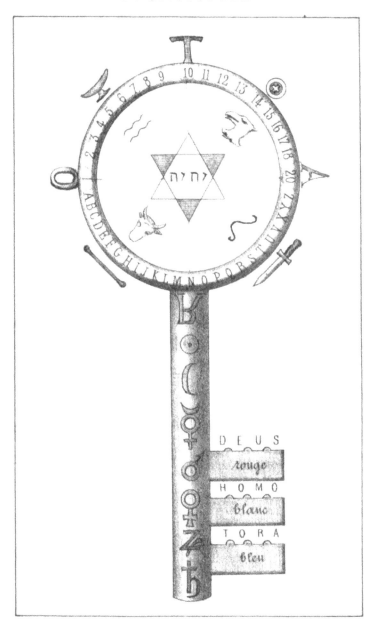

Clé absolue des sciences occultes

*donnée par Guillaume Postel et complétée par Eliphas Lévi*

## The sign of the great arcanum (G.A.)

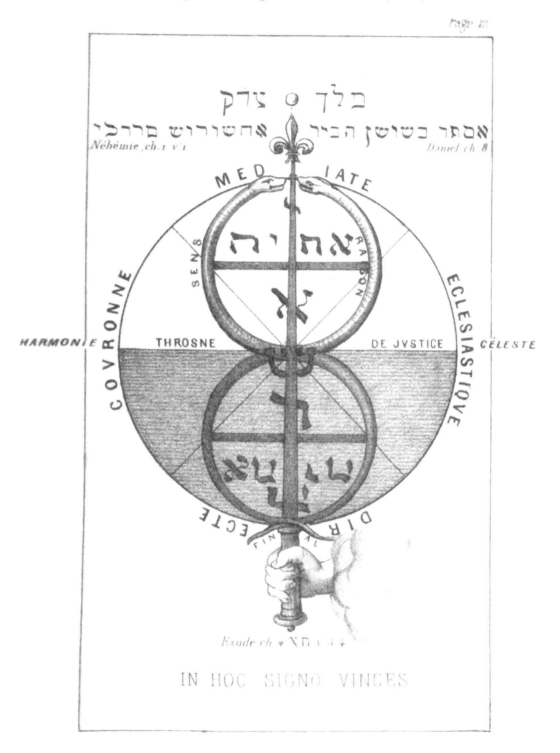

Le signe du grand arcane.
G∴A∴

## Great pentacle pulled from the vision of Saint John

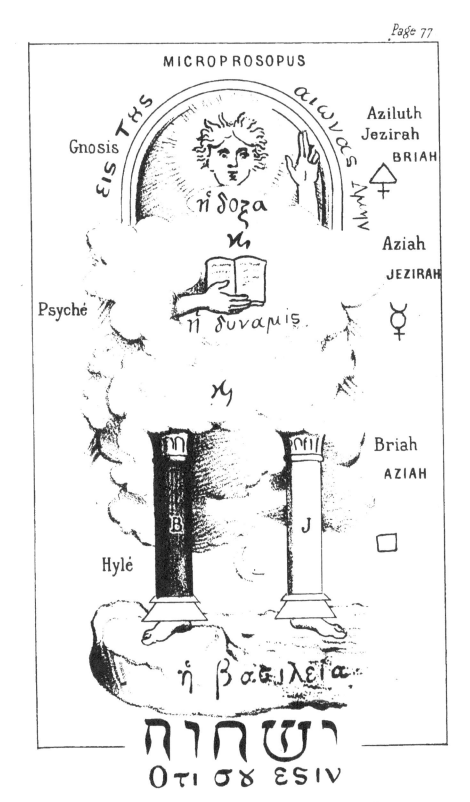

Grand pantacle tiré de la vision de St. Jean.

## The tenth key of the Tarot

La dixième clé du Tarot.

## First pentacle, the white star.

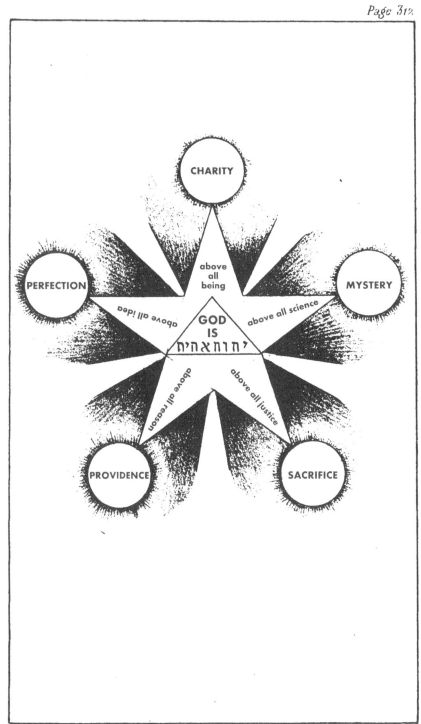

The star of the three magi

## Second pentacle, the black star.

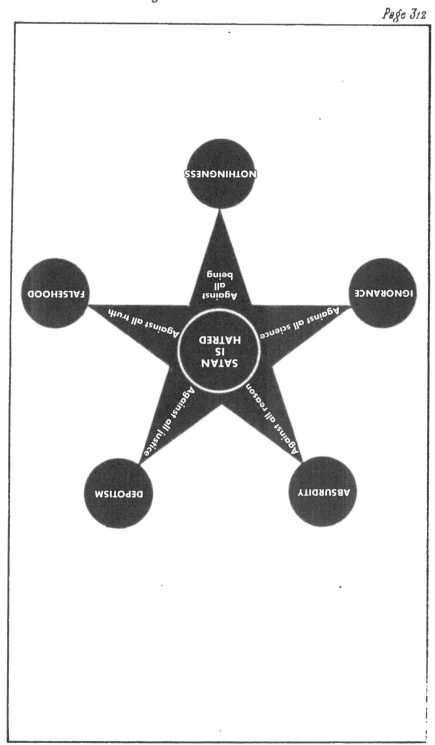

The evil star

## Third pentacle, the red star.

Page 312

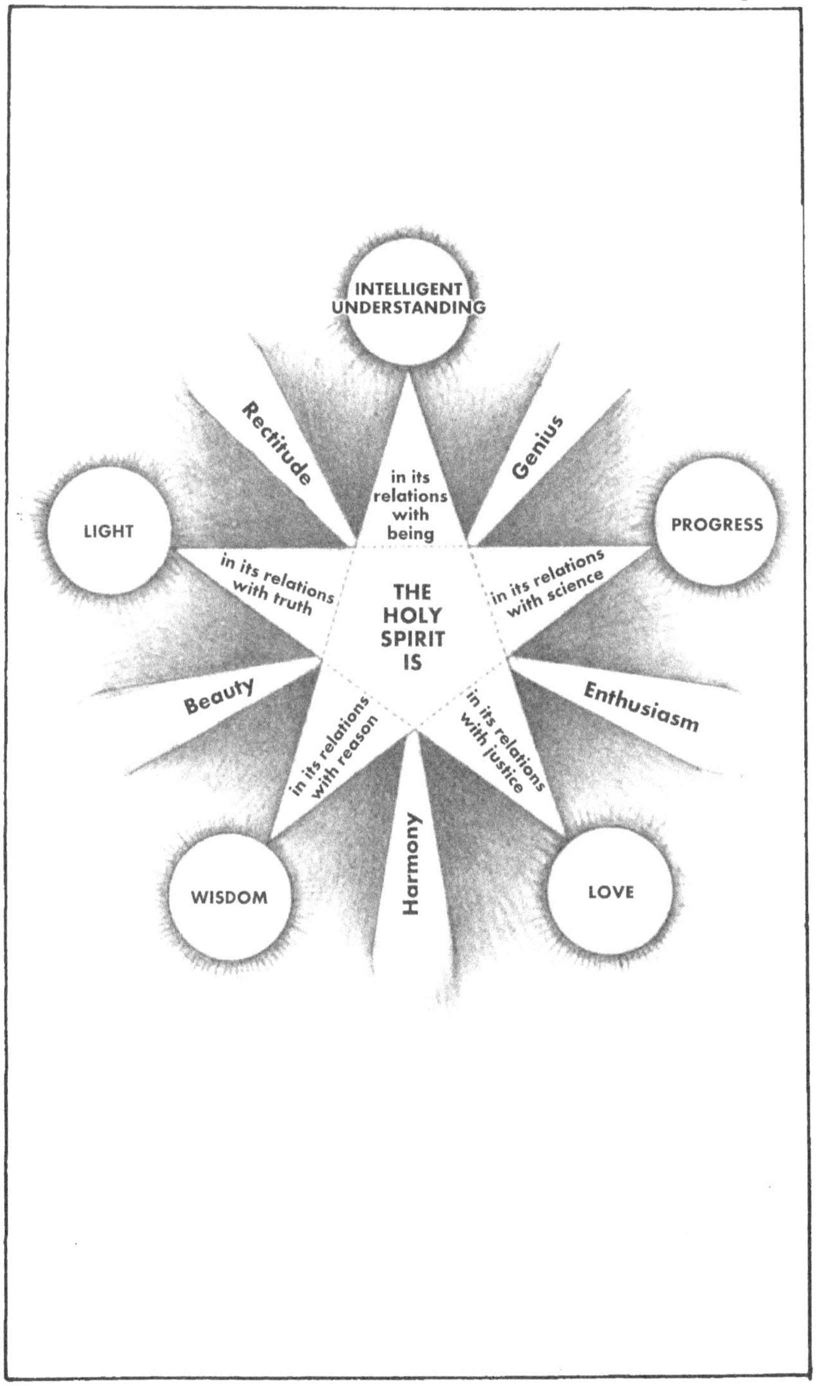
INTELLIGENT UNDERSTANDING
Rectitude
Genius
LIGHT
PROGRESS
in its relations with being
in its relations with truth
THE HOLY SPIRIT IS
in its relations with science
Beauty
Enthusiasm
in its relations with reason
in its relations with justice
Harmony
WISDOM
LOVE

Pentagram of the divine Paraclete

## The Key of the Great Arcanum

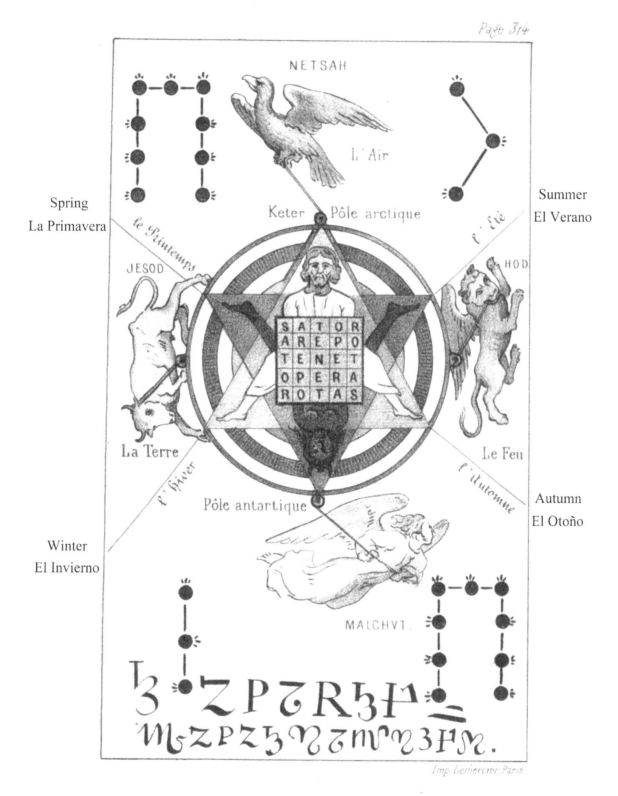

Editor's Appendix

## The Key of the Great Arcanum [Modified]

[Editor's Note: this image has been edited. The words "MALCHVT" and "JESOD" have exchanged places, since Malkuth is Earth (the Bull) and Jesod is Water. Also some writing has been removed from the bottom of the image that was in an Esoteric Alphabet from Johannes Trithemius. ]

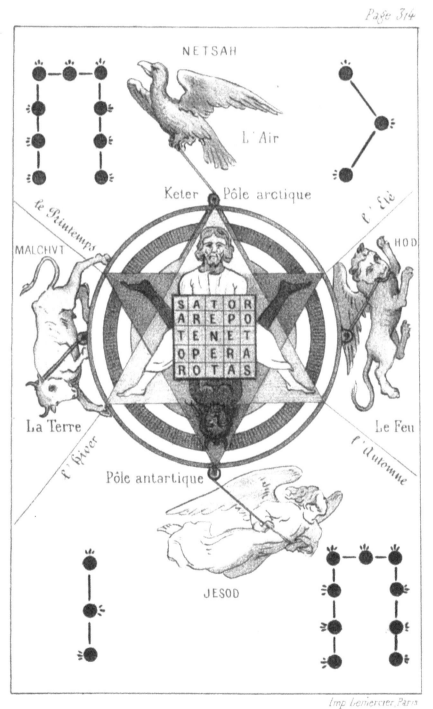

La clé du grand arcane

## The Sephiroth with the divine names

Key of theological notions according to the Hebrews

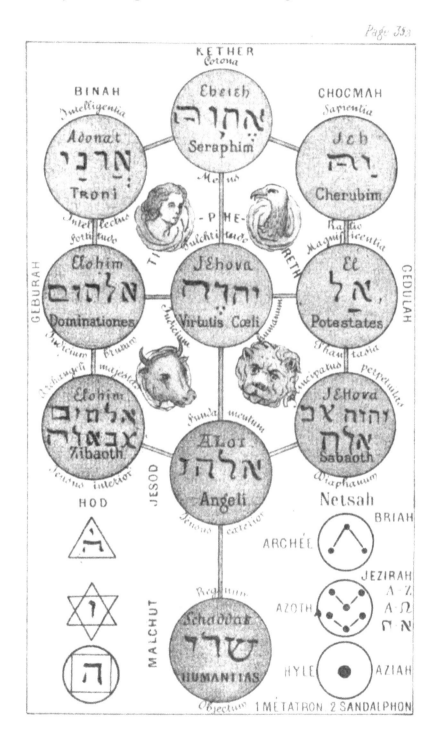

Les Séphiroth avec les noms divins
Clé des notions théologiques suivant les Hébreux.

## The Metallic Sephiroth
[Note that Netzah and Hod are reversed]

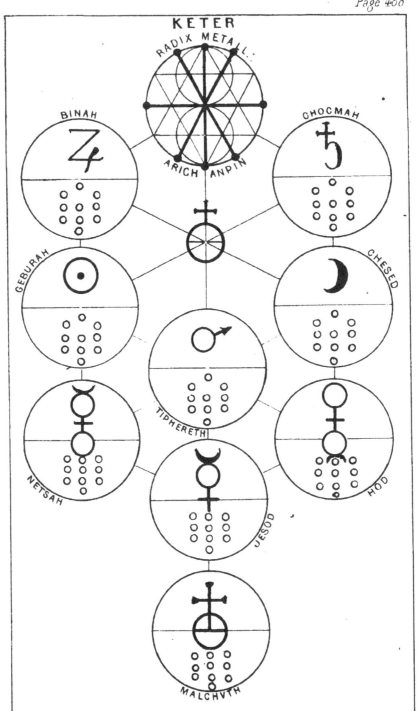

Les Séphiroth métalliques.

## The first three figures of Flamel

Les trois premieres figures de Flamel

## Fourth figure of Flamel

Dissolution of the birthing stone and fixation of mercury.

## Fifth figure of Flamel

The hermetic rose coming out of the mercurial stone
under the influence of the universal spirit.

## Sixth figure of Flamel

The budding rosebush at the hollow oak
the occult source and the seekers of gold.

## Seventh figure of Flamel

Dissolution of metallic germs represented by the innocent [children] that Herod kills

## The Mysteries of the temple of Solomon

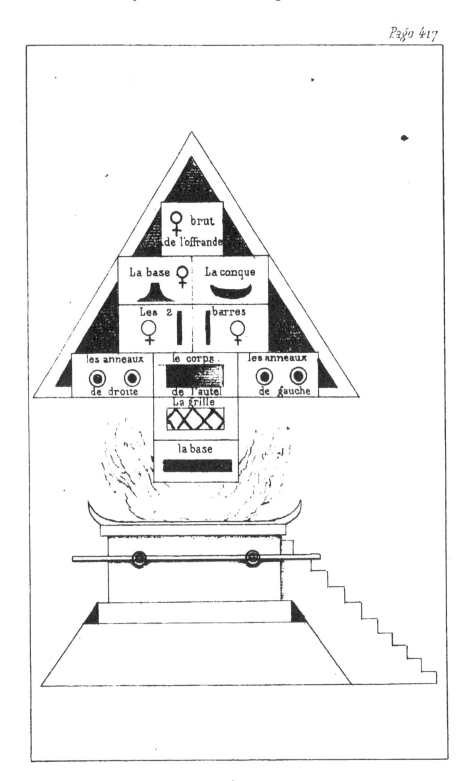

Les mystères du temple de Salomon.

## The Metallic Statue according to the Prophet Daniel

La statue métallique
suivant le Prophète Daniel.

# Some Drawings by Eliphas Levi from *Major Keys and the Clavicles of Solomon* or the 'Holy Clavicles' manuscript sent to the Baron Spédalieri *(November 1861)*[19]

### MAJOR KEYS AND CLAVICLES OF SOLOMON

Eliphas Lévi

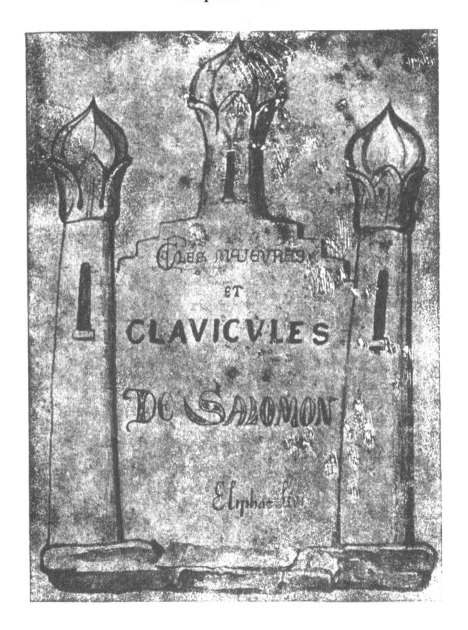

---

[19] First published in 1895, the rest of the images/drawings from this manuscript are given in *The Occult and Kabalistic Philosophy of Eliphas Levi, Volume 2* (which are related to the 36 Talismans of the nine hierarchies, or nine orders of angels)

## AZILUTH, JEZIRAH, BRIAH
### [The 3 Worlds]

## The Sacred Tau or the Universal Key

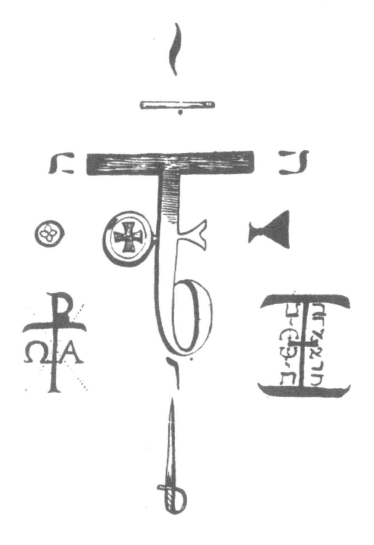

## The Shem HaMephorash

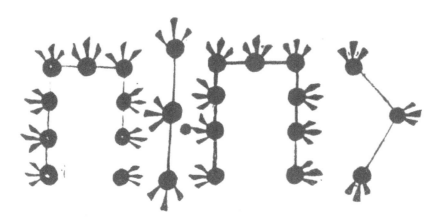

# The Sacred Letters, corresponding to the simple figures of the Tarot

יי  יה הה

The king of the scepter[20]

The king of the cup

The queen of the scepter

The queen of the cup

The father

The husband of the mother

The wife of the father

Mistress of herself

Malachim

**The Kings**

**The queens**

וי  וה הה

The king of the sword

The king of the circle[21]

The queen of the sword

The queen of the circle

The prince of love

The creating father

Princess of love

Mistress of the children

  יה הה

The knight of the scepter

The knight of the cup

The page of the scepter

The page of the cup

Conqueror of power

Conqueror of happiness

Slave of man

Slave of woman

**The knights**

**The pages**

  וה הת

The knight of the sword

The knight of the circle

The page of the sword

The page of children or of the circles

Conqueror of love

Conqueror of works

Slave of love

[Slave of children or works]

---

[20] Editor's note: The "scepter" refers to the suit of Clubs
[21] Editor's note: The "circles" refers to the suit of Pentacles

Editor's Appendix

# The Sacred Numbers

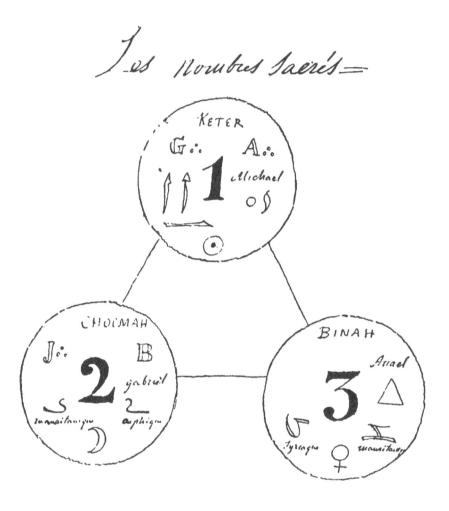

| Sephiroth | KETER | CHOCMAH | BINAH |
|---|---|---|---|
| Number | 1 | 2 | 3 |
| Masonic Association | G∴ A∴ (*Grand Architecte* Great Architect) | J∴ B[∴] (Jachin & Boaz) | |
| Angel & Planet | Michael & Sun | Gabriel & Moon | Anael & Venus |
| Symbol(s) | ☉ ♌ | | △ |
| Letter(s) | [*syriaque?* syriac?]   [?] | *mauritanique* mauritanic   *cuphique* cuphic | *syriaque* syriac   *mauritanique* mauritanic |

220

## [The Sacred Numbers (continued)]

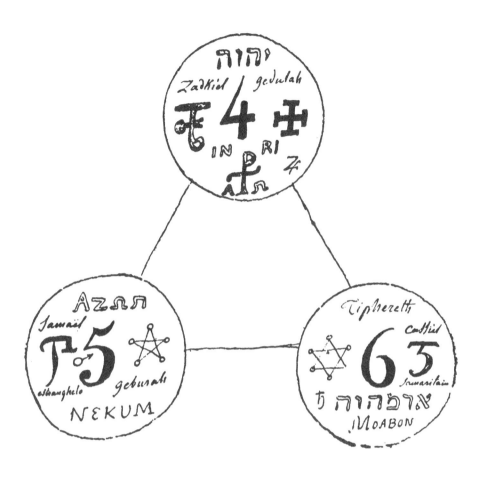

| Sephiroth | Gedulah [or Chesed] | Geburah | Tiphereth |
|---|---|---|---|
| Number | 4 | 5 | 6 |
| Masonic Association | יהוה<br>INRI | NEKUM | MOABON |
| Angel & Planet | Zadkiel & Jupiter | Samael & Mars | Cassiel & Saturn |
| Symbol(s) | | | |
| Letter(s) | | *estranghelo*<br>estranghela | *Samaritain*<br>Samaritan |

## [The Sacred Numbers (continued)]

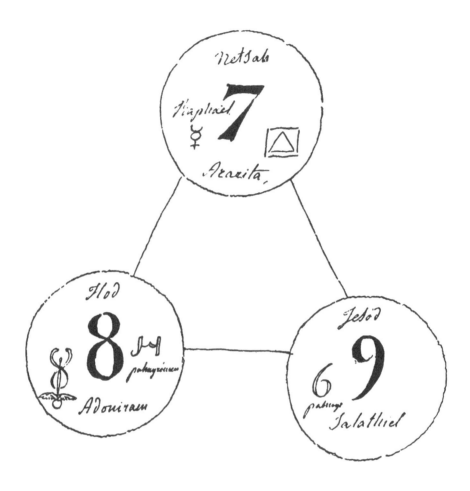

| Sephiroth | Netsah | Hod | Jesod |
|---|---|---|---|
| Number | 7 | 8 | 9 |
| Masonic Association | Ararita | Adoniram | Salathiel |
| Angel & Planet | Raphael & Mercury | | |
| Symbol(s) | △ | ☿ | |
| Letter(s) | | *palmyrénien* palmyrene | [?] |

## [The Sacred Numbers (continued)]

| Sephiroth | Malchut |
|---|---|
| Number | 10 |
| Masonic Association | |
| Angel & Planet | |
| Symbol(s) | [Snake biting its tail]<br><br>[4 Animals (corresponding to the 4 elements)] |
| Letter(s) | |

# Some Drawings by Eliphas Levi from *The Ritual of the Sanctum Regnum* or the Ritual from the Trithemius manuscript sent to the Baron Spédalieri *(November 1861)*

**GOD IS MAN AND MAN IS GOD
IN THE VERB MADE FLESH**

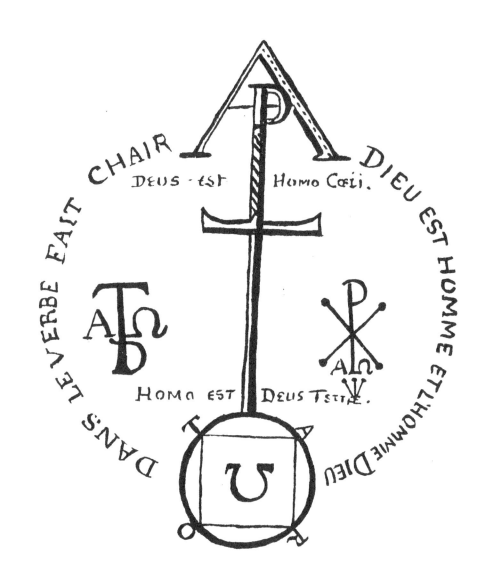

# The Cherub of Jekeskiel [or Ezekiel]

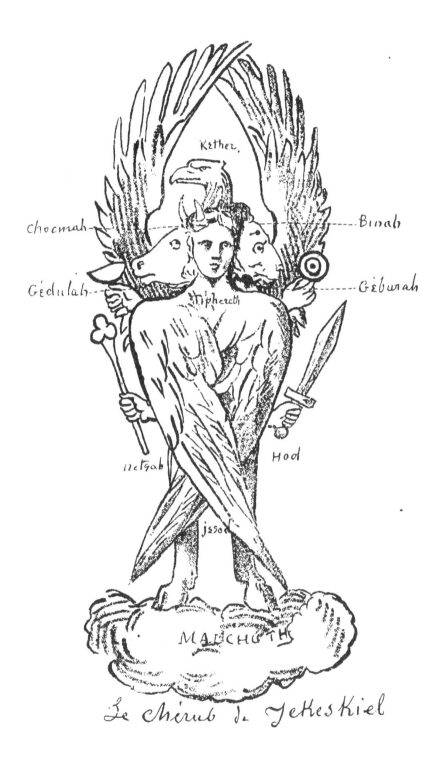

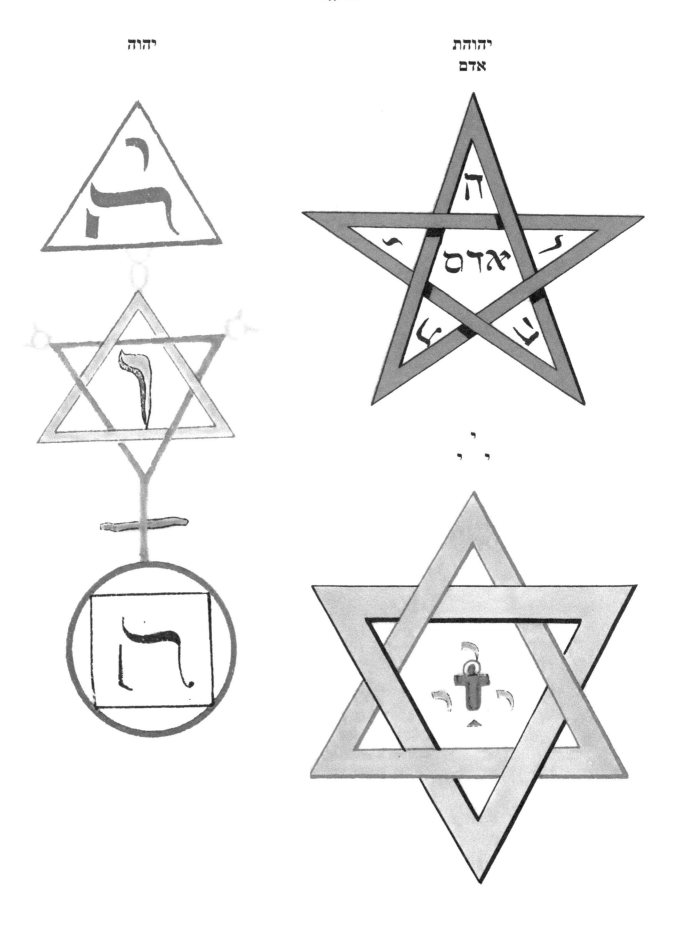

## [Sword of the Sephiroth]

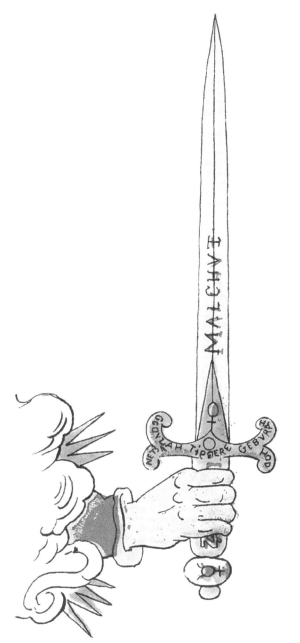

## [Azoth]

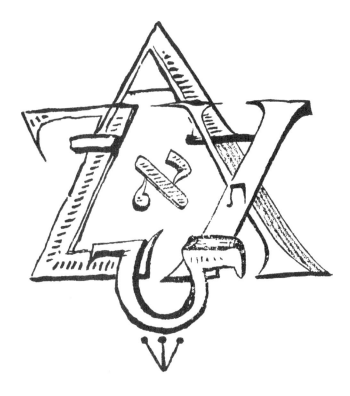

## [The Wheel of Ezekiel]

Electricity, Heat, Magnetism, Light

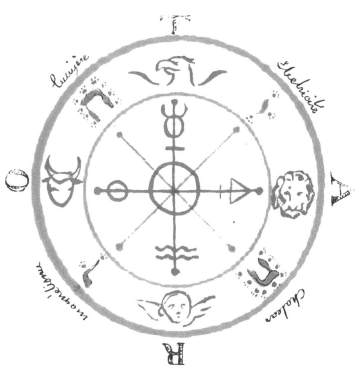

# Some Drawings by Eliphas Levi from *The Mysteries of the Kabalah (1860s)*[22]

## First Part – The Prophesy of Ezekiel

[1st Fig.] The great seal of Ezekiel taken from the magical calendars of Tycho-Brahé and of Duchanteau.

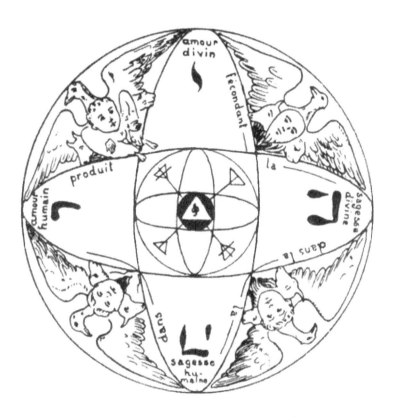

[2nd Fig.] The vision of Ezekiel.
[ י divine love  fecundates
ה human wisdom  in
ו human love  producing
ה divine wisdom ]

---

[22] First published in 1920, it is unclear when exactly this text was written. The images/drawings were not numbered in the book, but we have numbered them here in order of appearance.

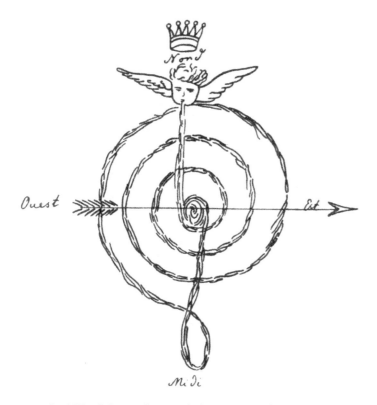

[3rd Fig.] Impulse[23] of the principle motor.

[4th Fig.] Vision of the fire that swirls[24].

[5th Fig.] Coagulation of the light and [the] formation of the electric astral kernel[25].

[6th Fig.] The forces, by combining together, produce the elementary forces

---

[23] Literally 'Impulsion' means "impetus, pulse; impulse, drive"
[24] Literally 'tourbillonne' means "whirl, swirl, eddy, flutter"
[25] Literally 'noyau' means "stone, pit; nucleus, core; kernel"

Editor's Appendix

[7th Fig.] ASSYRIAN KABALAH (*Sculpture of Nineveh*)
The victorious intelligence [or intelligent understanding] of force/strength.
The fire regulated and vanquished by the water.

[10th Fig.] TWENTY FIRST KEY OF THE TAROT[26]
The crown, the tetragram: living in movement and stability. Universal synthesis.

[8th Fig.] SCULPTURE OF NINEVEH
Man of inspiration:
The etheric water or universal matter.

[11th Fig.] INDIAN INITIATION
Vishnu in the center of the Universe

---

[26] Editor's note: This would correspond to the final card (#22) in this study guide.

**[9th Fig.] ASSYRIAN FRAGMENT**
Force/Strength taming[27] matter.
The fire penetrating the terrestrial cortex

**[12th Fig.] EGYPTIAN INITIATION**
The great Sphinx of Thebes.

**[13th Fig.]** The Ark of the Covenant and the Cherubim.

**[14th Fig.]** The Ark of the Covenant (side).

---

[27] Literally 'domptant' means "tame, manage, master, gentle, school"

Editor's Appendix

[15th Fig.] THE PENTACLE OF THE LIGHTENING[28]
Explaining the movement of comets,
mysterious illnesses, storms and miracles.

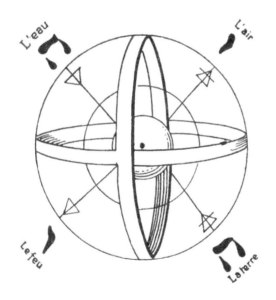

[16th Fig. י air ה water ו fire ה earth ]

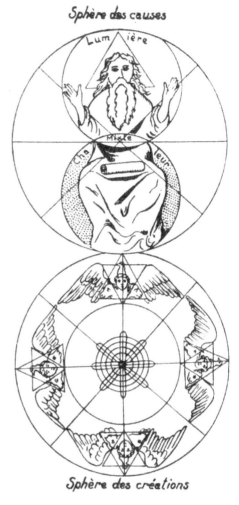

[17th Fig.] SPHERE OF CAUSES
[Light Mixture Heat]
SPHERE OF CREATIONS

---

[28] Literally 'FOUDRES' means "lightning, flash or streak of light in the sky caused by the discharge of an electric spark in a thundercloud"

[18th Fig.] From this upside-down and fallen star, Lucifer the chief of demon is made.

Rempham or the upside-down blazing star, from which a donkey's head is made.

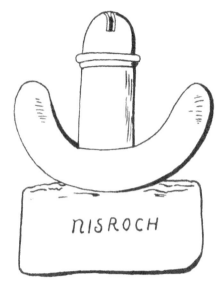

[26th Fig.] Nisroch. The Phallus.

[19th Fig.] Nibbas, the same as Anubis. – The sacerdotal science. – Black magic. – The demon Samaxia or Belial.

[20th Fig.] Thartac or Onochoetites. – The Shiva of the Indians. – Matter fecundated. – Ignorant Faith. – The fatal life. – The devil Astaroth.

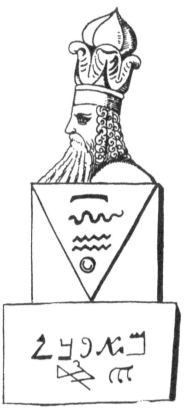

[21st Fig.] Marcolis. – The cubic stone. – Stability. – Fatality. – Moloch.

[22nd Fig.] Azima, the same as Mendes or Beelphegor. The scape goat. – Physical love.

[24th Fig.] Nergal. – The rooster of the Sabbath. – Abraxas. – The serpent of Mars. – The philosophical dragon.

[25th Fig.] Succoth Benoth. Nature. – The black hen of the sorcerers.

Editor's Appendix

[23rd Fig.] Anamelech, the same as Pegasus. – The verb of beauty. – The king of analogies.

[27th Fig.] Adramelech.
The peacock.
The proud world.
[Adramelech.
Creation and its luxury
The world and its pride.]

235

The following table prioritizes the preceding idols [so as to help] comprehend how the divine notions were [so] soon degraded by re-clothing[29] the hieroglyphic and idolatrous forms of impure worship and we will now comprehend the visions or allegorical descriptions of Ezekiel concerning the temple of the true God.

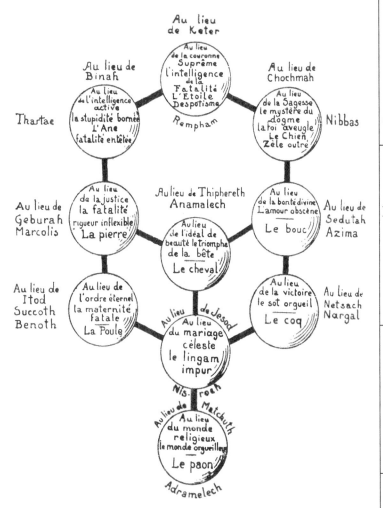

[28th FIG. The Klipoth Explained]

[Editor's note: Here Levi gives an explanation of the Klipoth or inverse Sephiroth:]

| Instead of Binah: Thartae | Instead of Kether: Rempham | Instead of Chokmah: Nibbas |
|---|---|---|
| Instead of the Supreme crown, the active intelligence [or intelligent understanding], narrow-minded[30] stupidity<br><br>The Donkey Complete fatality | Instead of the Supreme crown, the intelligent understanding of the fatality<br><br>The Star of Despotism | Instead of Wisdom, the mystery of the dogma, blind faith<br><br>The exaggerated[31] Zealous Dog |
| Instead of Geburah: Marcolis | Instead of Tiphereth: Anamalech | Instead of Gedulah: Azima |
| Instead of justice, fatality, inflexible rigor<br><br>The stone | Instead of the ideal of beauty, the triumph of the beast<br><br>The horse | Instead of divine goodness/ kindness, obscene love<br><br>The goat |
| Instead of Hod: Succoth Benoth | Instead of Yesod: Nisroch | Instead of Netsach: Nargal |
| Instead of the eternal order, Fatal maternity<br><br>The Hen | Instead of the celestial marriage, the impure lingam.<br><br>[The Phallus] | Instead of victory, the blind fool<br><br>The Rooster |
|  | Instead of Malkuth: Adramelech<br><br>Instead of the religious world, the proud world.<br><br>The peacock |  |

---

[29] Literally 'revêtant' means "cloth, don, array; dress, robe, face, endue; invest, line, panel"
[30] Literally 'bornée' means "narrow minded; hidebound, thick witted; obtuse, parochial; narrow, restricted"
[31] Literally 'outré' means "beyond, further; overdone, exaggerated, excessive"

Editor's Appendix

**[29th Fig.] TALISMAN OF THE ANCIENT GNOSTICS**
The spirit which awakens: The double serpent – water.
Matter subjugated[32] or the tamed willpower: The horse – earth.
Force/Strength and action: The lion – fire.
The changing and passing form: The rooster – air.

**HERMETIC SYMBOL**
The terrestrial and aerial central fire put into activity by the water

**[32nd Fig.] ANOTHER AMULET**
(more ancient, attributed to the disciples of Socrates)

Here form is explained through the ram, sign of universal generation and of spring.

The rooster: light – intelligence – fire.
The horse: earth – imagination –willpower.
The ram: air – spring – form.
The man: flesh – blood – water.

**[30th Fig.] ANCIENT GREEK MEDALLION**
The eagle – air: Inspiration
The man – earth: Thinking.
The woman – water: Love.
The lion – fire: Life and its passions.

**HERMETIC SYMBOL**
The mystery of the central fire produced by the combination of the earth, of the air, and of the water.

**[31st Fig.] BASILIDIAN AMULET**
The rooster – intelligence [or intelligent understanding].
The horse – imagination or willpower.
The man – reason.
The sheep – fatal instincts.

The initials mean:
L  lux [light].
T  terra [earth].
F  forma [form].
C  caro [flesh].

---

[32] Literally 'soumise' means "submit, subjugate; tame, present"

[33rd Fig.] **THE PENTACLE OF RESURRECTION**
Tablet of life and death.
Death reproducing[33] life.

[34th Fig.] **BIRTH[34] FROM DEATH**
IMAGE OFTEN REPRODUCED IN THE
SACRED HIEROGLYPHICS

[35th Fig.] **MASONIC SYMBOL.**
Death engendering[35] life.

[36th Fig.] **THE TEMPLE OF SOLOMON**
As it is found represented in the ancient
shekels[36] of Israel.

---

[33] Literally 'reproduisant' means "reproduce, replicate, copy, repeat"
[34] Literally 'enfantement' means "labor, childbirth, birth, mothering"
[35] Literally 'engendrant' means "give rise to, father; generate, breed; engender, procreate; germinate"
[36] Literally 'Sicles' means "Shekel, coin and monetary unit of Israel; silver coin of the ancient Hebrews"

# Editor's Appendix

**[37ᵗʰ Fɪɢ.] THE EDIFICE OF THE TEMPLE**
According to the Bible and the Talmud.

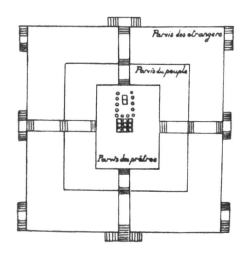

**[38ᵗʰ Fɪɢ.] GENERAL PLAN OF THE TEMPLE AND OF ITS PRECINCTS**[37]

Closed door which is only opened to the Messiah.
Plan of the temple, according to Flavius Joseph and the Talmud.

**[39ᵗʰ Fɪɢ.] GENERAL PICTURE OF THE TEMPLE**

The temple with its galleries and its precincts, according to all the ancient monuments.

**[40ᵗʰ Fɪɢ.] Pomegranate and the cap**[38].

---

[37] Literally 'ENCEINTES' means "pregnant, expecting; precinct, compound, enclosure, inclosure, speaker"
[38] Literally 'chapiteau' means "capital; marquee; head, big top"

[41st Fig.] SEA OF BRASS
Colossal cauldron serving as [a] reservoir for the temple.

[42nd Fig.] THE TAV IN MODERN HEBREW
Reunion of the four letters of the Shema

[43rd Fig.] THE HIERATIC[39] TAV
Such as it is found in the ancient Shekels of Israel

[44th Fig.] THE EXOTERIC TAV
Such as it is found in the ancient Shekels of Israel

[45th Fig.] THE SACRED TAV AND THE VULGAR TAV
According to Rabbi Azarias.

[46th Fig.] THE VULGAR TAV IN PRIMITIVE HEBREW
According to the manuscripts of the Library of the Vatican.

---

[39] Literally 'HIÉRATIQUE' means "hieratic, priestly"

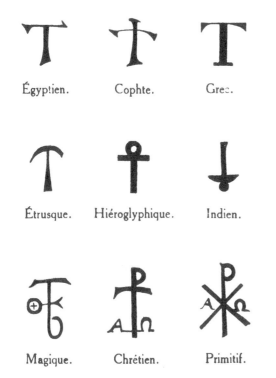

[47th Fig. Other forms of the Tav or Tau]

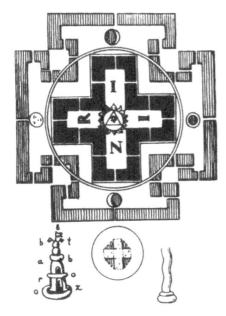

**[48th Fig.] THE PHILOSOPHICAL CROSS or THE PLAN OF THE TEMPLE ACCORDING TO EZEKIEL**

"It is according to this figure of the sacred Tav that the prophet traced the plan of the temple of the future. The last five chapters of his book are consecrated to making the description [of that temple]. The temple is the image of the universe, it corresponds to the pentacle of the animals and of the wheels…"

[53rd Fig.] The entrance of the temple of Ezekiel according to masonic documents.

"The prophecy of Ezekiel is the work of a reformer, it is what we would call in our times a palingenetic[40] poem. The author reveals first the mysteries of creation, he describes the equilibrated forces of nature and then develops the kabalistic theory of the divine ideal, conquered by the image and by the resemblance of the mysteries of nature…"

---

[40] Literally 'palingénésique' means "palingenetic, of or relating to palingenesis (a concept of rebirth or re-creation; its meaning stems from Greek palin, meaning again, and genesis, meaning birth.)"

[49th Fig.] We have seen that the first triangle, that of Solomon, represents a triangle [with] the point up.

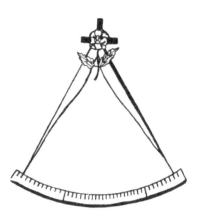

[50th Fig.] Symbol which corresponds to that of the masonic compass, image of Providence the laws of which are exact like numbers and precise like geometry.

[51st Fig.] New form of the masonic jewel analogous to the famous pentacle known under the name of Seal of Solomon.

The jewel of [the] master in high masonry.

[52nd Fig.] Ezekiel gives to his new Temple the figure of an upside-down triangle, symbol analogous to that of the masonic compass, image of the true science which corresponds in all points with divine exactitude

In such [a way] that the hieroglyphic form of the ancient temple is united with that of the [new] temple…

# Second Part – The Apocalypse or Revelation of Saint John

[54th Fig.]

[Forgiveness, through accepted pain is the master of fatal forces

The unity of Being is in the peace of pure hearts

The volitional verb of justice and truth overturns the instinct of all the idols

The Trinity of the spirit of the just equilibrates all according to the order of harmonies]

[55th Fig. In the beginning was the Verb and the Verb was...]

[56th Fig.] First Seal.
THE SEAL OF SAINT JOHN

[57th Fig.] THE SECOND SEAL

[58th Fig.] The third seal.

**HEAVEN OPEN**

[round and round]

The four animals, the stone of jasper, the 24 elders, etc.

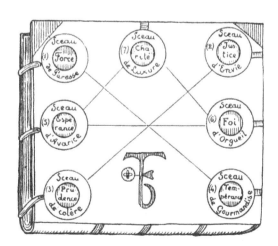

[59th Fig.] THE BOOK OF THE TRUTH

with its seven seals.

[60th Fig.] THE FOURTH SEAL

[61st Fig. The Fifth Seal] THE PAIN OF HEAVEN
THE SOULS OF THE MARTYRS

[62nd Fig.] THE SIXTH SEAL

THE BLACK SUN, THE BLOODY MOON
AND THE STARS THAT FALL

[63rd Fig.] Seventh Seal
THE CONSUMPTION

[SILENCE IN HEAVEN]

God rests after having created humanity a second time.

[64th Fig.] THE MOON AMONG THE SEVEN PLANETS

after a coin of the Faustine Empire.

[65th Fig.] THE FIRST TRUMPET

[Sun Sunday]

THE ANGEL MICHAEL

[66th Fig.] THE SECOND TRUMPET

[Moon Monday]

THE ANGEL GABRIEL

[67th Fig.] THIRD TRUMPET

[Mercury now ??? falling is for Jupiter]

THE ANGEL RAPHAEL

[68th Fig.] FOURTH TRUMPET

[Jupiter]

THE ANGEL SACHIEL-MELECH

[69th Fig.] FIFTH TRUMPET

[Venus]

THE ANGEL ANAEL

[70th Fig.] SIXTH TRUMPET

THE ANGEL CASSIEL

[73rd Fig.] The beast or brutal instinct.

[75th Fig.] The temporal empire of the beast.

The realized Synthesis of evil.

**[71st Fig.] THE RELIGIOUS GENIE OF MAN**

SEVENTH TRUMPET

[Aziluth

Yetzirah
John's Gospel

Briah]

THE INSPIRING ANGEL

Great pentacle of the eternal light under the attributes of the Sun and of man – the synthesis of the unity which corresponds to the 7 paths of the analysis.

**[72nd Fig.] THE RELIGIOUS GENIE OF WOMAN**

(Seventh Trumpet)

GREAT PENTACLE OF THE LIGHT REFLECTED UNDER THE ATTRIBUTES OF THE MOON AND OF WOMAN.

[77th Fig.] The mysterious lamb.

The solar ram: image of the new revelation.

Truth and sweetness[41].

The Host of the Sacrifice.

[74th Fig.] The corrupt priest.

The preacher of Satan.

[76th Fig.] The vision of Daniel

The four forms of the infernal Sphinx.

[78th Fig. The number of the beast]

---

[41] Literally 'douceur' means "softness, gentleness; smoothness, meekness, clemency; geniality, mildness; sweetness, mellowness"

[79th Fig.] THE FIRST CUP

Michael proclaims the glory of God alone.

[80th Fig.] THE SECOND CUP

The angel of the sea proclaims the unity of life.

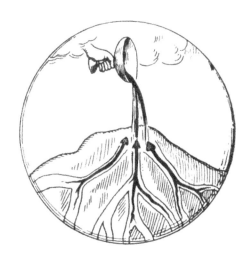

[81st Fig.] THIRD CUP

The angel Raphael proclaims the unity of the truth.

[82nd Fig.] FOURTH CUP

The angel of the sun proclaims the unity of light.

[83rd Fig.] FIFTH CUP

The angel Sachiel-Melech proclaims the unity of power.

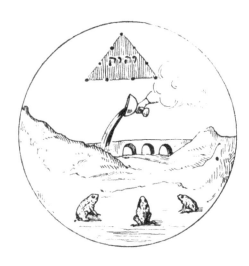

[84th Fig.] SIXTH CUP

The angel Samael proclaims the unity of justice.

[85th Fig.] SEVENTH CUP

The angel of Saturn proclaims the unity of the eternal reign.

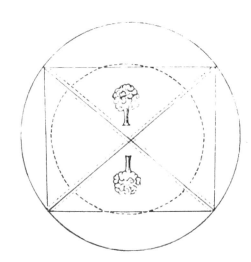

[86th Fig.] The plan of Eden and of the new Jerusalem.

Key of the pentacles, of hieroglyphic letters and of sacred numbers.

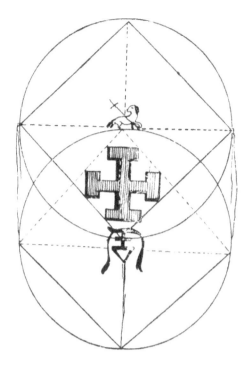

[87th Fig.] Elevation of the cube in the cylinder.

Quadrature and synthesis of the Church.

The first hieratic figure
The unity of God

The figure of the divine tetragram
The cross of the templars,

The tetragrammatic synthesis
The unity of the four divine attributes
Creation realized.

[88th Fig. The Tetragram as a Triangle, Cross and Square]

[89th Fig.] The sacred tetragram or the Shema

with its four hieroglyphics and their analogies.

Editor's Appendix

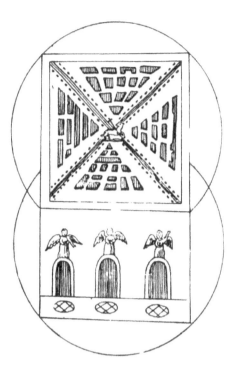

[90th Fig.] **Plan and elevation of the new Jerusalem**

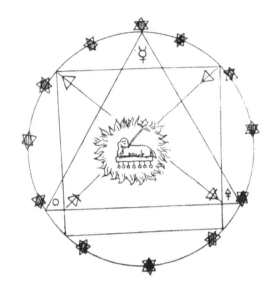

[91st Fig.] **Universal pentacle of the light.**

**Plan of the masonic temple.**

**Universal seal of Hermes.**

# The Minor Arcana
# from the writings of Eliphas Levi

"...Egypt from our standpoint is the cradle of the sciences and of wisdom; since it clothed[42] the dogma of the first Zoroaster with images, not only more rich, [but] also more exact and more pure, than those of India.

The sacerdotal art and the royal art made[43] adepts through initiation, and initiation was not enclosed within the egotistic limits of castes...

...The absolute hieroglyphic science had as [its] foundation an alphabet where all the deities were letters, all letters [were] ideas, all ideas [were] numbers, [and] all numbers [were] perfect signs.

This hieroglyphic alphabet was what Moses used to make the great secret of his kabalah, and which he took from the Egyptians; since, according to the "Sepher Yetzirah", it came from Abraham: this alphabet is the famous book of Thoth, [and it was] suggested by Count de Gebelin that it was preserved until our [present] day under the form of that bizarre card game which is called the tarot; misinterpreted then by Etteilla, with whom even a persevering[44] study of over thirty years could not substitute[45] [for his] lack of common sense nor for the first teaching[46] which he was missing...

...The alphabet of Thoth is only the original of our tarot in a roundabout[47] way.

The tarot that we have is of jewish origin and the sorts of figures are not older than the reign of Charles VII[48].

The cards of Jacquemin Gringonneur are the first tarots that we know of, but the symbols which he reproduced are of the highest antiquity.

This game was an attempt by some astrologers of that time to restore the king to reason with the help of the this key, of the oracles (who's answers result from the varied combination of signs) are always exact like mathematics and measured like the harmonies of nature.

But one must already be reasonable in order to know how to make use of an instrument of science and of reason; the poor king, fallen into childishness[49], only saw children's games in the paintings of Gingonneur, and made a card game from the mysterious alphabet of the kabalah..."

-from Ch. 4 of Book 1 of *History of Magic*

---

[42] Literally 'revêtit' means "cloth, don, array; dress, robe, face, endue; invest, line, panel"
[43] Literally 'formèrent' means "shape, form; train, discipline, fix; groom, develop; mold, make"
[44] Literally 'persévérance' means "perseverance, singleness, obstinacy"
[45] Literally 'suppléer' means "substitute, fill in, compensate"
[46] Literally 'éducation' means "education, schooling; upbringing, training; teaching"
[47] Literally 'détournée' means "roundabout, circuitous, devious, oblique, backdoor"
[48] Charles VII (1403-1461), called the Victorious or the Well-Served, was a monarch of the House of Valois who ruled as King of France from 1422 to his death.
[49] Literally 'enfance' means "childhood, girlhood, boyhood, infancy"

"...We have to talk here about the Tarot from the kabalistic point of view... This hieroglyphic book is composed of a kabalistic alphabet and of a wheel or circle of four decades, specified by four symbolical and typical figures, each having for its ray[50] a ladder of four progressive figures representing Humanity: man, woman, youth and child; master, mistress, soldier and page[51]...

...Let's now go to the four suits, that is to say, to the Clubs[52] [or Staffs/Wands], Cups, Swords, and Circles or Pentacles, vulgarly called Coins.

These figures are the hieroglyphs of the tetragram [ יהוה ]: thus, the Club [or Staff/Wand] is the Egyptian phallus or Hebrew yod [ י ]; the Cup is the cteis or primitive heh [ ה ]; the Sword is the conjunction of both, or the lingam, represented in hebrew before the captivity by vau [ ו ], and the Circle or Pentacle, image of the world, is the final heh [ ה ] of the divine name.

Now let us take a Tarot and reunite four by four all its pages [in order to] form the Wheel or ROTA of William Postel; let us group the four aces, the four twos, etc., and we will then have ten packs of cards giving the hieroglyphic explanation of the triangle of divine names on the scale of the denary which we have given above.

One can then read them thus, by relating each number to a corresponding Sephira:

יהוה

Four signs of the name which contain all the names.

1 KETHER.
The four aces.
The crown of God carrying four florets[53].

2 CHOKMAH.
The four twos.
His wisdom pours out[54] and forms four rivers.

3 BINAH.
The four threes.
From his intelligence [or intelligent understanding] he gives four proofs[55].

4 CHESED.
The four fours.
From mercy he is four benefactions[56].

5 GEBURAH.
The four fives.
His rigor punishes four crimes[57] four times.

---

[50] Literally 'rayon' means "ray, beam; radius; section, department, shelf; shaft, bracket; responsibility"
[51] Literally 'valet' means "manservant; jack, knave; valet"
[52] Literally 'bâton' means "stick, baton, wand, staff, club, pole, cane"
[53] Literally 'fleurons' means "flower, fleuron, floret, finial (small ornamental object at the top of a column or gable, etc.)"
[54] Literally 'épanche' means "unburden, outpour, free or relieve of a burden (weight, worry, etc.)"
[55] Literally 'preuves' means "evidence, proof; substantiation"
[56] Literally 'bienfaits' means "benefaction, kindness"
[57] Literally 'forfaits' means "felony, crime, infamy, withdrawal; contract, agreement; package deal, combined deal"

6 TIPHERETH
The four sixes.
Through four pure rays his beauty is revealed.

7 NETZAH.
The four sevens.
Let's celebrate four times his eternal victory.

8 HOD.
The four eights.
He triumphs four times in his eternity.

9 JESOD.
The four nines.
His throne is supported upon four foundations.

10 MALKUTH.
The four tens.
His unique kingdom is four times the same
And conforms to the florets of the divine diadem.

One can see through this simple arrangement the kabalistic sense of each plate[58].

Thus, for example, the five of clubs [or staffs/wands] rigorously signifies [the] geburah of Yod [ ׳ ], that is to say, the justice of the Creator or the wrath of man; the seven of cups signifies the victory of mercy or the triumph of woman; the eight of swords signifies eternal conflict or [eternal] equilibrium; and so forth for the others.

One can therefore comprehend how the ancient pontiffs proceeded to make the oracle speak: the plates randomly thrown always give a new kabalistic meaning, but rigorously true in their combinations, which alone were accidental[59]; and, as the faith of the ancients attributed nothing to chance, they read the answers of Providence in the oracles of the Tarot, which were called Theraph or Theraphims by the Hebrews, as the erudite kabalist Gaffarel (one of the magicians employed by Cardinal Richelieu) saw[60].

As for the figures, here is a last pair of verses[61] to explain them:

KING, QUEEN, KNIGHT, PAGE.

Husband[62], young man, child, [and] all [of] humanity;

Through these four rungs[63], unity is recovered[64].

---

[58] Literally 'lame' means "blade, sword; wave; runner; shaft; lamella; lamina"
[59] Literally 'fortuite' means "fortuitous; casual; incidental, adventitious, accidental"
[60] Literally 'pressenti' means "sense (in advance), have a premonition of; approach, contact, foresee; presurmise"
[61] Literally 'distique' means "distich, couplet (a pair of successive lines of verse, especially a pair that rhyme and are of the same length)"
[62] Literally 'époux' means "husband, spouse, mate, consort; spouses"
[63] Literally 'échelons' means "levels; rungs, spokes; grades, tiers, degrees, echelons"
[64] Literally 'remonte' means "get hold of, set up, reset; pick up, pull up, put up; recover; ascend, wind up, rewind; boost, work up, turn up; reassemble"

At the end of Ritual [of High Magic] we will give other details and complete documents about the marvelous book of the Tarot, and we will demonstrate that it is the primitive book, the key of all prophecies and all dogmas, in a word, the inspiration from inspired books, what neither [the] Court de Gebelin in his science, nor Etteilla or Alliette in his unique[65] intuitions, have presented.

The ten sephiroth and the twenty-two tarots form what the kabalists call 'the thirty-two paths of the absolute science'..."

- from Ch. 10 of *Dogma of High Magic*

"...the 22 keys of the Tarot ... explain all the numbers.

Thus, the juggler [or magician], or key of unities, explains the four aces with their quadruple progressive significance in the three worlds and in the first principle.

Thus the ace of pentacles or of circles is 'the soul of the world'; the ace of swords is 'militant intelligence [or intelligent understanding]'; the ace of cups is 'magnetizing[66] intelligence [or intelligent understanding]'; the ace of clubs is 'creative intelligence [or intelligent understanding]'; they are also the principles of movement, of progress, of fecundity and of power.

Each number, multiplied by a key, gives another number which (explained in turn by the keys) completes the philosophical and religious revelation contained in each sign.

Now, each of the 56 cards can be multiplied in turn by the 22 keys; a series of combinations will [be the] result, giving all the most astonishing[67] conclusions[68] of revelation and of light.

It is a truly philosophical machine, which keeps the mind from wandering[69], all while leaving it its initiative and its liberty; it is mathematics applied to the absolute, it is the alliance of the positive to the ideal, it is a lottery of thoughts all rigorously just like numbers, [and] finally it is perhaps what human genius has never conceived, all at the same time [while being] the simplest and greatest [conception of human genius]..."

- from Ch. 22 of *Ritual of High Magic*

"Let us now recover[70] the sources of true science by returning to the holy kabalah, or [to the] tradition of the children of Seth, taken from Chaldea by Abraham, taught to the Egyptian priesthood by Joseph, collected[71] and refined[72] by Moses, concealed beneath symbols in the Bible, revealed by the Savior to saint John, and again contained completely in the hieratic figures (analogous to those of all antiquity) in the Revelation of this apostle...

---

[65] Literally 'singulières' means "singular, single, uncommon, strange, odd, weird"
[66] Literally 'aimante' means "magnetic, operating via magnetic means; attractive; loving, affectionate, passionate"
[67] Literally 'surprenants' means "surprising, startling, amazing, odd, astonishing, astounding"
[68] Literally 'résultats' means "result, end, outcome; issue, effect; offspring, product, purpose, upshot; match"
[69] Literally 'égarer' means "mislead; mislay, misplace; stray"
[70] Literally 'Remontons' means "get hold of, set up, reset; pick up, pull up, put up; recover; ascend, wind up, rewind; boost, work up, turn up; reassemble"
[71] Literally 'recueillie' means "gather, collect; garner, obtain, take in; reflect, meditate, contemplate"
[72] Literally 'épurée' means "filter, refine, chasten"

...It has been said in our "dogma of high magic" that the name Jehovah [ יהוה ] resolves into seventy-two explicatory names, called *Shemahamphorash* [ שם המפורש[73] ].[74] The art of employing these seventy-two names and of finding in them the keys of the universal science is what the kabalists have called the *clavicles* of Solomon.

In fact, at the end of the collections of evocations and prayers that carry this title, one ordinarily finds seventy-two magical circles, making thirty-six talismans.

This is four times nine, that is to say the absolute number multiplied by the quaternary.

These talismans each carry two of the seventy-two names with the emblematic sign of their number and that of the four letters of the name Jehovah [ יהוה ] to which they correspond.

From this have originated the four emblematic decades of the tarot: the club[75] [or staff/wand], representing the yod [ י ]; the cup, the heh [ ה ]; the sword, the vau [ ו ]; and the pentacle, the final heh [ ה ].

To the tarot has been added the complement of the tens, which synthetically repeats the character of unity.

Popular traditions of magic say that the possessor of the clavicles of Solomon can converse with spirits of all orders and can make [them] obedient through all the natural powers.

Now, these clavicles, often times lost, then recovered, are none other than the talismans of the seventy-two names and the mysteries of the thirty-two hieroglyphic paths reproduced by the tarot.

With the aid of these signs and through their infinite combinations (like those of the numbers and of the letters), one can, in fact, arrive at the natural and mathematical revelation of all the secrets of nature, and [then] enter, consequently, into communication with the entire hierarchy of intelligences and of the genii..."

-from Ch. 7 of Book 1 of *History of Magic*

"...As for the numbers from one to ten, you will find their explanation repeated four times with the symbols of [the] club[76] [or staff/wand] or scepter of the father, [the] cup or delights of the mother, [the] sword or battle of love, and [the] coins[77] or fecundity[78].

---

[73] Editor's note: The 'Shem-hamphorash' or 'Shema Hamphorash' is a corruption of the Hebrew term "Shem HaMephorash" which literally means "the explicit Name [of God]" and is used to refer to a name or names of God without actually pronouncing it or them.
[74] Editor's note: This seems to be referring to the Preliminary Discourse, where it says: "...the synthesis of all the dogmas brings us back to only one symbolism, which is that of the kabalah and of the magi. ... We [can] now understand sacred mathematics which multiplies seventy-two times the divine tetragram [ יהוה ] to form the imprints of the thirty-six talismans of Solomon, Brought back by deep studies in the antique theology of Israel, we bend ourselves in front of the high truths of the kabalah, and we hope that the wise Israelites, in their turn, will recognize that they were separated from us only through a misunderstanding."
[75] Literally 'bâton' means "stick, baton, wand, staff, club, pole, cane"
[76] Literally 'bâton' means "stick, baton, wand, staff, club, pole, cane"
[77] Literally 'deniers' means "funds, monies, capital"
[78] Literally 'fécondité' means "fertility, fecundity, fruitfulness, fruition"

## Editor's Appendix

The Tarot is in the hieroglyphic book of the thirty-two paths, and its summary explanation is found in the book attributed to the patriarch Abraham, which is called [the] *Sepher-Yetzirah*. The scholar[79] Court de Gebelin was the first to discover[80] the importance of the Tarot, which is the great key to the hieratic[81] hieroglyphs.

... Spanish cards still carry the principal signs of the primitive Tarot and they are used to play the game of 'hombre' or man, [a] vague reminiscence of the primitive use of a mysterious book containing regulating judgments[82] for all human divinities.

The most ancient Tarots were medallions which have since become talismans. The clavicles or little keys of Solomon were composed of thirty-six talismans carrying seventy-two engravings analogous to the hieroglyphic figures of the Tarot.

These figures, altered by copyists, are still to be found on ancient clavicle manuscripts which exist in libraries. One of these manuscripts exists in the 'Bibliotheque Nationale' and another in the 'Bibliotheque de l'Arsenal'. The only authentic manuscripts of the clavicles are those which give the series of thirty-six talismans with the seventy-two mysterious names, the others, however ancient they may be, belong to the dreams of black magic and contain nothing more than mystifications. For the explanation of the Tarot, see my *Dogma and Ritual of high magic*..."

-from the 3rd Lesson of Levi's *The Elements of the Kabalah*

"Court de Gebelin saw in the twenty-two keys of the Tarot the representation of the egyptian mysteries and he attributed their invention to Hermes or Mercury Trismegistus, who was also called Thaut or Thoth.

It is certain that the hieroglyphs of the Tarot can be found on the ancient monuments of Egypt; it is certain that the signs of this book (traced in synoptic[83] series[84] on steles or on metal plates[85] similar to the isiac tablet of Bembo[86]) were separately reproduced on engraved stones or on medallions which later became amulets and talismans.

Thus one separates the pages of the infinite book into diverse combinations in order to assemble them, transpose them and arrange[87] them in an always new way in order to obtain the inexhaustible[88] oracles of the truth.

I have[89] one of these ancient talismans which was brought to me from Egypt by a traveler who was one of my friends. It represents the binary of Cycles or vulgarly the two of pentacles[90] [or coins]. It is the figurative expression of the great law of polarity and equilibrium producing harmony through the analogy of opposites; here is how this symbol is shown in the tarot S which we have and which is still sold in our times.

---

[79] Literally 'savant' means "scientist, scholar; expert, savant"
[80] Literally 'deviné' means "guess, divine; infer, sense; riddle"
[81] Literally 'hiératiques' means "hieratic, priestly"
[82] Literally 'arrêts' means "arrest, stopping, cessation; halt, stop; break, pause, standstill; stand, end; stand off, letup; bus stop"
[83] Literally 'synoptiques' means "synoptic (pertaining to or constituting a synopsis, presenting a similar point of view; of or pertaining to the first three gospels in the New Testament: Matthew, Mark and Luke)"
[84] Literally 'ensembles' means "ensemble, whole; collection, aggregate; set; body, series"
[85] Literally 'tables' means "table; board"
[86] Editor's note: Levi discusses this tablet in Ch. 4 of Book 1 of his *History of Magic*.
[87] Literally 'disposer' means "arrange, set; lay, dispose; place, put out; array, apply"
[88] Literally 'inépuisables' means "inexhaustible, bottomless, endless, unfailing, unflagging"
[89] Literally 'possède' means "possess, own; have; master, have a thorough knowledge of"
[90] Literally 'deniers' means "funds, monies, capital"

The medallion that I have is a little rough[91], about the size of a silver five-franc piece, but thicker. The two polaric cycles are shown exactly as in our italian tarot, a lotus flower with a halo or a nimbus[92]. The astral current which separates and at the same time attracts the two polaric seats[93] is represented in our egyptian talisman by the goat [of] Mendes placed between two vipers analogous to the serpents of the caduceus.

On the reverse side of the medallion, one sees an adept or egyptian priest who, having substituted himself for Mendes between the two cycles of universal equilibrium, is leading the goat, now simply a docile animal under the staff[94] [or wand] of the man [who is the] imitator of God, down a long avenue planted with trees.

The ten numeric signs, the twenty-two letters of the alphabet and the four astronomical signs of the seasons are the summary[95] of the whole Kabalah.

Twenty-two letters and ten numbers give the thirty-two paths of the Sepher Yetzirah: four gives the merkabah [ מרכבה or chariot of Ezekiel] and the shem-hamphorash[96] [or tetragram יהוה ]. It is as simple like a child's game and [yet] complicated like the most arduous[97] problems of pure mathematics. It is innocent[98] and profound like the truth and like nature. These four elementary and astronomical signs are the four forms of the sphinx and the four animals of Ezekiel and of saint John..."

-from the 7th Lesson of Levi's *The Elements of the Kabalah*

"...Begin with the number 1 and the letter Aleph [ א ], the juggler[99] [or magician] of the tarot, the ace of clubs[100] [or staffs/wands] or the staff[101] of Moses, the first chapter of my *Dogma* and of my *Ritual*, the first chapter of the book of Saint Martin: *Natural table of correspondences*, etc.[102], the first of the sephiroth or Kether, and make a summary of all this which you will send me, I will put you back on the path if you are lost you. We will proceed in the same [way] for other numbers..."

-from Letter #7 to the Baron Spédalieri

---

[91] Literally 'fruste' means "rough, uncouth, coarse; gross"
[92] Literally 'nimbe' means "nimbus, aureole, gloriole, halo"
[93] Literally 'foyers' means "home; hall; hearth, fireplace; seat, center; focus, focal point"
[94] Literally 'bâton' means "stick, baton, wand, staff, club, pole, cane"
[95] Literally 'le sommaire et le résumé' means "the summary and the abstract"
[96] Editor's note: The 'Shem-hamphorash' or 'Shema Hamphorash' is a corruption of the Hebrew term "Shem HaMephorash" [ שם המפורש ] which literally means "the explicit Name [of God]" and is used to refer to a name or names of God without actually pronouncing it or them.
[97] Literally 'ardus' means "arduous, difficult, hard; stiff, strenuous, uphill"
[98] Literally 'naïf' means "innocent, ingenuous, naive; simple, artless; simple minded, unsophisticated; unworldly"
[99] Editor's note: this is 'the Magician' card in English.
[100] Literally 'bâton' means "stick, baton, wand, staff, club, pole, cane"
[101] Literally 'verge' means "stick, wand; penis, male sexual organ"
[102] Louis Claude de Saint-Martin: "Natual Table of correspondences that exist between God, Man and the Universe" (1782).

# Compiled Information about the Minor Arcana:

|    | Card Name        | Association                                                                                                       | Source                                                                                                              |
|----|------------------|-------------------------------------------------------------------------------------------------------------------|---------------------------------------------------------------------------------------------------------------------|
| 23 | King of Clubs    | [White] יי, The father                                                                                            | *Major Keys and the Clavicles of Solomon*                                                                           |
| 24 | Queen of Clubs   | [Black] יה, The wife of the father                                                                                | *Major Keys and the Clavicles of Solomon*                                                                           |
| 25 | Knight of Clubs  | [White] יו, Conqueror of power                                                                                    | *Major Keys and the Clavicles of Solomon*                                                                           |
| 26 | Page of Clubs    | [Black] יה, Slave of man                                                                                          | *Major Keys and the Clavicles of Solomon*                                                                           |
| 27 | Ten of Clubs     | Arcanum 10 ( י ) and the Malkuth of Yod [ י ]                                                                     | Ch.10 of *Dogma of High Magic*                                                                                      |
| 28 | Nine of Clubs    | Arcanum 9 ( ט ) and the Yesod of Yod [ י ]                                                                        | Ch.10 of *Dogma of High Magic*                                                                                      |
| 29 | Eight of Clubs   | Arcanum 8 ( ח ) and the Hod of Yod [ י ]                                                                          | Ch.10 of *Dogma of High Magic*                                                                                      |
| 30 | Seven of Clubs   | Arcanum 7 ( ז ) and the Netzah of Yod [ י ]                                                                       | Ch.10 of *Dogma of High Magic*                                                                                      |
| 31 | Six of Clubs     | Arcanum 6 ( ו ) and the Tiphereth of Yod [ י ]                                                                    | Ch.10 of *Dogma of High Magic*                                                                                      |
| 32 | Five of Clubs    | Arcanum 5 ( ה ) and the Geburah of Yod [ י ]; the justice of the Creator or the wrath of man                      | Ch.10 of *Dogma of High Magic*                                                                                      |
| 33 | Four of Clubs    | Arcanum 4 ( ד ) and the Chesed of Yod [ י ]                                                                       | Ch.10 of *Dogma of High Magic*                                                                                      |
| 34 | Three of Clubs   | Arcanum 3 ( ג ) and the Binah of Yod [ י ]                                                                        | Ch.10 of *Dogma of High Magic*                                                                                      |
| 35 | Two of Clubs     | Arcanum 2 ( ב ) and the Chockmah of Yod [ י ]                                                                     | Ch.10 of *Dogma of High Magic*                                                                                      |
| 36 | Ace of Clubs     | Arcanum 1 ( א ) and the Kether of Yod [ י ]; Creative intelligence [or intelligent understanding]; the staff of Moses | Ch.10 of *Dogma of High Magic*, Ch.22 of *Ritual of High Magic* and Letter #7 to the Baron Spédalieri             |
| 37 | King of Cups     | [White] הי, The husband of the mother                                                                             | *Major Keys and the Clavicles of Solomon*                                                                           |
| 38 | Queen of Cups    | [Black/White] הה, Master/Mistress of herself                                                                      | *Major Keys and the Clavicles of Solomon*                                                                           |
| 39 | Knight of Cups   | [White] הו, Conqueror of happiness                                                                                | *Major Keys and the Clavicles of Solomon*                                                                           |
| 40 | Page of Cups     | [Black] הה, Slave of woman                                                                                        | *Major Keys and the Clavicles of Solomon*                                                                           |
| 41 | Ten of Cups      | Arcanum 10 ( י ) and the Malkuth of Heh [ ה ]                                                                     | Ch.10 of *Dogma of High Magic*                                                                                      |
| 42 | Nine of Cups     | Arcanum 9 ( ט ) and the Yesod of Heh [ ה ]                                                                        | Ch.10 of *Dogma of High Magic*                                                                                      |
| 43 | Eight of Cups    | Arcanum 8 ( ח ) and the Hod of Heh [ ה ]                                                                          | Ch.10 of *Dogma of High Magic*                                                                                      |
| 44 | Seven of Cups    | Arcanum 7 ( ז ) and the Netzah of Heh [ ה ]; the victory of mercy or the triumph of woman                         | Ch.10 of *Dogma of High Magic*                                                                                      |
| 45 | Six of Cups      | Arcanum 6 ( ו ) and the Tiphereth of Heh [ ה ]                                                                    | Ch.10 of *Dogma of High Magic*                                                                                      |
| 46 | Five of Cups     | Arcanum 5 ( ה ) and the Geburah of Heh [ ה ]                                                                      | Ch.10 of *Dogma of High Magic*                                                                                      |
| 47 | Four of Cups     | Arcanum 4 ( ד ) and the Chesed of Heh [ ה ]                                                                       | Ch.10 of *Dogma of High Magic*                                                                                      |
| 48 | Three of Cups    | Arcanum 3 ( ג ) and the Binah of Heh [ ה ]                                                                        | Ch.10 of *Dogma of High Magic*                                                                                      |
| 49 | Two of Cups      | Arcanum 2 ( ב ) and the Chockmah of Heh [ ה ]                                                                     | Ch.10 of *Dogma of High Magic*                                                                                      |
| 50 | Ace of Cups      | Arcanum 1 ( א ) and the Kether of Heh [ ה ]; magnetizing intelligence [or intelligent understanding]; Love, space | Ch.10 of *Dogma of High Magic*, Ch.22 of *Ritual of High Magic* and Letter #105 to the Baron Spédalieri            |

| | Card Name | Association | Source |
|---|---|---|---|
| 51 | King of Swords | [Black/White] וי, Prince of love | *Major Keys and the Clavicles of Solomon* |
| 52 | Queen of Swords | [Black] וה, Princess of love | *Major Keys and the Clavicles of Solomon* |
| 53 | Knight of Swords | [White] וו, Conqueror of love | *Major Keys and the Clavicles of Solomon* |
| 54 | Page of Swords | [Black] וה, Slave of love | *Major Keys and the Clavicles of Solomon* |
| 55 | Ten of Swords | Arcanum 10 ( י ) and the Malkuth of Vau [ ו ] | Ch.10 of *Dogma of High Magic* |
| 56 | Nine of Swords | Arcanum 9 ( ט ) and the Yesod of Vau [ ו ] | Ch.10 of *Dogma of High Magic* |
| 57 | Eight of Swords | Arcanum 8 ( ח ) and the Hod of Vau [ ו ]; eternal conflict or [eternal] equilibrium | Ch.10 of *Dogma of High Magic* |
| 58 | Seven of Swords | Arcanum 7 ( ז ) and the Netzah of Vau [ ו ] | Ch.10 of *Dogma of High Magic* |
| 59 | Six of Swords | Arcanum 6 ( ו ) and the Tiphereth of Vau [ ו ] | Ch.10 of *Dogma of High Magic* |
| 60 | Five of Swords | Arcanum 5 ( ה ) and the Geburah of Vau [ ו ] | Ch.10 of *Dogma of High Magic* |
| 61 | Four of Swords | Arcanum 4 ( ד ) and the Chesed of Vau [ ו ] | Ch.10 of *Dogma of High Magic* |
| 62 | Three of Swords | Arcanum 3 ( ג ) and the Binah of Vau [ ו ] | Ch.10 of *Dogma of High Magic* |
| 63 | Two of Swords | Arcanum 2 ( ב ) and the Chockmah of Vau [ ו ] | Ch.10 of *Dogma of High Magic* |
| 64 | Ace of Swords | Arcanum 1 ( א ) and the Kether of Vau [ ו ]; militant intelligence [or intelligent understanding] | Ch.10 of *Dogma of High Magic*, Ch.22 of *Ritual of High Magic* |
| 65 | King of Pentacles | [White] הי, The creating father | *Major Keys and the Clavicles of Solomon* |
| 66 | Queen of Pentacles | [Black] הה, Master/Mistress of the children | *Major Keys and the Clavicles of Solomon* |
| 67 | Knight of Pentacles | [White] הו, Conqueror of works | *Major Keys and the Clavicles of Solomon* |
| 68 | Page of Pentacles | [Black] הה, [Slave of children or works] | *Major Keys and the Clavicles of Solomon* |
| 69 | Ten of Pentacles | Arcanum 10 ( י ) and the Malkuth of Heh [ ה ] | Ch.10 of *Dogma of High Magic* |
| 70 | Nine of Pentacles | Arcanum 9 ( ט ) and the Yesod of Heh [ ה ] | Ch.10 of *Dogma of High Magic* |
| 71 | Eight of Pentacles | Arcanum 8 ( ח ) and the Hod of Heh [ ה ] | Ch.10 of *Dogma of High Magic* |
| 72 | Seven of Pentacles | Arcanum 7 ( ז ) and the Netzah of Heh [ ה ] | Ch.10 of *Dogma of High Magic* |
| 73 | Six of Pentacles | Arcanum 6 ( ו ) and the Tiphereth of Heh [ ה ] | Ch.10 of *Dogma of High Magic* |
| 74 | Five of Pentacles | Arcanum 5 ( ה ) and the Geburah of Heh [ ה ] | Ch.10 of *Dogma of High Magic* |
| 75 | Four of Pentacles | Arcanum 4 ( ד ) and the Chesed of Heh [ ה ] | Ch.10 of *Dogma of High Magic* |
| 76 | Three of Pentacles | Arcanum 3 ( ג ) and the Binah of Heh [ ה ] | Ch.10 of *Dogma of High Magic* |
| 77 | Two of Pentacles | Arcanum 2 ( ב ) and the Chockmah of Heh [ ה ] | Ch.10 of *Dogma of High Magic* |
| 78 | Ace of Pentacles | Arcanum 1 ( א ) and the Kether of Heh [ ה ]; the soul of the world | Ch.10 of *Dogma of High Magic*, Ch.22 of *Ritual of High Magic* |

Editor's Appendix

# Compiled Information from Eliphas Levi about the 4 Letters of the Tetragram [ יהוה ] and the 10 Sephiroth of the Kabalah related with the 4 Suits of the Minor Arcana:

| Letters of the Tetragram (or Tetragrammaton) | Ch. 10 of *Dogma of High Magic* & Ch. 22 of *Ritual of High Magic* | 3rd Lesson of *The Elements of the Kabalah* | Letters #70, 153, 156 & 50 to the Baron Spédalieri | Synthesis |
|---|---|---|---|---|
| Yod  י | the Club [or Staff/Wand] is the Egyptian phallus; Creative/Creator | [the] club [or staff/wand] or scepter of the father | **Father; Atziluth** : Light of glory | Club/Staff/Wand or Scepter, Phallus, Man, Father; *Atziluth*, etc. |
| Heh  ה | the Cup is the cteis; Magnetizing[103] | [the] cup or delights of the mother | **Son; Briah** : Light of universal, astral and magnetic life. The world of causes. | Cup, Cteis, Woman, Mother; Son, *Briah*, etc. |
| Vau  ו | the Sword is the conjunction of both or the lingam; Militancy | [the] sword or battle of love | **Holy Spirit; Yetzirah** : Visible, celestial, terrestrial and igneous light. The world of thoughts or ideas. | Sword, Conjunction, Battle, Love; Holy Spirit, *Yetzirah*, etc. |
| Heh  ה | the Circle or Pentacle, image of the world | and [the] coins[104] or fecundity[105] | **Creation; [ Assiah :]** The world of forms. | Circle/Coin or Pentacle, the World, Fertility; Creation, *Assiah*, etc. |

"…One can see through this simple arrangement the kabalistic sense of each plate. Thus, for example:

- the 5 of Clubs [or staffs/wands] rigorously signifies [the] geburah of Yod [ י ],
    - that is to say, the justice of the Creator or the wrath of man;
- the 7 of Cups signifies
    - the victory of mercy or the triumph of woman;
- the 8 of Swords signifies
    - eternal conflict or [eternal] equilibrium;

and so forth for the others…"

-from Ch. 10 of *Dogma of High Magic*

---

[103] Literally 'aimante' means "magnetic, operating via magnetic means; attractive; loving, affectionate, passionate"
[104] Literally 'deniers' means "funds, monies, capital"
[105] Literally 'fécondité' means "fertility, fecundity, fruitfulness, fruition"

# Editor's Appendix

| | Names of the Sephiroth | Ch. 10 of *Dogma of High Magic* | 2nd & 4th Lessons of *The Elements of the Kabalah* | Letters #70, 60, 113, 103. 153, 171, 169 to the Baron Spédalieri |
|---|---|---|---|---|
| 1 | **Kether** | The Crown, the equilibrating power. | Supreme power; Crown | Omnipotence |
| 2 | **Chokmah** | Wisdom, equilibrated in its unchangeable order by the initiative of understanding. | Absolute wisdom; Immutable Wisdom | Wisdom |
| 3 | **Binah** | Active Understanding[106], equilibrated by Wisdom. | Infinite Understanding; Creative Understanding | Active Liberty; Intelligent Understanding |
| 4 | **Chesed** | Mercy, second conception of Wisdom, always benevolent[107], because it is strong. | Goodness | Mercy |
| 5 | **Geburah** | The Rigor[108] necessitated by Wisdom itself and by goodness. To suffer evil is to hinder good. | Justice or Rigor | Force/Strength |
| 6 | **Tiphereth** | Beauty, the luminous conception of equilibrium in forms, intermediary between the crown and the kingdom, mediating principle between the creator and the creation. (Do we not find such a sublime idea here of poetry and of its sovereign priesthood!) | Beauty | Beauty or the Absolute Ideal; Tiphereth is the Shekinah (the 'light of glory') of Kether |
| 7 | **Netzah** | Victory, that is to say, the eternal triumph of understanding and justice. | Victory; Victorious Movement | The Counsel which renders one Victorious |
| 8 | **Hod** | The Eternity of the victories of the spirit over matter, of the active over the passive, [and] of life over death. | Eternity; Great Eternal Repose | Fear of God |
| 9 | **Yesod** | The Foundation, that is to say, the basis of all belief and all truth, this is what we call the ABSOLUTE in philosophy. | Fecundity[109]; Continual Birthing[110] | Yesod is the visible light of Shekinah; the Law of Creation |
| 10 | **Malkuth** | The Kingdom, it is the universe, it is the whole of creation, the work and mirror of God, the proof of supreme reason, the formal consequence which forces us to re-ascend[111] to virtual premises, the enigma who's word is God, that is to say, supreme and absolute reason. | Reality; the immensity which populates the Universe | Creation; the Kingdom |

---

[106] Literally 'Intelligence' means "Intelligence, cleverness; wit, brilliance, cunning; understanding"
[107] Literally 'bienveillante' means "benevolent, benign; kind, kindly, gentle"
[108] Literally 'Rigueur' means "harshness, rigor; severity, sternness, strictness; tightness, toughness; stringency"
[109] Literally 'fécondité' means "fertility, fecundity, fruitfulness, fruition"
[110] Literally 'enfantment' means "labor, childbirth"
[111] Literally 'remonter' means "get hold of, set up, reset; pick up, pull up, put up; recover; ascend, wind up, rewind; boost, work up, turn up; reassemble"

Editor's Appendix

# Speculation of the Editors regarding Levi's Minor Arcana Associations:

"...The talismans, numbering 36, correspond to the nine hierarchies, or better [said] to the nine orders of angels, divided into four hierarchical degrees: they represent the clubs[112] [or staffs/wands], the cups, the swords and the circles [or pentacles] like the hieroglyphics of the Tarot. The seventy-two names which correspond are the ternary rays of the twenty-four pearls which form the letters of the sacred tetragram [ יהוה ]: they are the finials[113] of the apocalyptic crown of the twenty-four elders[114]..."

-from Letter #2 to the Baron Spédalieri

"...The four unities, which are but one, are expressed by the four letters of the divine Tetragram [ יהוה ] and represented hieroglyphically by the club [or staff/wand], the cup, the sword and the coins[115] [or pentacles] of the Tarot..."

-from Letter #12 to the Baron Spédalieri

|    | Card Name | Letter of the Tetragram | Additional Association | Origin of Association |
|----|-----------|------------------------|------------------------|----------------------|
| 23 | King of Clubs | י | י | Ch.10 of *Dogma of High Magic* |
| 24 | Queen of Clubs | י | ה | Ch.10 of *Dogma of High Magic* |
| 25 | Knight of Clubs | י | ו | Ch.10 of *Dogma of High Magic* |
| 26 | Page of Clubs | י | ה | Ch.10 of *Dogma of High Magic* |
| 27 | Ten of Clubs | י | Element Earth | Editors' Speculation based on a Figure given by Levi[116] |
| 28 | Nine of Clubs | י | Talisman 9 of 36 | Letter #2 to the Baron Spédalieri |
| 29 | Eight of Clubs | י | Talisman 8 of 36 | Letter #2 to the Baron Spédalieri |
| 30 | Seven of Clubs | י | Talisman 7 of 36 | Letter #2 to the Baron Spédalieri |
| 31 | Six of Clubs | י | Talisman 6 of 36 | Letter #2 to the Baron Spédalieri |
| 32 | Five of Clubs | י | Talisman 5 of 36 | Letter #2 to the Baron Spédalieri |
| 33 | Four of Clubs | י | Talisman 4 of 36 | Letter #2 to the Baron Spédalieri |
| 34 | Three of Clubs | י | Talisman 3 of 36 | Letter #2 to the Baron Spédalieri |
| 35 | Two of Clubs | י | Talisman 2 of 36 | Letter #2 to the Baron Spédalieri |
| 36 | Ace of Clubs | י | Talisman 1 of 36 | Letter #2 to the Baron Spédalieri |

---

[112] Literally 'bâton' means "stick, baton, wand, staff, club, pole, cane"
[113] Literally 'fleurons' means "finial (in Architecture), small ornamental object at the top of a column (or gable, etc.)"
[114] See Revelations 4:4 "And round about the throne were four and twenty seats: and upon the seats I saw four and twenty elders sitting, clothed in white raiment; and they had on their heads crowns of gold."
[115] Literally 'denier' refers to "silver coins". The denier was a Frankish coin created by Charlemagne in the Early Middle Ages which served as the model for many of Europe's currencies.
[116] See the 'Absolute Key of the Occult Sciences', which is the Frontispiece from *Key to the Great Mysteries* (p.197 in this book)

| | **Card Name** | **Letter of the Tetragram** | **Additional Association** | **Origin of Association** |
|---|---|---|---|---|
| 37 | King of Cups | ה | י | Ch.10 of *Dogma of High Magic* |
| 38 | Queen of Cups | ה | ה | Ch.10 of *Dogma of High Magic* |
| 39 | Knight of Cups | ה | ו | Ch.10 of *Dogma of High Magic* |
| 40 | Page of Cups | ה | ה | Ch.10 of *Dogma of High Magic* |
| 41 | Ten of Cups | ה | Element Water | Editors' Speculation based on a Figure given by Levi[117] |
| 42 | Nine of Cups | ה | Talisman 18 of 36 | Letter #2 to the Baron Spédalieri |
| 43 | Eight of Cups | ה | Talisman 17 of 36 | Letter #2 to the Baron Spédalieri |
| 44 | Seven of Cups | ה | Talisman 16 of 36 | Letter #2 to the Baron Spédalieri |
| 45 | Six of Cups | ה | Talisman 15 of 36 | Letter #2 to the Baron Spédalieri |
| 46 | Five of Cups | ה | Talisman 14 of 36 | Letter #2 to the Baron Spédalieri |
| 47 | Four of Cups | ה | Talisman 13 of 36 | Letter #2 to the Baron Spédalieri |
| 48 | Three of Cups | ה | Talisman 12 of 36 | Letter #2 to the Baron Spédalieri |
| 49 | Two of Cups | ה | Talisman 11 of 36 | Letter #2 to the Baron Spédalieri[118] |
| 50 | Ace of Cups | ה | Talisman 10 of 36 | Letter #2 to the Baron Spédalieri |
| 51 | King of Swords | ו | י | Ch.10 of *Dogma of High Magic* |
| 52 | Queen of Swords | ו | ה | Ch.10 of *Dogma of High Magic* |
| 53 | Knight of Swords | ו | ו | Ch.10 of *Dogma of High Magic* |
| 54 | Page of Swords | ו | ה | Ch.10 of *Dogma of High Magic* |
| 55 | Ten of Swords | ו | Element Fire | Editors' Speculation based on a Figure given by Levi[119] |
| 56 | Nine of Swords | ו | Talisman 27 of 36 | Letter #2 to the Baron Spédalieri |
| 57 | Eight of Swords | ו | Talisman 26 of 36 | Letter #2 to the Baron Spédalieri |
| 58 | Seven of Swords | ו | Talisman 25 of 36 | Letter #2 to the Baron Spédalieri |
| 59 | Six of Swords | ו | Talisman 24 of 36 | Letter #2 to the Baron Spédalieri |
| 60 | Five of Swords | ו | Talisman 23 of 36 | Letter #2 to the Baron Spédalieri |
| 61 | Four of Swords | ו | Talisman 22 of 36 | Letter #2 to the Baron Spédalieri |
| 62 | Three of Swords | ו | Talisman 21 of 36 | Letter #2 to the Baron Spédalieri[120] |
| 63 | Two of Swords | ו | Talisman 20 of 36 | Letter #2 to the Baron Spédalieri |
| 64 | Ace of Swords | ו | Talisman 19 of 36 | Letter #2 to the Baron Spédalieri |
| 65 | King of Pentacles | ה | י | Ch.10 of *Dogma of High Magic* |
| 66 | Queen of Pentacles | ה | ה | Ch.10 of *Dogma of High Magic* |

---

[117] See the 'Absolute Key of the Occult Sciences', which is the Frontispiece from *Key to the Great Mysteries* (p.197 in this book)
[118] Compare the 'Primitive Egyptian Tarots' from *History of Magic* (on p.193 in this book) and the figure Levi gives for this Pentacle.
[119] See the 'Absolute Key of the Occult Sciences', which is the Frontispiece from *Key to the Great Mysteries* (p.197 in this book)
[120] Compare Figure 6 from *Ritual of High Magic* (on p.169 in this book) and the figure Levi gives for this Pentacle.

|    | **Card Name** | **Letter of the Tetragram** | **Additional Association** | **Origin of Association** |
|----|---|---|---|---|
| 67 | Knight of Pentacles | ה | ו | Ch.10 of *Dogma of High Magic* |
| 68 | Page of Pentacles | ה | ה | Ch.10 of *Dogma of High Magic* |
| 69 | Ten of Pentacles | ה |  Element Air | Editors' Speculation based on a Figure given by Levi[121] |
| 70 | Nine of Pentacles | ה | Talisman 36 of 36 | Letter #2 to the Baron Spédalieri |
| 71 | Eight of Pentacles | ה | Talisman 35 of 36 | Letter #2 to the Baron Spédalieri |
| 72 | Seven of Pentacles | ה | Talisman 34 of 36 | Letter #2 to the Baron Spédalieri |
| 73 | Six of Pentacles | ה | Talisman 33 of 36 | Letter #2 to the Baron Spédalieri |
| 74 | Five of Pentacles | ה | Talisman 32 of 36 | Letter #2 to the Baron Spédalieri |
| 75 | Four of Pentacles | ה | Talisman 31 of 36 | Letter #2 to the Baron Spédalieri |
| 76 | Three of Pentacles | ה | Talisman 30 of 36 | Letter #2 to the Baron Spédalieri |
| 77 | Two of Pentacles | ה | Talisman 29 of 36 | Letter #2 to the Baron Spédalieri and the 7th Lesson to Mr. Montaut[122] |
| 78 | Ace of Pentacles | ה | Talisman 28 of 36 | Letter #2 to the Baron Spédalieri and Ch. 1 of *Dogma of High Magic*[123] |

---

[121] See the 'Absolute Key of the Occult Sciences', which is the Frontispiece from *Key to the Great Mysteries* (p.197 in this book)

[122] Levi mentions in Lesson #7 of his ... that "It is certain that the hieroglyphs of the Tarot can be found on the ancient monuments of Egypt; it is certain that the signs of this book ... were separately reproduced on engraved stones or on medallions which later became amulets and talismans. ... I have one of these ancient talismans which was brought to me from Egypt by a traveler who was one of my friends… It represents the binary of Cycles or vulgarly the two of pentacles [or coins]. It is the figurative expression of the great law of polarity and of equilibrium producing harmony through the analogy of opposites; here is how this symbol is shown in the tarot which we have and which is still sold in our times."

[123] This is the yin-yang symbol that is actually right before Ch.1, in Figure 2 'The Esoteric sacerdotal formula of reprobation'. The description of this figure says "...Above we see the ace of pentacles from the chinese Tarot...". Levi also mentions the pentacle in Letter #13 to the Baron Spédalieri, saying "...There are, then, two Alephs [ א ] ; the white aleph and the black aleph; the black is the shadow of the white and the white is the light of the black. ...This is what the Chinese express through the pentacle of Confucius..."

Editor's Appendix

# Compare what Samael Aun Weor says about the Tarot and Minor Arcana:

"...In this path we will have to live all the 12 Hours of which the Great Sage Apollonius spoke about. The Black Magician "Papus" tried to disfigure the 12 Hours of Apollonius with teachings of Black Magic, liquidating all the millions of kabalistic volumes that drift in the world.

We arrived at the conclusion that: all Kabalah is reduced to the 22 Major Arcana of the Tarot and 4 Aces, which represent the 4 Elements of Nature. On such a simple thing, scholars have written millions of volumes and theories that would turn anyone "crazy[124]" who had the bad taste of becoming intellectualized with that whole arsenal.

The worst of it is that, in questions of Kabalah, the Black Magicians seized[125] what they found, in order to disfigure the teaching and lead the world astray. The works of Papus are legitimate black magic.

The Tarot is a book as ancient as the ages, and is intimately related with the Wisdom of the Planetary Gods. This book is the Tarot deck and consists[126] of 78 plates[127], divided into 22 called Major Arcana, [and] 56 denominated Minor Arcana.

The 4 Aces represent the Elements of Nature.[128]

THE **ACE OF SWORDS** SYMBOLIZES THE **FIRE.**

THE **ACE OF CUPS** SYMBOLIZES THE **WATER.**

THE **ACE OF PENTACLES**[129] SYMBOLIZES THE **AIR.**

THE **ACE OF CLUBS**[130] SYMBOLIZES THE **EARTH**

All the 56 plates of the Minor Arcana are based on these 4 Aces, and on the 10 numbers of our decimal system. In the 22 Major Arcana, for example, a 4 of Clubs is none other than Arcanum "4", the Emperor and the symbol of the Ace of Clubs repeated 4 times; the same [thing] happens with the 56 plates of the Minor Arcana. Intuitively interpret these cards combining the Natural Element with the Major Arcana and the problem will be resolved.

For example: a 6 of Pentacles would be interpreted [by] combining Arcanum 6 with the Element Air, or "Soul[131]", symbolized by the Pentacles; this would say: "A Love Affair", and so on successively.

---

[124] Literally 'loco' means "mad, crazy, insane; madman, lunatic, maniac, one who is mentally deranged; idiot, half wit"
[125] Literally 'apoderaron' means "seized, took possession; authorize, empower"
[126] Literally 'consta' means "be known; be on record; feature; know"
[127] Literally 'lamina' means "sheet, plate, lamina; lamella"
[128] Compare the associations given in the top part of the 'Absolute Key of the Occult Sciences', the Frontispiece from *Key to the Great Mysteries* (on p.197 in this book), where the Swords are associated with the sign of Leo or Fire; the Cups are associated with Water; the Pentacles are associated with the eagle or Air; and the Clubs/Staffs/Wands are associated with the bull or Earth.
[129] Literally 'OROS' means "Gold, Gold Medals; Diamonds; Pentacles"
[130] Literally 'BASTOS' means "Clubs, Wands"
[131] Literally 'Alma' means "soul, spirit; heart; lifeblood; sacred, holy, worthy of reverence; sanctified, consecrated"

There are two kinds of Kabalists: Intellectual Kabalists and Intuitive Kabalists. The Intellectual Kabalists are Black Magicians; the Intuitive Kabalists are White Magicians.

Many times the Sidereal Gods answer us by showing us a card of the Tarot; then we [should] intuitively comprehend the answer which has been given to us. By merely looking at a card of the Tarot, the Intuitive Kabalists comprehend what destiny reserves for them.

On a certain occasion I consulted a Planetary Genie about the convenience of making a trip, for which I was not prepared economically; the Planetary Genie showed me 3 cards. One of them was a King of Pentacles, everything beautifully embroidered with gold; I understood with my heart and made my trip, and everything went very well.

When humanity was judged before me, I saw the Tarot extended in lines of 7 cards, and when a certain card of the 6th line was shown, the Gods judged the Great Prostitute (humanity) and considered her unworthy[132]. The sentence of the Gods was: "To the Abyss, to the Abyss, to the Abyss, to the Abyss." (the number of humanity is 666).

The White Magician prays to the Gods, throws his cards on the table with closed eyes; and beseeching his God, picks up a card, observes it, and makes the forecast with his intuition. Each card of the Tarot is, by itself, a total forecast. The exercises of Sagittarius are to awaken Clairvoyance and to see and comprehend all these things.

The Kabalists of Intuition understand everything with the Heart. The Intellectual Kabalists want to resolve everything with the Animal Mind. The Kabalist of Intuition is only guided by the Voice of Silence, the Intimate.

These cards of the Tarot are the language of the Superior Worlds of Light. These cards of the Tarot are the Occult Wisdom of the Sidereal Gods.

The 12 Hours of Apollonius are the Path of Initiation. [It is] horrifying to see how men have accumulated so many theories on this book so simple and sublime like God.

The 78 plates of the Tarot are like 78 ineffable Hieroglyphs shining in this pyramid of five angles which is called man $1 + 2 + 3 + 4 = 10$; the entire progress of the student is based on these numbers..."

- from Ch. 9 (Sagittarius) of *Zodical Course* by Samael Aun Weor

---

[132] Literally 'indigna' means "discreditable; unfit; worthless, unworthy"

Editor's Appendix

# The Esoteric Egyptian Tarot from Eliphas Levi's Descriptions

The following Tarot cards were originally drawn by Gabriel Goulinat and first appeared in *Le Tarot Divinatoire* (1909). They have been modified by the Editors to incorporate the elements emphasized by Levi in his writings (including the Talismans from his *Major Keys and the Clavicles of Solomon*) and the associations of the Editors (see 'Speculation' above).

Levi only gave Talismans for cards #1-9 for each suit[133], so card #10 for each suit has been associated with one of the 4 Elements (again, see 'Speculation' above). Additionally, the Talismans for Swords 8 & 9 as well as all Talismans for the Pentacles 1-9 have been either created or modified with the information Levi provided. Sometimes he says they should be decorated "...with signs particular to the will of the operator..." in which case we have chosen shapes and symbols that reflect the corresponding number in order to be as general as possible. For more information about the Names or Explanations of the Talismans, see *Clefs Majeures et Clavicules de Salomon* (1895) or *The Kabalistic and Occult Philosophy of Eliphas Levi*, Volume 2.

## Major Arcana

Plate, Glyph or Symbolic Representation associated with the Card (drawn by Goulinat)

Hebrew letter (Top) and Estrangela letter (Bottom) associated with the Card

Name associated with the Card — The Magician / Le Bateleur

Number associated with the Card — 1

## Minor Arcana

Hebrew Number associated with the Card, related to the Suit (ex: Ace = 1 = Aleph), if any

Plate, Glyph or Symbolic Representation associated with the Card (drawn by Goulinat)

Levi's Kabalistic Talismans associated with the Card [or, when unavailable, then those created by Editors, if any]

Levi's Name or Explanation associated with the Talismans or Card [or, when unavailable, then those suggested by the Editors] — The First Principle / Le Premier Principe

Number associated with the Card — 36

Name associated with the Card — Ace of Clubs / As de Bâton

Levi's Kabalistic Correspondences associated with the Card: Letter of the Tetragram corresponding to the Suit (Right) and the Sephiroth or Letter associated with the Card (Left)

---

[133] Levi says "One must observe that the tens which are found in the tarot are not featured on the talismans; because the ten, being the synthesis of the unity, is virtually contained within the unity of each number" (see 'Notes on Letter #2' in *The Kabalistic and Occult Philosophy of Eliphas Levi*, Volume 2)

ז
ן  The Chariot
   Le Chariot      7

ח
ח  Justice
   La Justice     8

ט
ט  The Hermit
   L'Hermite      9

י  The Wheel of Fortune
י  La Roue de Fortune   10

כ
כ  Strength
   La Force      11

ל
ל  Hanged Man
   Le Pendu     12

Editor's Appendix

Death / La Mort — 13

Temperance / La Temperance — 14

The Devil / Le Diable — 15

The House of God / La Maison de Dieu — 16

The Star / L'Etoile — 17

The Moon / La Lune — 18

The Sun
Le Soleil
19

Judgement
Le Judgement
20

The Lunatic
Le Fou
(0) 21

The World
Le Monde
(21) 22

23 King of Clubs
Roi de Bâton
The Father
Le Père

24 Queen of Clubs
Dame de Bâtons
The Wife of the Father
L'Épouse du Père

Conqueror of Power
Conquérant de Puissance

**25** Knight of Clubs
Chevalier de Bâton

Slave of Man
Esclave de l'Homme

**26** Page of Clubs
Valet de Bâton

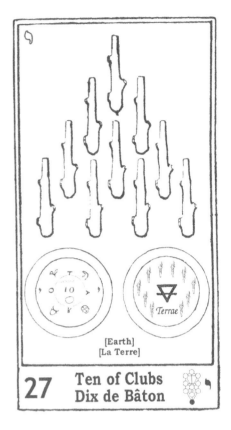

[Earth]
[La Terre]

**27** Ten of Clubs
Dix de Bâton

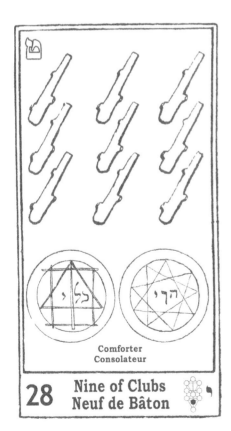

Comforter
Consolateur

**28** Nine of Clubs
Neuf de Bâton

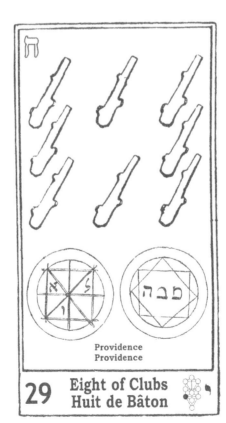

Providence
Providence

**29** Eight of Clubs
Huit de Bâton

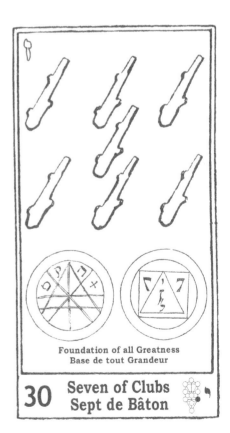

Foundation of all Greatness
Base de tout Grandeur

**30** Seven of Clubs
Sept de Bâton

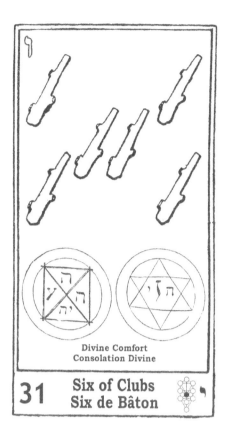
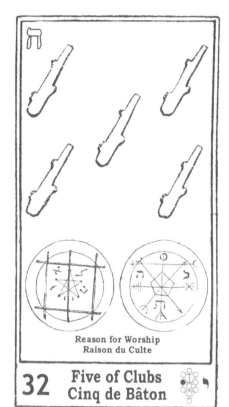
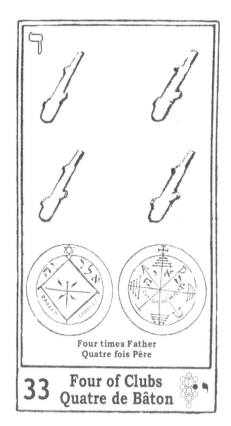
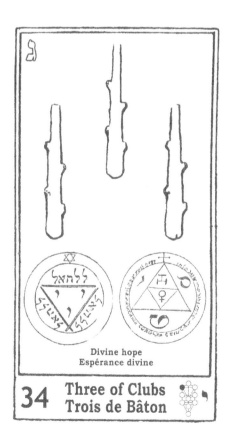
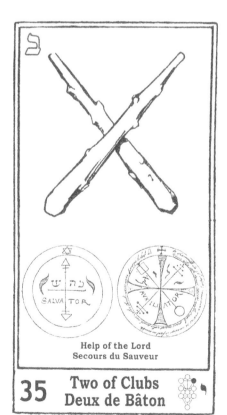
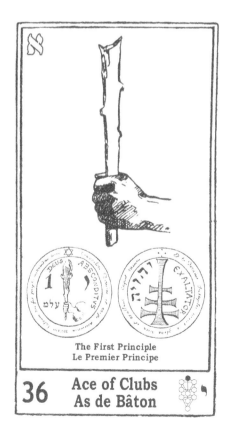

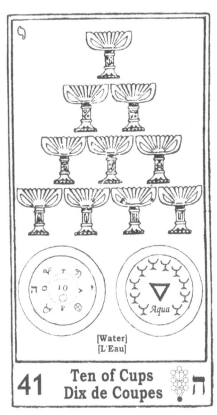
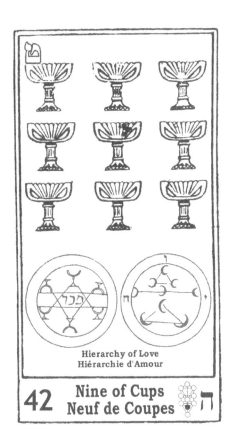

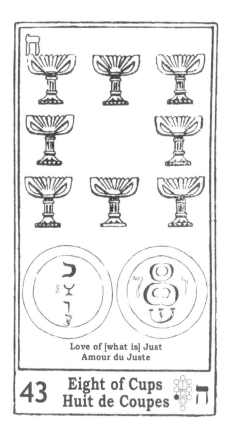

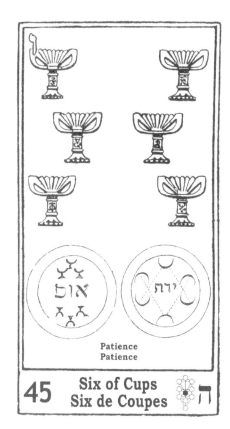
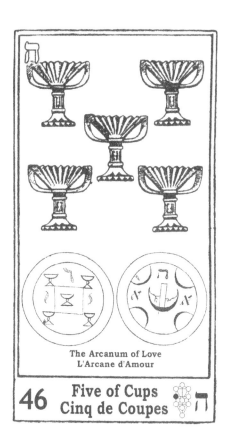
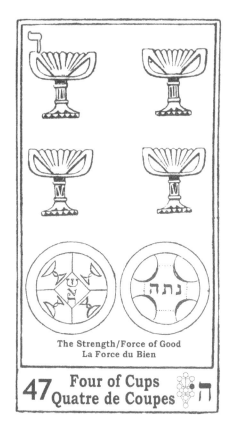
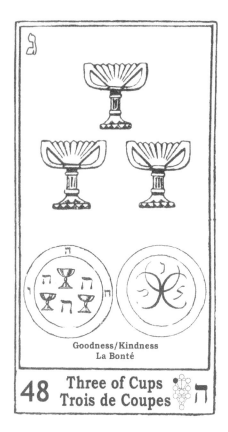

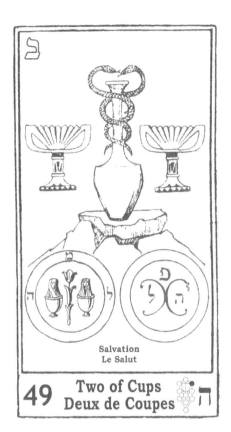

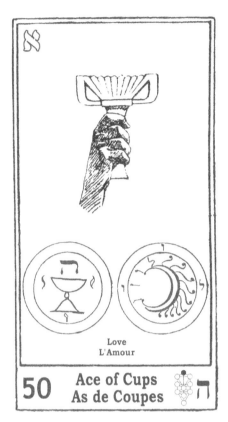

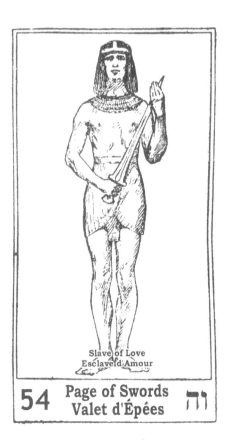

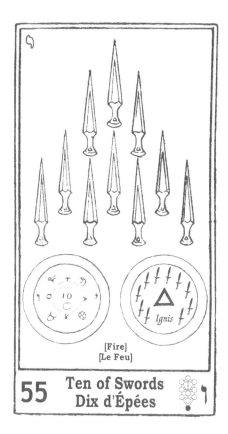
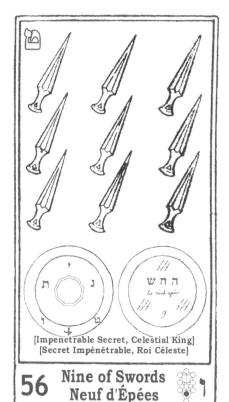
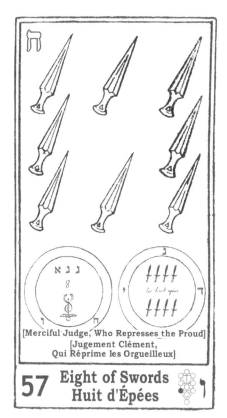
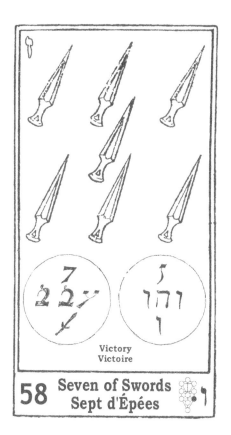
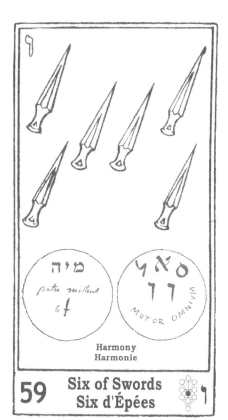
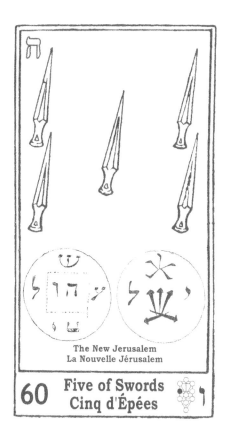

Editor's Appendix

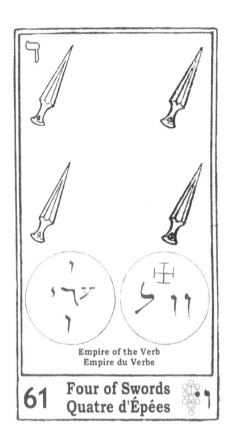
61  Four of Swords
    Quatre d'Épées
    Empire of the Verb
    Empire du Verbe

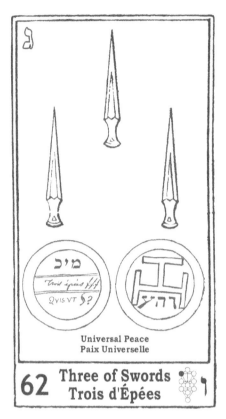
62  Three of Swords
    Trois d'Épées
    Universal Peace
    Paix Universelle

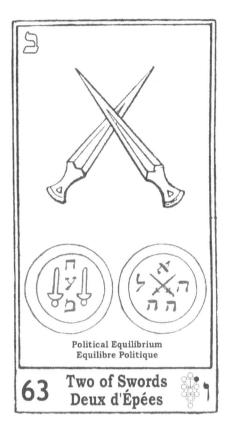
63  Two of Swords
    Deux d'Épées
    Political Equilibrium
    Equilibre Politique

64  Ace of Swords
    As d'Épées
    Force which Fecundates
    Force qui Féconde

65  King of Pentacles
    Roi de Deniers
    The Creating Father
    Le Père Créateur

66  Queen of Pentacles
    Dame de Deniers
    Master/Mistress of the Children
    Maîtresse des Enfants

**67** Knight of Pentacles / Chevalier de Deniers

Conqueror of Works / Conquérant des Œuvres

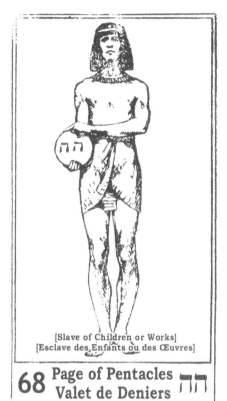

**68** Page of Pentacles / Valet de Deniers

[Slave of Children or Works] / [Esclave des Enfants ou des Œuvres]

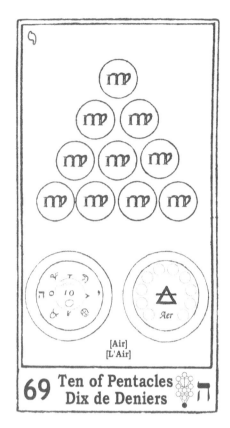

**69** Ten of Pentacles / Dix de Deniers

[Air] / [L'Air]

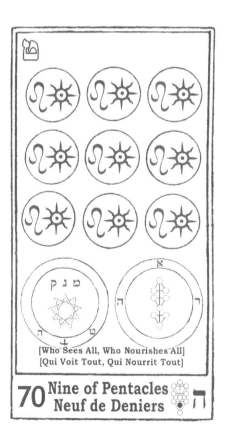

**70** Nine of Pentacles / Neuf de Deniers

[Who Sees All, Who Nourishes All] / [Qui Voit Tout, Qui Nourrit Tout]

**71** Eight of Pentacles / Huit de Deniers

[Liberal, Fountain of Wisdom] / [Libéral, Fontaine de la Sagesse]

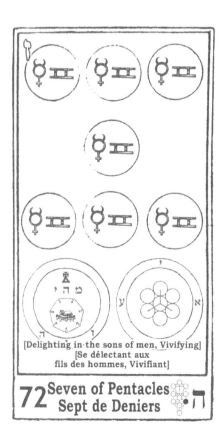

**72** Seven of Pentacles / Sept de Deniers

[Delighting in the sons of men, Vivifying] / [Se délectant aux fils des hommes, Vivifiant]

Editor's Appendix

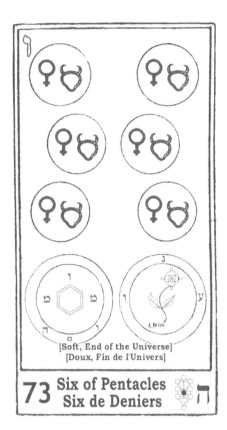
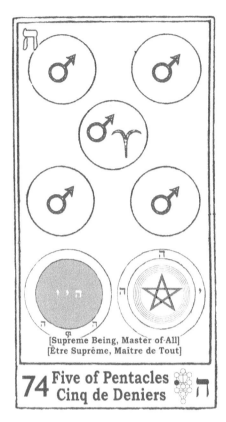
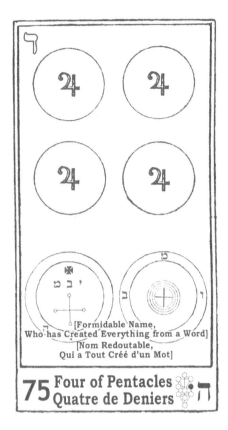
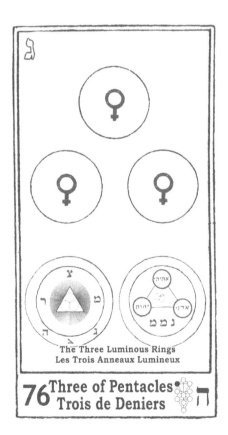
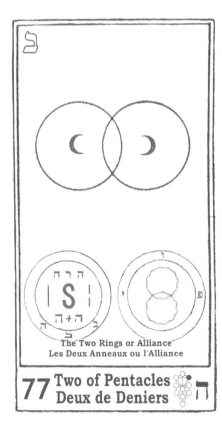
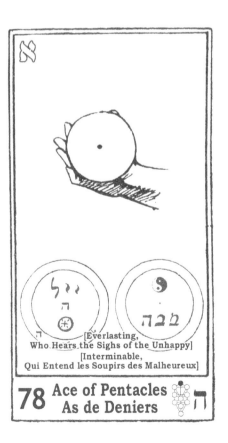

284

Editor's Appendix

| Court Cards: | | ה Pentacles/Coins | ו Swords | ה Cups | י Clubs/Wands |
|---|---|---|---|---|---|
| Kings | י | 65. The Creating Father | 51. The Prince of Love | 37. Husband of the Mother | 23. The Father |
| Queens | ה | 66. Master or Mistress of the Children | 52. Princess of Love | 38. Master or Mistress of Herself | 24. Wife of the Father |
| Knights | ו | 67. Conqueror of Works | 53. Conqueror of Love | 39. Conqueror of Happiness | 25. Conqueror of Power |
| Pages | ה | 68. [Slave of Children or Works] | 54. Slave of Love | 40. Slave of Woman | 26. Slave of Man |
| Synthesis of Court Cards: | | Creation, Children, Works | Love | Mother, Happiness, Woman | Father, Power, Man |
| Numbered Cards: | | | | | |
| Tens | י | 69. [Air] | 55. [Fire] | 41. [Water] | 27. [Earth] |
| Nines | ט | 70. [Who Sees all, Who Nourishes all] | 56. [Impenetrable Secret, Celestial King] | 42. Hierarchy of Love | 28. Comforter |
| Eights | ח | 71. [Liberal, Fountain of Wisdom] | 57. [Merciful Judge, Who represses the proud] | 43. Love of [what is] Just | 29. Providence |
| Sevens | ז | 72. [Delighting in the Sons of Men, Vivifying] | 58. Victory | 44. Science of Love | 30. Foundation of all Greatness |
| Sixes | ו | 73. [Soft, End of the Universe] | 59. Harmony | 45. Patience | 31. Divine Comfort |
| Fives | ה | 74. [Supreme Being, Master of All] | 60. The new Jerusalem | 46. The Arcanum of Love | 32. Reason for Worship |
| Fours | ד | 75. [Formidable Name, Who has Created Everything from a Word] | 61. Empire of the Verb | 47. The Strength/ Force of Good | 33. Four times Father |
| Threes | ג | 76. The Three Luminous Rings | 62. Universal Peace | 48. Kindness | 34. Divine hope |
| Twos | ב | 77. The Two Rings or Alliance | 63. Political Equilibrium | 49. Salvation | 35. Help of the Lord |
| Ones | א | 78. [Everlasting, Who Hears the Sighs of the Unhappy] | 64. Force which Fecundates | 50. Love | 36. The First Principle |
| Synthesis of Numbered Cards: | | **Seeing and Nourishing, Fountain, Vivifying, Soft, Creating Everything From a Word, Alliance, Everlasting.** | **Celestial Royalty, Merciful Judge, Victory, New Jerusalem, Harmony, Empire, Peace, Equilibrium, Fecundating.** | **Love, [what is] Just, Science, Patience, Strength/Force of Good, Kindness, Salvation.** | **Comforter, Foundation of Greatness, Reason for Worship, Hope, Help, First Principle.** |

# Some Objects for Reference

In Ch.14 of *Occult Masonry* (1853) by Jean Marie Ragon, he says the following:

> "MAGISM is the science of sciences, or rather it is the assembly of all the human sciences or knowledge; which is why, in ancient times, the magi were the most learned philosophers; in fact, a magus must be initiated into the principal sciences: 1st the preparatory science is the knowledge of ancient languages, the kabalistic signs, numbers, alphabets, talismanic and other hieroglyphs, [that are] used in occultism..."[134]

This section has been created to serve as a reference or lookup. The material is from different books and may or may not be accurate. The Editors have tried their best to gather materials of interest to the Student of Kabalah and Esotericism, but in the end: this material is just a compilation of what other authors have written. Awaken your Consciousness and become an Intuitive Kabalist.

---

[134] This quote is from p.117 of *Esoteric Studies in Masonry Volume 1: France, Freemasonry, Hermeticism, Kabalah and Alchemical Symbolism* which contains further extracts from the writings of J.M. Ragon.

# ALPHABETS.

*Tab. XXVI p. 146.*

| Modern Gothic | Old English | Set Chancery | Common Chancery | Court Hand | Secretary | Francic. Ex M.S Cotton. Cal. A.7. | SECRET ALPHABETS | | RUSSIAN. | | | |
|---|---|---|---|---|---|---|---|---|---|---|---|---|
| | | | | | | | | | Figure Antq./Mod. | | Name | Power |
| A | A a | A a | A a | A a | A a | λΛ a | ZI a | К a | Ᾱ A | As | a |
| B | B b | B b | G b | F b | B b | B b | † b | ʃ b | Б Б | Booke | b |
| C | C c | C c | C c | C c | C c | CL c | Ϗ c | Ϟ c | В В | Vadi | v or f |
| D | D d | D d | ʒ d | ʃ d | D d | OD d | Π d | ‡ d | Г Г | Glaghol | gh |
| E | E e | E e | C e | t e | E e | E E e | CO e | ⚹ e | Д Д | Dobra | d |
| F | F f | F f | ff f | ff f | ff f | f f | ℔ f | k f | Ě E | Yest | e or ye |
| G | G g | B g | G g | d g | Gg g | CG g | P g | Ꮞ g | Ж Ж | Sevetie | g |
| H | H h | Ꮟ h | b h | B h | Lɔh h | ƄH h | Λ h | b h | S S | Zielo | z |
| I | J i j | F ij | q ij | Ꮱ ij | JG ij | I i | m i | l i | З З | Zemle | z |
| K | K k | K k | k k | k k | k k | K K k | ϕ k | ‡ k | И И | Eie | i or e |
| L | L l | L l | C l | ſ l | L l | LL l | Ӿ l | ⅃ l | Ї I | E | i or e |
| M | M m | M m | y m | m | M m | MCO m | Π m | ⚡ m | K K | Kavko | k or c |
| N | N n | N n | h n | P n | N n | NN n | Γ n | ϕ n | Λ Λ | Ludee | l |
| O | O o | O o | O o | O o | O o | OO o | Ͷ o | X o | M M | Muislete | m |
| P | P p | P p | p p | p p | P p | P p | V p | ⅄ p | Н H | Nash | n |
| Q | Q q | Q q | Q q | Q q | Q q | qQ q | Λ q | ⌂ q | O O | Ohn | o w o |
| R | R r | R r | F r | B r | R r | R r | Ͷ r | X r | П П | Pokoy | p |
| S | S s | S s | G s | G s | S s | S s | Ψ s | V s | ρ P | Rise | r |
| T | T t | T t | T t | T t | T t | T t | 7 t | И t | C C | Slovo | s |
| U | U u v | V u v | S u v | V u v | U u v | U A u | 6 u | Λ u | T T | Tverdo | t |
| W | W w | W w | S w | B w | W w | W w | Q w | Ω w | У У | Eek | u oo |
| X | X x | X x | X x | Y x | X x | X X x | φ x | ⨉ x | Ф Ф | Phert | f ph |
| Y | Y y | Y y | Y y | Y y | Y y | Y Y y | Ͱ y | b y | X X | Kher | ch |
| Z | Z z | z z | z z | z z | z z | Ꮓz z | Ψ z | Z z | Ц Ц | Tse | ts |
| | | | | | | | | | Ч Ч | Tcherf | tch |
| | | | | | | | | | Ш Ш | Shaw | sh |
| | | | | | | | | | Щ Щ | Stshaw | stsh |
| | | | | | | | | | Z Ъ | Yerr | |
| | | | | | | | | | Ы ЬІ | Yerui | ui |
| | | | | | | | | | Ь Ь | Yeer | e |
| | | | | | | | | | Ѣ Ѣ | Yat | ye |
| | | | | | | | | | Э Э | Xe | x |
| | | | | | | | | | Ю Ю | Kji | |
| | | | | | | | | | Я Я | Pse | ps |
| | | | | | | | | | Θ Θ | Tita | th |
| | | | | | | | | | V V | Eijetfa | v |

*Longmate sculp.*

From *The Origin and Progress of Writing* (1784) by Thomas Astle

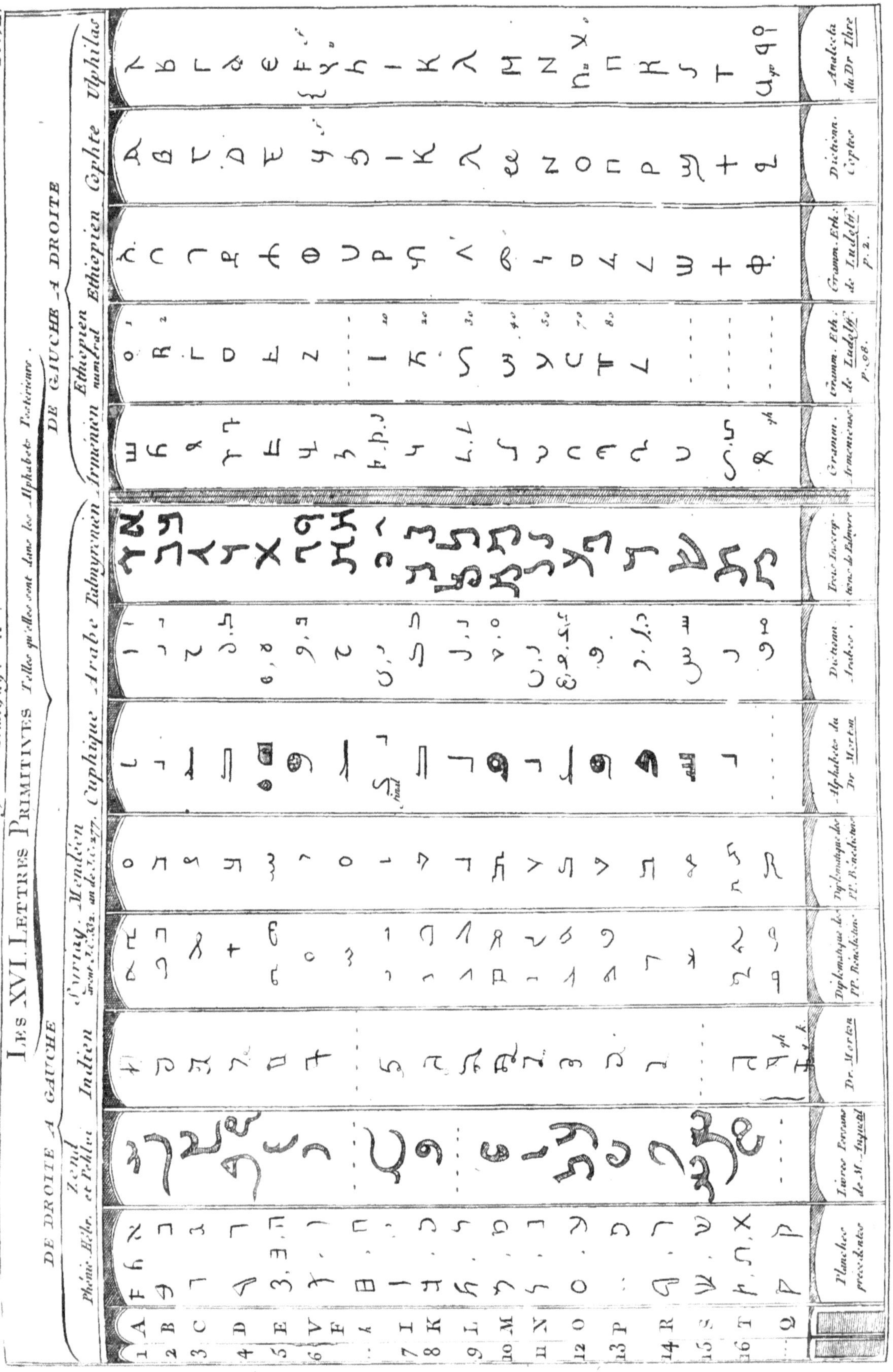


From *Monde Primitive* Vol. 3 (1777) by Antonie Court de Gébelin

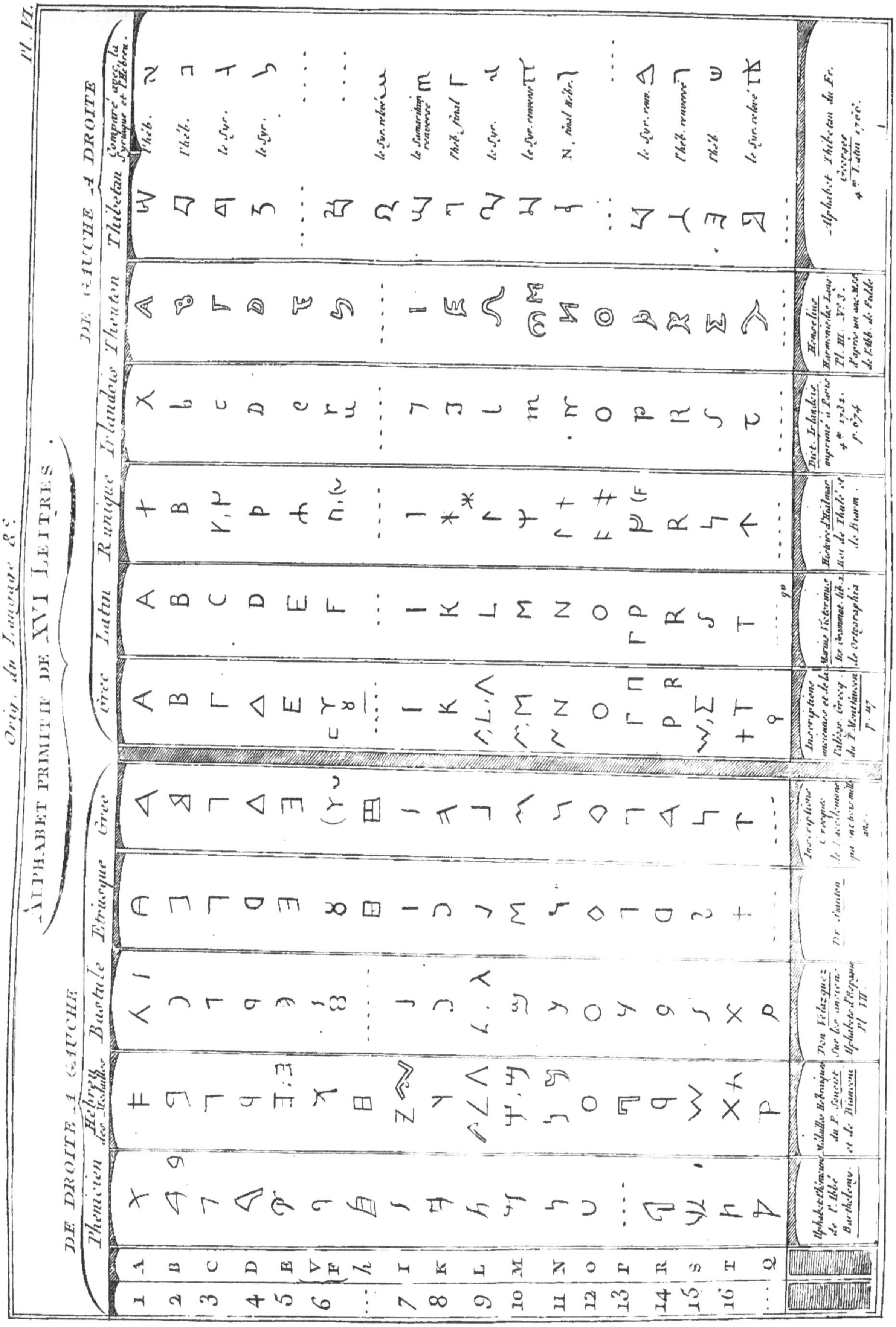


From *Monde Primitive* Vol. 3 (1777) by Antonie Court de Gébelin

## PLATE XXXV

| Number. | Sound. | Assyrian. | Babylonian. | Akkadian. | Syrian. | Syllable. | Greek. | Phoenician. | Letter. | Hebrew. |
|---|---|---|---|---|---|---|---|---|---|---|
| 1 | AU | | | | | | | | A | א |
| 2 | AB | | | | | | | | B | ב |
| 3 | GAU | | | | | | | | G | ג |
| 4 | DU | | | | | | | | D | ד |
| 5 | E | | | | | | | | E | ה |
| 6 | BU | | | | | | | | V | ו |
| 7 | UZ | | | | | | | | Z | ז |
| 8 | KHAV | | | | | | | | Ḥ | ח |
| 9 | UṬ | | | | | | | | Ṭ | ט |
| 10 | YA | | | | | | | | I | י |
| 11 | GUV | | | | | | | | K | כ |
| 12 | LU | | | | | | | | L | ל |
| 13 | MI | | | | | | | | M | מ |
| 14 | NU | | | | | | | | N | נ |
| 15 | SAN | | | | | | | | Ś | ס |
| 16 | 'A | | | | | | | | O | ע |
| 17 | PI | | | | | | | | P | פ |
| 18 | UŚ | | | | | | | | Ṣ | צ |
| 19 | GU | | | | | | | | Q | ק |
| 20 | ER | | | | | | | | R | ר |
| 21 | SA | | | | | | | | S | ש |
| 22 | TA | | | | | | | | T | ת |

ORIGIN OF ALPHABET

From *The Illustrated Bible Dictionary* (1908) by William Coleman Piercy

Editor's Appendix

## PLATE XXXVI

| Hebrew | Number | Syllable | Ionian | Sabean | Numidian | Phoenician | Punic | Israel | Samaritan | Aramaic | Palmyra | Square | Sound |
|---|---|---|---|---|---|---|---|---|---|---|---|---|---|
| א | 1 | ⋉ | A | ⅄ |  | ⋉ | ⊤ | ⊤ | ⊬ | ⊬ | ⋊ | ⋊ | A |
| ב | 2 | ◩ | B | R |  | 9 | 9 | 9 | 9 | 9 | ꭹ | ꭹ | B |
| ג | 3 | ⌐ | Γ | ⅂ | ⋀ | ⋀ | ⋀ | ⅂ | ⊤ | ⋀ | ⅃ | ⅃ | G |
| ד | 4 | ◊ | ◁ | ⋈ | ⋀ | ⋀ | ⋀ | ⋀ | ⋃ | ⋃ | ⋃ | ⅂ | D |
| ה | 5 | E | E | Y | ☰ | ⋣ | ⋣ | ⋣ | ⋣ | ⋤ | ⊓ | ⊓ | E |
| ו | 6 | ⸁ | F | ↓ | = | ⅃ | ⅃ | ⊬ | ⋎ | ⅃ | ⅃ | ⅃ | V |
| ז | 7 | ⊥ | Z | H | ⋈ | Z | H | ⊞ | ⋈ | ⊬ | ⅃ | ⅃ | Z |
| ח | 8 | ♯ | H | ⅏ | ⊒ | ⊟ | ⋈ | ⊟ | ⊟ | ⊞ | ⊬ | ⊬ | Ḥ |
| ט | 9 | ⊕ | ⊕ | ⅏ | ⌁ | ⊕ | ⸁ |  | ⋃ | ⋃ | ⋃ | ⋂ | Ṭ |
| י | 10 | ⋎ | ⋎ | P | ⋎ | ⋎ | ⋎ | ⋎ | ⋎ | ⋎ | > | ⋎ | I |
| כ | 11 | K | K | ⅃ | π | ⅃ | ⅃ | ⋎ | ⋎ | ⅃ | ⋎ | ⅃ | K |
| ל | 12 | ⋒ | ⋀ | ⋀ | ⋀ | ⋀ | ⋀ | ⋀ | ⋀ | ⋀ | ⋀ | ⋀ | L |
| מ | 13 | ⋀⋀ | M | ⋈ | ⅃ | ⋎ | ⋎ | ⋎ | ⋎ | ⋎ | ⋎ | ⋎ | M |
| נ | 14 | ⋎ | N | ⋎ | ⅃ | ⋎ | ⋎ | ⋎ | ⋎ | ⋎ | ⋎ | ⋎ | N |
| ס | 15 | ⋇ | ⋣ | ⋈ |  | ⋎ | ⋎ |  | ⋈ | ⋃ | ⋃ | ⋃ | S |
| ע | 16 | ◯ | O | ▽ | · | ◯ | ◯ | ◯ | ▽ | Y | Y | Y | O |
| פ | 17 | ⌐ | Γ |  | ⊙ | ⋃ | ⋃ | ⋃ | ⊐ | ⅃ | ⅃ | ⅃ | P |
| צ | 18 | ⋜ | M | ⊠ | ⊠ | ⋈ | ⋈ | ⋈ | m | ⋎ | ⋎ | ⋎ | Ṣ |
| ק | 19 | P | ⋑ | Φ | ⅲ | P | P | P | ⋃ | P | P | P | Q |
| ר | 20 | ⋔ | R | ⋎ | ⋀ | 9 | 9 | 9 | 9 | ⋎ | ⋎ | ⋎ | R |
| ש | 21 | ⋎ | Ɛ | ⋓ | ⋓ | ⋓ | ⋏ | ⋓ | ⋓ | ⊬ | ⊬ | ⋎ | S |
| ת | 22 | ⋏ | T | ) | + | ⊢ | ⋏ | ⋈ | ⊤ | ⊓ | .H | ⊓ | T |

EARLY ALPHABETS.

From *The Illustrated Bible Dictionary* (1908) by William Coleman Piercy

## Première partie. Planche I.

## ALPHABET SYRIAQUE.

| N°ˢ d'ordre | Lettres isolées | Lettres jointes | | | hébr. | Signes de transcription | Noms des lettres | Valeur numér. |
|---|---|---|---|---|---|---|---|---|
| 1 | ܐ | ܐ | | | א | ' ou rien | ܟܦ ou ܐܠܦ aleph ou âlaph | 1 |
| 2 | ܒ | ܒ | ܒ | ܒ | ב | b, bh | ܒܝܬ beth | 2 |
| 3 | ܓ | ܓ | ܓ | ܓ | ג | g, gh | ܓܡܠ gâmal | 3 |
| 4 | ܕ | ܕ | | | ד | d, dh | ܕܠܬ dâlath | 4 |
| 5 | ܗ | ܗ | | | ה | h | ܗܐ hé | 5 |
| 6 | ܘ | ܘ | | | ו | w | ܘܘ waw | 6 |
| 7 | ܙ | ܙ | | | ז | z | ܙܝܢ zaïn | 7 |
| 8 | ܚ | ܚ | ܚ | ܚ | ח | ḥ | ܚܝܬ ḥeth | 8 |
| 9 | ܛ | ܛ | ܛ | ܛ | ט | ṭ | ܛܝܬ ṭeth | 9 |
| 10 | ܝ | ܝ | ܝ | ܝ | י | y | ܝܘܕ youdh | 10 |
| 11 | ܟ | ܟ | ܟ | ܟ | כ | k, kh | ܟܦ kâph | 20 |
| 12 | ܠ | ܠ | ܠ | ܠ | ל | l | ܠܡܕ lâmadh | 30 |
| 13 | ܡ | ܡ | ܡ | ܡ | מ | m | ܡܝܡ mim | 40 |
| 14 | ܢ | ܢ | ܢ | ܢ | נ | n | ܢܘܢ noun | 50 |
| 15 | ܣ | ܣ | ܣ | ܣ | ס | s | ܣܡܟܬ semkath | 60 |
| 16 | ܥ | ܥ | ܥ | ܥ | ע | ʿ | ܥܐ ʿé | 70 |
| 17 | ܦ | ܦ | ܦ | ܦ | פ | p, ph | ܦܐ pé | 80 |
| 18 | ܨ | ܨ | | | צ | ṣ | ܨܕܐ ṣâdhé | 90 |
| 19 | ܩ | ܩ | ܩ | ܩ | ק | q | ܩܘܦ qoph | 100 |
| 20 | ܪ | ܪ | | | ר | r | ܪܝܫ riš | 200 |
| 21 | ܫ | ܫ | ܫ | ܫ | ש | š | ܫܝܢ šin | 300 |
| 22 | ܬ | ܬ | | | ת | t, th | ܬܘ tau | 400 |

From *Traité de Grammaire Syriaque* (1881) by Rubens Duval

## Première partie. Planche II.

### TABLEAU SYNOPTIQUE DES ALPHABETS SYRIAQUES.

| Palmyrien | Estrangelâ | Cursif jacobite | Cursif nestorien | Syro-palestinien |
|---|---|---|---|---|

Plate 1.

**PHŒNICIAN, HEBREW & GREEK ALPHABETS.**

From *Phœnicia* (1855) by John Kenrick

## Editor's Appendix

| | | 1. Phoenician written from right to left. | 2. Right to left { Sigean Inscript. above 500 B.C. | 3. Left to right | 4. Attic Greek. | 5. Gothic invented by Ulphilas about A.D. 370. | 6. Latin, more than four centuries before Christ. | 7. Saxon formed from the Roman in the 6th and following centuries. |
|---|---|---|---|---|---|---|---|---|
| | A | ⊼ | Λ | Λ | Λ | λ | A | A λ ᴧ a |
| | B | ⊴ | ᗺ | B | B | Ⲃ | B | B ʙ ƀ |
| G or | C | ┥ | Λ | Λ | Γ | Γ | ⲄⲤc | Ⲥ c |
| | D | ⊲ | Δ | ∇ | Δ | ⲇ | D | D Ð Δ δ |
| | E | ⊰ | ⋣ | Ǝ | E | ⲉ | E | E є ℮ e |
| F or | V | ⋎ | ⋎ | F | F | Ⲋ | F | F Ꝼ |
| | G | · | · | · | · | Ç | C | Ⲅ Ⳝ ᵹ ᵹ̇ |
| | Z | ⋜ | · | · | Z | Ꙉ | Z | Z |
| | H | ⊟ | H | H | H | ђ | H | Ⲏ h h |
| | TH | · | ⊕ | ⊕ | Θ | ѱ | · | T h ҕ ƥ |
| | I | ⌠ | J | ⌠ | I | ï or I | I | J 1 |
| | K | ⋏ | ⋊ | K | K | К | K | K k |
| | L | ⋏ | ⌐ | Ⅴ | Λ | λ | L | L ł 1 |
| | M | ⋈ | ⋎ | ⋎ | M | M | M | ⲙ ⲙ ᵯ |
| | N | ⋎ | Ϥ | ⋎ | N | N | N | N ɲ n |
| | X | · | · | · | ☰ | · | · | · |
| | O | ▽ | O | O | O | ჲ | O | O |
| | P | ⌡ | ⌐ | Γ | Π | Π | P | P p |
| | Q | ⲣ | · | · | ⲣ | ☉ | Q | · |
| | R | ⲣ | ⲣ | P | P | К | ʀʀ | ʀ ʀ ᴘ |
| | S | ₃ | Z | ⋊ | ∑ | S | ş | ſ ſ ʃ ᴛ |
| | T | ⊤ | T | T | T | T | T | T Ⲧ ⲧ |
| U,Y,& W | · | ⋎ | ⋎ | ⋎ | nⱴ.a | ⋎ʏ | ⲣⲩⲣⲩ̇ |
| | PH | · | ɸ | ɸ | ɸ | · | · | · |
| | CH | · | ✝ | ✝ | ⲭ | X | X | X |
| | PS | · | · | · | ⲯ | · | · | · |
| | O | · | Ω | O | Ω | · | · | · |
| | | Astle & Henley { | Chishull { | | Morton & Bernard { | Hickes & Bernard { | Bernard { | Hickes & Bernard { |

From *The Elements of Anglo-Saxon Grammar* (1823) by Joseph Bosworth

### Table showing the Correspondence between the Phoenician, Greek, and Roman Alphabets.

| I. Phoenician Alphabet and Numerical Value. | II. Full No. of Greek Letters (earliest form [1]). | | III. Classical Greek Alphabet. | IV. Numerals corresponding. | V. Roman Alphabet. | |
|---|---|---|---|---|---|---|
| | | | | | Characters. | Probable Pronunciation. |
| 1 Aleph = 1 | Alpha | A | A | 1 | A | *ah* |
| 2 Beth = 2 | Beta | B | B | 2 | B | *b* |
| 3 Gimel = 3 | Gamma | ᛚ Γ | Γ | 3 | C = K | *k* (*c* in *cat*) |
| 4 Daleth = 4 | Delta | ▷ Δ[2] | Δ | 4 | D | *d* |
| 5 He = 5 | E | ⴲ E | Ε ψιλόν | 5 | E | *ay* (*a* in *whale*) |
| 6 Vau = 6 | Vau | F | | 6 (ϛ′) | F (older Ⅰ') | *f* |
| 7 Zain = 7 | Zeta | I | Z | 7 | (G) | *g* (in *give*) |
| 8 Heth = 8 | Heta | H Β | H | 8 | H = ' | *h* (in *hat*) |
| 9 Teth = 9 | Theta | ⊗ | Θ | 9 | | |
| 10 Jod = 10 | Iota | ⟩ | I | 10 | I {vowel / consonant} | *ee* (in *feet*) / *y* (in *yes*) |
| 11 Kaph = 20 | Kappa | K | K | 20 | (K) | *k* |
| 12 Lamed = 30 | Lambda | V Λ | Λ | 30 | L (old ⌐) | *l* |
| 13 Mim = 40 | Mu | M | M | 40 | M | *m* |
| 14 Nun = 50 | Nu | N | N | 50 | N | *n* |
| 15 Samech = 60 | Sigma | ⊞ | Ξ | 60 | | |
| 16 Ayin = 70 | Ŏ | O | Ο μικρόν | 70 | O | *o* |
| 17 Pe = 80 | Pi | Γ | Π | 80 | P (Γ inscr.) | *p* |
| 18 Tsade = 90 | | M | | | | |
| 19 Koph = 100 | Koppa | Ọ | | 90 (Ọ) | Q (old Ọ) | *k* |
| 20 Resch = 200 | Rho | R P | P | 100 | R (old R)[3] | *r* |
| 21 Shin = 300 | Xi | Ƹ | Σ | 200 | S | *s* |
| 22 Thau = 400 | Tau | T | T | 300 | T | *t* |
| | Υ | Y V | Υ | 400 | V vowel | *oo* (in *fool*) |
| | Phi | Φ | Φ | 500 | V consonant | *w*, or Fr. *ou* in *oui* |
| | Chi | Ψ Ψ X | X | 600 | X = Ξ | *x* |
| | Psi | (caret) | Ψ | 700 | (Y) } later introductions to represent Gk. *v*, *ζ*. | |
| | Ō | Ω | Ω μέγα | 800 | (Z) } | |
| | | | | 900 ( ⟩) | | |

[1] The Greek characters are originally the Phoenician characters reversed to suit the mode of writing from left to right, which in Greece superseded the earlier right-to-left ('links läufig') writing of the Phoenicians. Examples of this latter method are found in the oldest Greek inscriptions: while in those of the sixth century B.C. is found a mixture of the two modes ('furchenförmig' or 'ridge-like') in which the writing is read backwards and forwards in alternate lines, e.g.

```
Ι Σ Τ Ι Α        i.e. Ἱστια(ῖος)
Ω Τ Ǝ Κ H             (ἀνέθ)ηκε τὠ-
Π Ο Λ Λ Ω             -πόλλω(νι)
```

[2] ▷ on Olympian inscriptions.
[3] This tailed R is found in the old Greek alphabet; e.g. on some inscriptions at Olympia.

From *A Manual of Comparative Philology* (1877) by Thomas Leslie Papillon

From *Mémoire sur l'origine égyptienne de l'alphabet phénicien* (1874)
by M. Le V^te Emmanuel de Rougé

From *Mémoire sur l'origine égyptienne de l'alphabet phénicien* (1874)
by M. Le V<sup>te</sup> Emmanuel de Rougé

# Tableau paléographique
## des formes cursives de l'Alphabet Égyptien prototypes des lettres phéniciennes

| Valeur | Hiéroglyphe | Hiératique | | | Démotique | |
| --- | --- | --- | --- | --- | --- | --- |
| | | Papyrus Prisse | XIXᵉ Dynastie | Basses époques | 1ᵉʳ Type | 2ᵉ Type |
| r | ⌒ | ໑ | ⌒ | ⌒ | ≡ | ʮ |
| r | 🦁 | 🦁 | 𝓁𝓁 | 𝓁𝓁 | ʏ ʏ | / |
| s | ⊥⊥ | ⊥ | ⊥⊥ | ⊥ | ≡ | ⊥ |
| š | ⋔ | ⋔ | ⋔ | ⋔ | 𝟹 𝟹 | 𝟹 𝟹 |
| t' | ∼ | ∼𝓈 | ∼𝓈 | ∼𝓈 | 𝟹 | 𝟽 |
| t' | 🦆 | ƛ | ƛ | ƛ | ? | ? |
| x | ⊘ | ● | ○ | ∞ | 6 | c, c |
| h | □ | ⊞ | ⊓ | □ | P | p, p, p |
| a | 🦅 | 2 | 2 | ɞ | 2 2 | ?2, 2, 2 |
| i | ‖ | ɣ | ‖ | ɣ | ɣ | ρ, ρ |
| f | — | 𝓎𝓎 | 𝓎 | / | ɣ | ɣ ɣ |

From *Mémoire sur l'origine égyptienne de l'alphabet phénicien* (1874)
by M. Le Vᵗᵉ Emmanuel de Rougé

# Egyptian Origin of the Phoenician Alphabet

| Associated Sound or Letter(s): | Egyptian Hieroglyphic: | Egyptian Hieratic Alphabet: | Egyptian Demotic Alphabet: | Ancient Egyptian Alphabet: | Phoenician Alphabet: | Ancient Phoenician Alphabet: | Ancient Greek Alphabet: | Hebrew Alphabet: |
|---|---|---|---|---|---|---|---|---|
| 1 A | | | | | | | | |
| 2 B | | | | | | | | |
| 3 G | | | | | | | | |
| 4 D | | | | | | | | |
| 5 H | | | | | | | | |
| 6 U/V | | | | | | | | |
| 7 Z | | | | | | | | |
| 8 Ch | | | | | | | | |
| 9 Th | | | | | | | | |
| 10 I/J/Y | | | | | | | | |
| 11 C/K | | | | | | | | |
| 12 L | | | | | | | | |
| 13 M | | | | | | | | |
| 14 N | | | | | | | | |
| 15 S | | | | | | | | |
| 16 O/E | | | | | | | | |
| 17 P | | | | | | | | |
| 18 Tz | | | | | | | | |
| 19 Q | | | | | | | | |
| 20 R | | | | | | | | |
| 21 Sh | | | | | | | | |
| 22 T | | | | | | | | |

Source: "Mémoire sur l'origine égyptienne de l'alphabet phénicien" (1874) by M. Le Vicomte Emmanuel de Rougé

# Hebrew Letters and their Origins

| Numeric Value | Kabalistic Value | Square Hebrew: | Hebrew Letter Name: | Hieratic (Priestly) Egyptian: | Pheonecian: | Primitive Semitic: | Punic: | Siloam: | Israelite: | Samaritan: |
|---|---|---|---|---|---|---|---|---|---|---|
| 1 | 1 | א | Aleph | | | | | | | |
| 2 | 2 | ב | Beth | | | | | | | |
| 3 | 3 | ג | Gimel | | | | | | | |
| 4 | 4 | ד | Dalet | | | | | | | |
| 5 | 5 | ה | Heh | | | | | | | |
| 6 | 6 | ו | Vau | | | | | | | |
| 7 | 7 | ז | Zayin | | | | | | | |
| 8 | 8 | ח | Cheth | | | | | | | |
| 9 | 9 | ט | Teth | | | | | | | |
| 10 | 10 | י | Yod/Jod | | | | | | | |
| 11 | 20 | כ | Kaf/Kaph | | | | | | | |
| 12 | 30 | ל | Lamed | | | | | | | |
| 13 | 40 | מ | Mem/Men | | | | | | | |
| 14 | 50 | נ | Nun | | | | | | | |
| 15 | 60 | ס | Samech | | | | | | | |
| 16 | 70 | ע | Ayin | | | | | | | |
| 17 | 80 | פ | Pei | | | | | | | |
| 18 | 90 | צ | Tzadik | | | | | | | |
| 19 | 100 | ק | Kuf/Qoph | | | | | | | |
| 20 | 200 | ר | Resh/Reish | | | | | | | |
| 21 | 300 | ש | Shin | | | | | | | |
| 22 | 400 | ת | Tav | | | | | | | |
| 23 | 500 | ך | final Kaph | | | | | | | |
| 24 | 600 | ם | final Mem | | | | | | | |
| 25 | 700 | ן | final Nun | | | | | | | |
| 26 | 800 | ף | final Pei | | | | | | | |
| 27 | 900 | ץ | final Tzadik | | | | | | | |

Sources: "The Alphabet: An Account of the Origin and Development of Letters" (1883) by Isaac Taylor and "Essai sur la Propagation de l'Alphabet Phénicien" (1875) by François LeNormant

# Hebrew, Chaldean and Syrian Alphabets

| Numeric Value | Kabalistic Value | Square Hebrew: | Hebrew Letter Name: | Samaritan Alphabet: | Chaldean Alphabet: | Nabathean Alphabet: | Syrian Alphabet: | Syrian Letter Name: |
|---|---|---|---|---|---|---|---|---|
| 1 | 1 | א | Aleph | | | | | A - Olaph; *Aloho* |
| 2 | 2 | ב | Beth | | | | | B - Beth; *Barnio* |
| 3 | 3 | ג | Gimel | | | | | G - Gomal; *Gaboro* |
| 4 | 4 | ד | Dalet | | | | | D - Dolath; *Daiono* |
| 5 | 5 | ה | Heh | | | | | H - He; *Hadoio* |
| 6 | 6 | ו | Vau | | | | | V - Vau; *Vagdo* |
| 7 | 7 | ז | Zayin | | | | | Z - Zain; *Zaiono* |
| 8 | 8 | ח | Cheth | | | | | Hh - Hheth; *Hhanono* |
| 9 | 9 | ט | Teth | | | | | Th - Theth; *Tobo* |
| 10 | 10 | י | Yod/Jod | | | | | I - Iudi; *Iohubo* |
| 11 | 20 | כ | Kaf/Kaph | | | | | C - Coph; *Cino* |
| 12 | 30 | ל | Lamed | | | | | L - Lomad; *Lmino* |
| 13 | 40 | מ | Mem/Men | | | | | M - Mim; *Morio* |
| 14 | 50 | נ | Nun | | | | | N - Nun; *Nubero* |
| 15 | 60 | ס | Samech | | | | | S - Somchath; *Sabro* |
| 16 | 70 | ע | Ayin | | | | | Ga - Gain; *Gobado* |
| 17 | 80 | פ | Pei | | | | | P - Pe, Phe; *Pharuquo* |
| 18 | 90 | צ | Tzadik | | | | | Zz - Zzode; *Zhbo* |
| 19 | 100 | ק | Kuf/Qoph | | | | | Q - Quoph; *Quadifo* |
| 20 | 200 | ר | Resh/Reish | | | | | R - Ris; *Romo* |
| 21 | 300 | ש | Shin | | | | | Sc - Schin; *Shihho* |
| 22 | 400 | ת | Tav | | | | | Th - Thau; *Tlithoiutho* |
| 23 | 500 | ך | final Kaph | | | | | |
| 24 | 600 | ם | final Mem | | | | | |
| 25 | 700 | ן | final Nun | | | | | |
| 26 | 800 | ף | final Pei | | | | | |
| 27 | 900 | ץ | final Tzadik | | | | | |

Sources: "The Alphabet: An Account of the Origin and Development of Letters" (1883) by Isaac Taylor and "Traicté des chiffres ou Secrètes manières d'escrire" (1587) by Blaise de Vigenère

# Syrio-Hebraic and Semetic Alphabets

| Numeric Value | Square Hebrew: | Hebrew Letter Name: | Syrian Alphabet: | Old Syriac, Primitive Chaldean or "Estrangela" Alphabet: | | | | Syriac Alphabet: | Syrio-Hebraic Alphabet: | Mauritanic Alphabet: | Cuphic Alphabet: |
|---|---|---|---|---|---|---|---|---|---|---|---|
| 1 | א | Aleph | | | | | | | | | |
| 2 | ב | Beth | | | | | | | | | |
| 3 | ג | Gimel | | | | | | | | | |
| 4 | ד | Dalet | | | | | | | | | |
| 5 | ה | Heh | | | | | | | | | |
| 6 | ו | Vau | | | | | | | | | |
| 7 | ז | Zayin | | | | | | | | | |
| 8 | ח | Cheth | | | | | | | | | |
| 9 | ט | Teth | | | | | | | | | |
| 10 | י | Yod/Jod | | | | | | | | | |
| 11 | כ | Kaf/Kaph | | | | | | | | | |
| 12 | ל | Lamed | | | | | | | | | |
| 13 | מ | Mem/Men | | | | | | | | | |
| 14 | נ | Nun | | | | | | | | | |
| 15 | ס | Samech | | | | | | | | | |
| 16 | ע | Ayin | | | | | | | | | |
| 17 | פ | Peh | | | | | | | | | |
| 18 | צ | Tzadik | | | | | | | | | |
| 19 | ק | Kuf/Qoph | | | | | | | | | |
| 20 | ר | Resh/Reish | | | | | | | | | |
| 21 | ש | Shin | | | | | | | | | |
| 22 | ת | Tav | | | | | | | | | |

Sources: "Alphabetum Chaldicum Antiquum Estranghelo Dictum" (1636) by Sac. Congr. de Propag. Fide, "Manuel Typographique" (1766) by Pierre Simon Fournier & Nicolas Gando, "Typographia" (1824) by John Johnson, and "Traicté des chiffres ou Secrètes manières d'escrire" (1587) by Blaise de Vigenère

# African, Middle Eastern and European Alphabets

| Numeric Value | Square Hebrew | Hebrew Letter Name | Samaritan Alphabet | Assyrian Alphabet | Ethiopic or Nubian Alphabet | Ethiopic or Nubian Letter Name | Gothic Alphabet | Ancient Greek Letter | Ancient Greek Letter Name |
|---|---|---|---|---|---|---|---|---|---|
| 1 | א | Aleph | | | | A | | Α α | Alpha |
| 2 | ב | Beth | | | | Ba | | Β β | Beta |
| 3 | ג | Gimel | | | | Ga | | Γ γ | Gamma |
| 4 | ד | Dalet | | | | Da | | Δ δ | Delta |
| 5 | ה | Heh | | | | Ha | | Ε ε | Epsilon |
| 6 | ו | Vau | | | | Va | | F ϝ | Wau |
| 7 | ז | Zayin | | | | Za | | Ζ ζ | Zeta |
| 8 | ח | Cheth | | | | Hhah | | Η η | Eta |
| 9 | ט | Teth | | | | Tha | | Θ θ | Theta |
| 10 | י | Yod/Jod | | | | Iud | | Ι ι | Iota |
| 11 | כ | Kaf/Kaph | | | | Ka | | Κ κ | Kappa |
| 12 | ל | Lamed | | | | La | | Λ λ | Lambda |
| 13 | מ | Mem/Men | | | | Ma | | Μ μ | Mu |
| 14 | נ | Nun | | | | Na | | Ν ν | Nu |
| 15 | ס | Samech | | | | Sa | | Ξ ξ | Xi |
| 16 | ע | Ayin | | | | A | | Ο σ | Omicron |
| 17 | פ | Pei | | | | Pa | | Π π | Pi |
| 18 | צ | Tzadik | | | | Tza | | ϡ | Sampi |
| 19 | ק | Kuf/Qoph | | | | Cha | | ϙ | Koppa |
| 20 | ר | Resh/Reish | | | | Ra | | Ρ ρ | Rho |
| 21 | ש | Shin | | | | Sha | | Σ σ | Sigma |
| 22 | ת | Tav | | | | Ta | | Τ τ | Tau |
| 23 | | | | | | Guo | | Υ υ | Upsilon |
| 24 | | | | | | Huo | | Φ φ | Phi |
| 25 | | | | | | Kuo | | Χ χ | Chi |
| 26 | | | | | | Chuo | | Ψ ψ | Psi |
| 27 | | | | | | | | Ω ω | Omega |

Source: "Traicté des chiffres ou Secrètes manières d'escrire" (1587) by Blaise de Vigenère

# Alphabet of the Magi and Esoteric Alphabets

| Numeric Value | Kabalistic Value | Square Hebrew | Hebrew Letter Name | Theseus Ambrosius Alphabet | Grimanian Alphabet | Alphabet of the Magi | Alphabet of the Magi Letter Name | Alphabet of Solomon | Geomantic & Astrologic Alphabet |
|---|---|---|---|---|---|---|---|---|---|
| 1 | 1 | א | Aleph | | | | A - Athoïm | | |
| 2 | 2 | ב | Beth | | | | B - Beïnthin | | |
| 3 | 3 | ג | Gimel | | | | G - Gomor | | |
| 4 | 4 | ד | Dalet | | | | D - Dinain | | |
| 5 | 5 | ה | Heh | | | | E - Eni | | |
| 6 | 6 | ו | Vau | | | | U/V - Ur | | |
| 7 | 7 | ז | Zayin | | | | Z - Zaïn | | |
| 8 | 8 | ח | Cheth | | | | H - Heletha | | |
| 9 | 9 | ט | Teth | | | | Th - Théla/Thala | | |
| 10 | 10 | י | Yod/Jod | | | | I/J/Y - Ioïthi | | |
| 11 | 20 | כ | Kaf/Kaph | | | | C/K - Caïtha | | |
| 12 | 30 | ל | Lamed | | | | L - Luzain | | |
| 13 | 40 | מ | Mem/Men | | | | M - Mataloth | | |
| 14 | 50 | נ | Nun | | | | N - Naïn | | |
| 15 | 60 | ס | Samech | | | | X - Xiron | | |
| 16 | 70 | ע | Ayin | | | | O - Olélath | | |
| 17 | 80 | פ | Pei | | | | F/P - Pilôn | | |
| 18 | 90 | צ | Tzadik | | | | Ts - Tsadi | | |
| 19 | 100 | ק | Kuf/Qoph | | | | Q - Quitolath | | |
| 20 | 200 | ר | Resh/Reish | | | | R - Rasith | | |
| 21 | 300 | ש | Shin | | | | S - Sichen | | |
| 22 | 400 | ת | Tav | | | | T - Thoth | | |
| 23 | 500 | ך | final Kaph | | | | | | |
| 24 | 600 | ם | final Mem | | | | | | |
| 25 | 700 | ן | final Nun | | | | | | |
| 26 | 800 | ף | final Pei | | | | | | |
| 27 | 900 | ץ | final Tzadik | | | | | | |

Source: "Traicté des chiffres ou Secrètes manières d'escrire" (1587) by Blaise de Vigenère and "Historie de la Magie" (1870) by Jean Baptiste Pitois

# Esoteric and Secret Hebrew Alphabets

| Numeric Value | Kabalistic Value | Square Hebrew | Hebrew Letter Name | Esoteric Hebrew Alphabets | Alphabet of the Magi | Scriptura Transitus Fluvii | Scriptura Malachim | Bartolocci's Other Esoteric Hebrew Alphabets |
|---|---|---|---|---|---|---|---|---|
| 1 | 1 | א | Aleph | | | | | |
| 2 | 2 | ב | Beth | | | | | |
| 3 | 3 | ג | Gimel | | | | | |
| 4 | 4 | ד | Dalet | | | | | |
| 5 | 5 | ה | Heh | | | | | |
| 6 | 6 | ו | Vau | | | | | |
| 7 | 7 | ז | Zayin | | | | | |
| 8 | 8 | ח | Cheth | | | | | |
| 9 | 9 | ט | Teth | | | | | |
| 10 | 10 | י | Yod/Jod | | | | | |
| 11 | 20 | כ | Kaf/Kaph | | | | | |
| 12 | 30 | ל | Lamed | | | | | |
| 13 | 40 | מ | Mem/Men | | | | | |
| 14 | 50 | נ | Nun | | | | | |
| 15 | 60 | ס | Samech | | | | | |
| 16 | 70 | ע | Ayin | | | | | |
| 17 | 80 | פ | Pei | | | | | |
| 18 | 90 | צ | Tzadik | | | | | |
| 19 | 100 | ק | Kuf/Qoph | | | | | |
| 20 | 200 | ר | Resh/Reish | | | | | |
| 21 | 300 | ש | Shin | | | | | |
| 22 | 400 | ת | Tav | | | | | |
| 23 | 500 | ך | final Kaph | | | | | |
| 24 | 600 | ם | final Mem | | | | | |
| 25 | 700 | ן | final Nun | | | | | |
| 26 | 800 | ף | final Pei | | | | | |
| 27 | 900 | ץ | final Tzadik | | | | | |

Source: "Bibliotheca Magna Rabbinica" (1675-1693) by Giulio Bartolocci and Carlo Giuseppe Imbonati and "Traicté des chiffres ou Secrètes manières d'escrire" (1587) by Blaise de Vigenère

# Ancient and Esoteric Greek Alphabets

| Serial Value | Greek Letter: | Greek Letter Name: | Old Greek Alphabets: | | | Jacobite Alphabet: | Cophite Alphabet: | Georgian Alphabet: | Alphabet of Apollonius Thianeen: | Alphabet of Virgil the Philosopher: |
|---|---|---|---|---|---|---|---|---|---|---|
| 1 | A α | Alpha | | | | | | | | |
| 2 | B β | Beta | | | | | | | | |
| 3 | Γ γ | Gamma | | | | | | | | |
| 4 | Δ δ | Delta | | | | | | | | |
| 5 | E ε | Epsilon | | | | | | | | |
| 6 | Z ζ | Zeta | | | | | | | | |
| 7 | H η | Eta | | | | | | | | |
| 8 | Θ ϑ | Theta | | | | | | | | |
| 9 | I ι | Iota | | | | | | | | |
| 10 | K κ | Kappa | | | | | | | | |
| 11 | Λ λ | Lambda | | | | | | | | |
| 12 | M μ | Mu | | | | | | | | |
| 13 | N ν | Nu | | | | | | | | |
| 14 | Ξ ξ | Xi | | | | | | | | |
| 15 | O σ | Omicron | | | | | | | | |
| 16 | Π π | Pi | | | | | | | | |
| 17 | P ρ | Rho | | | | | | | | |
| 18 | Σ σ | Sigma | | | | | | | | |
| 19 | T τ | Tau | | | | | | | | |
| 20 | Υ υ | Upsilon | | | | | | | | |
| 21 | Φ φ | Phi | | | | | | | | |
| 22 | X χ | Chi | | | | | | | | |
| 23 | Ψ ψ | Psi | | | | | | | | |
| 24 | Ω ω | Omega | | | | | | | | |

Source: "Traicté des chiffres ou Secrètes manières d'escrire" (1587) by Blaise de Vigenère

# Egyptian, Esoteric and Alchemical Letters

| Letter(s): | Egyptian Alphabet: | Egyptian Letter Name: | Phenician Alphabet: | Ionic Phenician Alphabet: | Esoteric Hieroglyphic Alphabet: | Alphabet of Secret Philosophy: | Hetrusque or Thoscan Alphabets: | Thebian Alphabet: | Alchemist's Alphabet: |
|---|---|---|---|---|---|---|---|---|---|
| 1 | A | Athiom | | | | | | | |
| 2 | B | Beinthin | | | | | | | |
| 3 | C | Chinoth | | | | | | | |
| 4 | D | Dinain | | | | | | | |
| 5 | E | Eny | | | | | | | |
| 6 | F | Fin | | | | | | | |
| 7 | G | Gomor | | | | | | | |
| 8 | H | Heletha | | | | | | | |
| 9 | I [J] | Iamin | | | | | | | |
| 10 | K | Kaita | | | | | | | |
| 11 | L | Luzain | | | | | | | |
| 12 | M | Miche | | | | | | | |
| 13 | N | Nain | | | | | | | |
| 14 | O | Olelath | | | | | | | |
| 15 | P | Pilon | | | | | | | |
| 16 | Q | Quyn | | | | | | | |
| 17 | R | Iron | | | | | | | |
| 18 | S | Sichen | | | | | | | |
| 19 | T | Thela | | | | | | | |
| 20 | V [U] | Vr | | | | | | | |
| 21 | X | Xiron | | | | | | | |
| 22 | Y | Yph | | | | | | | |
| 23 | Z | Zain | | | | | | | |
| 24 | Th | Thou | | | | | | | |
| 25 | Ch | | | | | | | | |
| 26 | Il | | | | | | | | |
| 27 | & | | | | | | | | |

Source: "Traicté des chiffres ou Secrètes manières d'escrire" (1587) by Blaise de Vigenère
and "Polygraphiae" (1561) by Johannes Trithemius

# Ancient Royal European Alphabets

| Serial Value | Letter(s) | Gothic Alphabet | Royal Artique Alphabet | | Another Artique Alphabet | | The Secret Royal Alphabets of Emperor Charlemagne | | | | | | | |
|---|---|---|---|---|---|---|---|---|---|---|---|---|---|---|
| 1 | A | | | | | | | | | | | | | |
| 2 | B | | | | | | | | | | | | | |
| 3 | C | | | | | | | | | | | | | |
| 4 | D | | | | | | | | | | | | | |
| 5 | E/É | | | | | | | | | | | | | |
| 6 | F | | | | | | | | | | | | | |
| 7 | G | | | | | | | | | | | | | |
| 8 | H | | | | | | | | | | | | | |
| 9 | I/J | | | | | | | | | | | | | |
| 10 | K | | | | | | | | | | | | | |
| 11 | L | | | | | | | | | | | | | |
| 12 | M | | | | | | | | | | | | | |
| 13 | N | | | | | | | | | | | | | |
| 14 | O/Ó | | | | | | | | | | | | | |
| 15 | P | | | | | | | | | | | | | |
| 16 | Q | | | | | | | | | | | | | |
| 17 | R | | | | | | | | | | | | | |
| 18 | S | | | | | | | | | | | | | |
| 19 | T | | | | | | | | | | | | | |
| 20 | U/V/W | | | | | | | | | | | | | |
| 21 | X | | | | | | | | | | | | | |
| 22 | Y | | | | | | | | | | | | | |
| 23 | Z | | | | | | | | | | | | | |
| 24 | & | | | | | | | | | | | | | |
| 25 | Th | | | | | | | | | | | | | |
| 26 | Ph | | | | | | | | | | | | | |
| 27 | Ch | | | | | | | | | | | | | |
| 28 | Ps/Sp | | | | | | | | | | | | | |
| 29 | Sch | | | | | | | | | | | | | |
| 30 | Sc/St | | | | | | | | | | | | | |

Source: "Traicté des chiffres ou Secrètes manières d'escrire" (1587) by Blaise de Vigenère and "Polygraphiae" (1561) by Johannes Trithemius

# Esoteric and Secret European Alphabets

| Serial Value | Letter(s) | Gothic Alphabet | An Ancient French Alphabet | Another Old French Alphabet | French Dorac Alphabet | Northmanic Alphabet | Johannes Trithemius Alphabet | Another Trithemius Alphabet |
|---|---|---|---|---|---|---|---|---|
| 1 | A | | | | | | | |
| 2 | B | | | | | | | |
| 3 | C | | | | | | | |
| 4 | D | | | | | | | |
| 5 | E/É | | | | | | | |
| 6 | F | | | | | | | |
| 7 | G | | | | | | | |
| 8 | H | | | | | | | |
| 9 | I/J | | | | | | | |
| 10 | K | | | | | | | |
| 11 | L | | | | | | | |
| 12 | M | | | | | | | |
| 13 | N | | | | | | | |
| 14 | O/Ó | | | | | | | |
| 15 | P | | | | | | | |
| 16 | Q | | | | | | | |
| 17 | R | | | | | | | |
| 18 | S | | | | | | | |
| 19 | T | | | | | | | |
| 20 | U/V/W | | | | | | | |
| 21 | X | | | | | | | |
| 22 | Y | | | | | | | |
| 23 | Z | | | | | | | |
| 24 | & | | | | | | | |
| 25 | Th | | | | | | | |
| 26 | Ph | | | | | | | |
| 27 | Ch | | | | | | | |
| 28 | Ps/Sp | | | | | | | |
| 29 | Sch | | | | | | | |
| 30 | Sc/St | | | | | | | |

Source: "Traicté des chiffres ou Secrètes manières d'escrire" (1587) by Blaise de Vigenère and "Polygraphiae" (1561) by Johannes Trithemius

# Meaning and Associations of Hebrew Letters

| Numeric Value | Kabalistic Value | Square Hebrew | Hebrew Letter Name | Hebrew Letter Meaning | Associated Egyptian Hieroglyphic | Egpytian Hieroglyphic Meaning | Associated Syrian Letter | Syrian Letter Meaning | Eliphas Levi's Associated Letter |
|---|---|---|---|---|---|---|---|---|---|
| 1 | 1 | א | Aleph | Ox | | Eagle | | God | A |
| 2 | 2 | ב | Beth | House | | Crane | | Creator | B |
| 3 | 3 | ג | Gimel | Camel | | Throne | | Powerful | C |
| 4 | 4 | ד | Dalet | Door | | Hand | | Judge | D |
| 5 | 5 | ה | Heh | Window/Look | | Meander | | Humble | E |
| 6 | 6 | ו | Vau | Hook | | Cerastes | | Promise | F |
| 7 | 7 | ז | Zayin | Weapons | | Duck | | Nourish | G |
| 8 | 8 | ח | Cheth | Fence | | Sieve | | Mercy | H |
| 9 | 9 | ט | Teth | Serpent? | | Tongs | | Good | I |
| 10 | 10 | י | Yod/Jod | Hand | | Parallels | | Liberal | K |
| 11 | 20 | כ | Kaf/Kaph | Palm of Hand | | Bowl | | Righteous | L |
| 12 | 30 | ל | Lamed | Ox-Goad/Spit | | Lioness | | Pacific | M |
| 13 | 40 | מ | Mem/Men | Water | | Owl | | Lord | N |
| 14 | 50 | נ | Nun | Fish | | Water | | Light | O |
| 15 | 60 | ס | Samech | Post | | Chairback | | Hope | P |
| 16 | 70 | ע | Ayin | Eye | | [no glyph] | | Governor | Q |
| 17 | 80 | פ | Pei | Mouth | | Shutter | | Saluter | R |
| 18 | 90 | צ | Tzadik | Javelin? | | Snake | | Crucified | S |
| 19 | 100 | ק | Kuf/Qoph | Knot? | | Angle | | Holy | T |
| 20 | 200 | ר | Resh/Reish | Head | | Mouth | | Very High | U |
| 21 | 300 | ש | Shin | Teeth | | Inundated Garden | | Glorious | X |
| 22 | 400 | ת | Tav | Mark | | Lasso | | Trinity | Z |

Sources: "The alphabet: an account of the origin and development of letters" (1883) by Isaac Taylor, "Traicté des chiffres ou Secrètes manières d'escrire" (1587) by Blaise de Vigenère, and "Dogma de la Haute Magie"(1855) by Éliphas Lévi

# Do you know these Esoteric Letters?

What are these Alphabets from page 105 of Volume 2 of Athanasius Kircher's *Oedipus Aegyptiacus* (1653)?

I. _____  II. _____
III. _____  IV. _____
V. _____  VI. _____

| Interpretatio. | Character duplex mysticus ab Angelis traditus. | Character temp. transfitus flum. R.Abr.Bal. | Characterum variæ formæ ex numis & Blaneutio extractæ. | Floridus character post transitum fluminis quem & Hebræum sive Samaritanum diximus. | Character Mosaicus Legis ex inscript: & Rabbinorum monumentis. | Assyrius sive Esdrzus |
|---|---|---|---|---|---|---|
| A | | | F F | | | |
| B | | | | | | |
| G | | | | | | |
| D | | | | | | |
| H | | | | | | |
| V | | | | | | |
| Z | | | | | | |
| Ch | | | | | | |
| T | | | | | | |
| I | | | | | | |
| C | | | | | | |
| L | | | | | | |
| M | | | | | | |
| N | | | | | | |
| S | | | | | | |
| Ngh | | | | | | |
| P | | | | | | |
| Tſ | | | | | | |
| Qk | | | P P | | P | |
| R | | | | | | |
| Sch | | | | | | |
| Th | | | | | | |
| | I | II | III | IV | V | VI |

# Do you know these Esoteric Letters?

What are these Alphabets from page 106 of Volume 2 of Athanasius Kircher's *Oedipus Aegyptiacus* (1653)?

VII. _____  VIII. _____

IX. _____  X. _____

XI. _____  XII. _____

XIII. _____

| Modernus character Samaritanus. | Character Syriacus modernus. | Literæ Phœnicum. | Literæ Coptæ modernæ. | Græcæ modernæ. | Latinæ modernæ. | Literæ Arabicæ modernæ. |
|---|---|---|---|---|---|---|
| | | | | A a | A a | |
| | | | | B β | B b | |
| | | | | Γ γ | G g | |
| | | | | Δ δ | D d | |
| | | | | | H h | |
| | | | | | V u | |
| | | | | Z ζ | Z z | |
| | | | | X χ | Ch | |
| | | | | Θ ϑ | Th | |
| | | | | I ι | I i | |
| | | | | K κ | K k | |
| | | | | Λ λ | L l | |
| | | | | M μ | M m | |
| | | | | N ν | N n | |
| | | | | Σ σ | S s | |
| | | | | | | |
| | | | | Π π | P p | |
| | | | | Z ζ | Z | |
| | | | | K κ | Q q | |
| | | | | P ρ | R r | |
| | | | | Σ σ | S ſ | |
| | | | | T τ | T t | |
| VII | VIII | IX | X | XI | XII | XIII |

315

# Daath Gnosis: Bilingual Translations

"The Book of the Virgin of Carmel" by Samael Aun Weor

"Universal Charity" by Samael Aun Weor

"Gnostic Christification" by Samael Aun Weor

"Logos Mantram Magic" by Krumm-Heller (Huiracocha)

"The Reconciliation of Science and Religion" by Eliphas Levi

"The Bible of Liberty" by Eliphas Levi

"The Initiatic Path in the Arcanum of the Tarot & Kabalah" by Samael Aun Weor

"Esoteric Course of Kabalah" by Samael Aun Weor

"Magic, Alchemy and the Great Work" by Samael Aun Weor

"Dogma of High Magic" by Eliphas Levi

"The Awakening of Man" by Samael Aun Weor

"Gnostic Rosicrucian Astrology" by Krumm-Heller (Huiracocha)

"The Kabalistic and Occult Philosophy of Eliphas Levi" Vol.1 by Eliphas Levi


"The Kabalistic and Occult Philosophy of Eliphas Levi" Vol.2 by Eliphas Levi *

"Gnostic Rosicrucian Kabalah" by Krumm-Heller (Huiracocha) *

"Ritual of High Magic" by Eliphas Levi *


\* Current projects for future publication from Daath Gnostic Publishing

# Daath Gnosis: Reprints[1]

"The Psychology of Man's Possible Evolution" by P.D. Ouspensky *(English-Español)*

"In Search of the Miraculous" Vol. 1 & 2 by P.D. Ouspensky *(English-Español)*

"Mystical Kabalah" by Dion Fortune *(English - Español)*

"Rito Memphis y Misraim Guias del Aprendiz, Compañero, y Maestro" by Memphis y Misraim Argentina *(Español)*

"The Theosophical ZOHAR" by Nurho de Manahar *(English)*

"The Oragean Version" by C. Daly King *(English)*

"La Science Cabalistique" by Lazare Lenain *(Français)* *

"The Fourth Way" by P.D. Ouspensky *(English - Español)* *

# Daath Gnosis: Study Guides

"Gnostic Egyptian Tarot Coloring Book" *(English - Español)*

"The Gnostic Kabalistic Verb" *(English - Español)*

"The Gnostic and Esoteric Mysteries of Freemasonry, Lucifer and the Great Work" *(English - Español)*

"The Kabalistic and Occult Tarot of Eliphas Levi" *(English)*

"Esoteric Studies in Masonry" Vol. 1 *(English - Français)*

"Esoteric Studies in Masonry" Vol. 2 *(English - Français)* *

\* Current projects for future publication from Daath Gnostic Publishing

---

[1] These are books which were 1) either originally in English and have been republished by Daath Gnosis in order to either make them bilingual or 2) provide access to difficult to find documents in their original language.

A word about "**Daath Gnostic Publishing – Art, Science, Philosophy and Mysticism (A.S.P.M)**" and our motivation:

> In an attempt to integrate the large amount of enlightening material on the subject of GNOSIS into the English language and to provide a way:
> - for non-English speakers to give lectures & assignments to English speaking students (and vice versa) and be able to reference specific topics or quotes, and
> - for English speakers to access materials previously unavailable in English (or not critically translated into English)
>
> we have decided to translate and publish these materials for the serious Gnostic Students.

Almost all our publications are bilingual, giving access to the original source material and the translation so that the reader can decide for themselves what the meaning of each sentence is.

We are also working on Study Guides that are a combination of Gnostic Materials from multiple sources which provide further insight when taken together.

Because of the need for a practical GNOSIS in these revolutionary times, we have focused on, and continue to benefit from, the writing and teachings of Samael Aun Weor. We encourage you to study his materials, they are wonderful.

In *Endocrinology and Criminology* (1959), at the end of Ch. 15, he says:

> "Before delivering ourselves to the development of occult powers, we need to study ourselves and make a persona-logical and psycho-pathological diagnosis of our own personality.
>
> After discovering our own particular Psycho-bio-typo-logical "I", it is necessary for us to reform ourselves with intellectual culture.
>
> A Pedagogic[2] Psychotherapy is necessary in order to reform ourselves.

> "Antes de entregarnos al desarrollo de los poderes ocultos necesitamos estudiarnos a sí mismos, y hacer un diagnóstico persona-lógico y psico-patológico de nuestra propia personalidad.
>
> Después de haber descubierto nuestro propio yo Psico-Biotipológico, necesitamos reformarnos con la cultura intelectual.
>
> Necesitamos una Psicoterapia Pedagógica para reformarnos.

---

[2] Pedagogy: 1) the function or work of a teacher; teaching. 2) the art or science of teaching; education; instructional methods.

| | |
|---|---|
| The four gospels of Jesus Christ are the best Pedagogic Psychotherapy.<br><br>It is necessary to totally study and practice all the teachings contained in the four gospels of Jesus Christ.<br><br>Only after reforming ourselves morally can we deliver ourselves to the development of the chakras, discs or magnetic wheels, of the astral body.<br><br>It is also urgent to study the best authors of Theosophy, Rosicrucianism, Psychology, Yoga, etc., etc." | Los cuatro evangelios del Cristo Jesús, son realmente la mejor Psicoterapia Pedagógica.<br><br>Es necesario estudiar y practicar totalmente todas las enseñanzas contenidas en los cuatro evangelios del Cristo-Jesús.<br><br>Sólo después de habernos reformado moralmente podemos entregarnos al desarrollo de los chacras, discos o ruedas magnéticas del cuerpo astral.<br><br>Es también urgente estudiar a todos los mejores autores de Teosofía, Rosacrucismo, Sicología, Yoguismo, etc., etc." |

In *The Seven Words* (1953), about a third of the way through, he says:

| | |
|---|---|
| "I dare to affirm that all the books which have been written in the world on Theosophism, Rosicrucianism, Spiritualism, etc., are completely antiquated for the new AQUARIAN Era, and therefore they should be revised in order to extract from them only what is essential.<br><br>Here I, AUN WEOR, deliver to humanity, the authentic message that the WHITE LODGE sends to humanity for the new AQUARIAN Era.<br><br>God has delivered to men the wisdom of the Serpent. What more do they want?<br><br>This science is not mine; this science is from God; my person is not worth anything; the work is everything, I am nothing but an emissary." | "Yo me atrevo a afirmar que todos los libros que se han escrito en el mundo sobre teosofismo, Rosacrucismo, espiritismo, etc., están ya completamente anticuados para la nueva Era ACUARIA, y por consiguiente deben ser revisados para extraer de ellos únicamente lo esencial.<br><br>Yo, AUN WEOR, aquí le entrego a la humanidad el auténtico mensaje que la LOGIA BLANCA envía a la humanidad para la nueva Era ACUARIA.<br><br>Dios le ha entregado a los hombres la sabiduría de la Serpiente. ¿Qué más quieren?<br><br>Esta ciencia no es mía; esta ciencia es de Dios; mi persona no vale nada, la obra lo es todo, yo no soy sino un emisario." |

So let us practice the Science of the Serpent, *la magia amorosa*, while we study and extract only what is essential from the Esoteric texts of the past, in order to synthesize the truth within ourselves.

If you are interested:
- in receiving a list of our currently available materials,
- or would like to suggest a better translation for anything we publish,
- or if you would like to take the responsibility and time to translate or proofread a chapter or a book (in English, French or Spanish),
- or would like to suggest or submit materials for publication,
- or would like to inquire about purchasing Gnostic Tarot Deck(s)

please send us an email at:
**GnosticStudies@gmail.com**

Or join our group for the latest updates:
**http://groups.yahoo.com/group/DaathGnosis/**

Daath דעת
Gnostic ☥
Publishing

Art - Arte
Science - Ciencia
Philosophy - Filosofía
Mysticism - Misticismo